W9-CFQ-477

BEATRICE PUBLIC LIBRARY
BEATRICE, NE 68310

The Lion Book of Family Prayers

BEATRICE PUBLIC LIBRARY
BEATRICE, NE 68310

For Alan

THE LION
BOOK OF

FAMILY PRAYERS

COMPILED BY

Mary Batchelor

A LION BOOK
Oxford · Batavia · Sydney

This collection copyright © 1992 Mary Batchelor
All copyright prayers appear by permission of the authors
Illustrations © 1992 Harriet Dell and Richard Allen

Published by
Lion Publishing plc
Sandy Lane West, Oxford, England
ISBN 0 7459 2065 9
Lion Publishing Corporation
1705 Hubbard Avenue, Batavia, Illinois 60510, USA
ISBN 0 7459 2065 9
Albatross Books Pty Ltd
PO Box 320, Sutherland, NSW 2232, Australia
ISBN 0 7324 0579 3

First edition 1992
All rights reserved

A catalogue record for this book is available
from the British Library

Library of Congress CIP Data applied for

Printed and bound in Spain

Contents

Prayers suitable for children and young people can be found throughout the collection: they are marked ◆

Our Father
who art in heaven,
hallowed be thy name;
thy kingdom come;
thy will be done;
on earth as it is in heaven.
Give us this day our daily bread.
And forgive us our trespasses,
as we forgive those who trespass
against us.
And lead us not into temptation;
but deliver us from evil.
For thine is the kingdom, the power,
and the glory, for ever and ever. Amen.

Introduction

What makes a good prayer? The answer depends on what we think prayer is. Prayer is talking and listening to God. As in a close human relationship, words are used to express love, to ask for help and to talk over what lies near to the heart. Of course, to say that is to assume that we *know* God. It is hoped that this collection of prayers will help us to begin such a relationship if it does not already exist, as well as encouraging it to develop and grow. Knowing God is not an optional extra but an essential part of what it means to be human. We are not fully alive until we are alive to God and in touch with him. When we pray we make contact with God, listen to him, get onto his wavelength and tell him everything that is in our minds.

We all know God in different ways, therefore every person's prayers are unique. No one else shares quite the same relationship with God. That is why personal, extempore prayer is so important. But we also have much in common as human beings, so written prayers can reflect the desires of many hearts, just as great love poetry expresses the feelings of thousands who are in love.

So a 'good' prayer should find an echo in our own hearts. It must seem to speak for us as well—or better—than if the words were our own. But prayer is not only an individual exercise. We pray together as congregations or groups sharing the same interests. So, where appropriate, set prayers must reflect the wider thoughts and feelings of the united group. A good prayer implies God's greatness, his otherness from us and his worthiness to be praised and respected. Our Father is in heaven, which means that he is great beyond our comprehension and good beyond our understanding.

But God *is* our Father and a good prayer helps us to feel close to him and in touch. Sometimes the words are majestic and the rhythms beautiful but when the words are conversational and the mood immediate the true spirit of prayer can still be captured.

A good prayer is honest and sincere. There is no room for pretence when we are talking to God who knows us through and through.

The condition for all prayer is that it should be offered through Jesus

Christ. We are sinful and earthbound. We have no right to God's ear and no access to his presence except through the way Jesus made open through his death on our behalf. We also ask in Jesus' name because he himself told us to do so. He promised that God would hear and answer such prayers.

I have tried to include in this book many of the differing moods and methods of prayer. I have culled prayers from other centuries and many different countries and traditions. There are few prayers from nonconformists, who use extempore prayer more often, so I have suggested ways in which the reader can be gently led along the path of extempore prayer too.

I have shortened some long prayers—the wisdom writer of the Old Testament reminds us that since God is in heaven and we are on earth, our words should be few. I have sometimes changed 'thou' and its difficult verbal forms to the 'you' we use almost universally today. Because prayer is listening as well as speaking to God, I have left pauses for quietness and receiving too.

I hope that the book will be useful in churches, schools, groups, families and also for the individual and for this reason I have tried to provide prayers for many of the situations of life. There are sure to be woeful gaps. There are also those whose contribution, because unknown, has not been acknowledged and for this I apologize. But no collection of prayers could hope to be complete. At least I trust that this book will help men and women and boys and girls to make and develop a personal relationship with God and Jesus Christ. I hope too that it will help us all—as prayer should do—to look at ourselves and our world more through the eyes of God.

◆ *A Time to be Silent* ◆

I am listening to what the Lord God is saying; he promises
peace . . .

FROM PSALM 85

Finding God in Quietness and Listening

We often rush into words of prayer. But we find God when we take time to be quiet, realizing that God is close and wanting to speak as well as to listen to us, though we may find listening hard at first.

Do not give up... When you first begin, you find only darkness and as it were a cloud of unknowing. You don't know what this means except that in your will you feel a simple, steadfast intention reaching out towards God... Reconcile yourself to wait in this darkness as long as is necessary, but still go on longing after him whom you love.

> From *The Cloud of Unknowing* (fourteenth century)

> To be there before you, Lord, that's all.
> To shut the eyes of my body,
> To shut the eyes of my soul,
> And be still and silent,
> To expose myself to you who are there, exposed to me.
> To be there before you, the Eternal Presence.

> *Michel Quoist*

In the rush and noise of life, as you have intervals, step within yourselves and be still. Wait upon God and feel his good presence; this will carry you through your day's business.

> *William Penn (1644–1718)*

Dear Lord and Father of mankind,
Forgive our foolish ways!
Reclothe us in our rightful mind;
In purer lives your service find,
In deeper reverence, praise.

Drop your still dews of quietness
Till all our strivings cease:
Take from our lives the strain and stress,
And let our ordered lives confess
The beauty of your peace.

John Greenleaf Whittier (1807–1892)

O Lord, my God,
grant us your peace; already, indeed, you have made us rich in all
things!
Give us that peace of being at rest,
that sabbath peace,
the peace which knows no end.

St Augustine (354–430)

O make my heart so still, so still,
When I am deep in prayer,
That I might hear the white mist-wreaths
Losing themselves in air!

Utsonomya San, Japan

Father in heaven, when the thought of you wakes in our hearts, let it not wake
like a frightened bird that flies about in dismay, but like a child waking from
its sleep with a heavenly smile.

Sören Kierkegaard (1813–1855)

Give unto us, O Lord, that quietness of mind in which we can hear you speaking to us, for your own name's sake.

> Lord, you have taught us in your word that there is a time to speak
> and a time to keep silence.
>
> As we thank you for the power of speech,
> we pray for the grace of silence.
>
> Make us as ready to listen as we are to talk,
> ready to listen to your voice in the quietness of our hearts
> and ready to listen to other people who need a sympathetic ear.
> Show us when to open our mouths and when to hold our peace
> that we may glorify you both in speech and in silence
> through Jesus Christ our Lord.
>
> *Frank Colquhoun*

O God, let me not interrupt you with my chatter. Let me listen, rather, to your still, small voice.

Geddes MacGregor

Speak, Lord, your servant is listening.

From 1 Samuel 3

O Lord, the Scripture says 'there is a time for silence and a time for speech.' Saviour, teach me the silence of humility, the silence of wisdom, the silence of love, the silence of perfection, the silence that speaks without words, the silence of faith.

Lord, teach me to silence my own heart that I may listen to the gentle movement of the Holy Spirit within me and sense the depths which are of God.

Frankfurt prayer (sixteenth century)

Sentence for personal meditation and prayer:

Be still and know that I am God.

There is no place where God is not,
Wherever I go, there God is.
Now and always he upholds me with his power
And keeps me safe in his love.

Author unknown

My spirit longs for thee
Within my troubled breast,
Though I unworthy be
Of so divine a guest.

Of so divine a guest
Unworthy though I be,
Yet has my heart no rest
Unless it come from thee.

John Byrom (1692–1763)

It is not far to go
for you are near,
It is not far to go
for you are here.
And not by travelling, Lord,
we come to you,
but by the way of love,
and we love you.

Amy Carmichael (1868–1951)

Coming Close to God through Jesus

Jesus said: No one comes to the Father, except by me.

From John 14

We have ... complete freedom to go into the Most Holy Place by means of the death of Jesus ... So let us come near to God with a sincere heart and sure faith, with hearts that have been purified from a guilty conscience.

From Hebrews 10

Lord Jesus, you are our way to the Father. We have no goodness of our own to make us fit for God's presence. We come humbly to the Father through the benefits of your death for us and through the victory of your resurrection and ascension. We come to him through you and give you praise and thanksgiving. Amen.

> Jesus, the very thought of thee
> With sweetness fills my breast;
> But sweeter far thy face to see,
> And in thy presence rest.
>
> Jesus, our only joy be thou,
> As thou our prize wilt be;
> Jesus, be thou our glory now,
> And through eternity.
>
> *Bernard of Clairvaux (1091–1153),*
> *translated by Edward Caswell (1814–1878)*

> We adore you, Lord Jesus Christ,
> in all the churches of the whole world
> and we bless you, for by means of your holy cross
> you have redeemed the world.
>
> *St Francis of Assisi (1182–1226)*

O Lord Jesus Christ, who art the way, the truth and the life, we pray thee not to suffer us to stray from thee, who art the way, nor to distrust thee, who art the truth, nor to rest on any other than thee, who art the life. Teach us to believe, what to do and wherein to take our rest.

Desiderius Erasmus (1467–1536)

Jesus, thou joy of loving hearts,
Thou fount of life, thou light of men,
From the best bliss that earth imparts,
we turn unfilled to thee again.

O Jesus, ever with us stay;
Make all our moments calm and bright;
Chase the dark night of sin away;
Shed o'er the world thy holy light.

Latin, probably eleventh century,
translated by Ray Palmer (1808–87)

Hail, hail, hail,
death, resurrection and return,
may happiness come!
Lord, you are resurrection and life.

You, crucifixion, are here!
You, resurrection, are here!
You, ascension, are here!
You, spirit-medicine of life, are here!

Prayer from Africa

O Christ our God, who are yourself the fulfilment of the law and the prophets, and did fulfil all the ordered purpose of the Father, always fill our hearts with joy and gladness, now and for ever, world without end.

Liturgy of St Chrysostom (347–407)

Whoever truly loves you, good Lord,
walks in safety down a royal road, far from the dangerous abyss;
and if he so much as stumbles, you, O Lord, stretch out
your hand.
Not one fall, or many, will cause you to abandon him
if he loves you
and does not love the things of this world,
because he walks in the vale of humility.

St Teresa of Avila (1515–1582)

Jesus! Your mercies are untold,
Through each returning day;
Your love exceeds a thousandfold
Whatever we can say.

Grant us, while here on earth we stay,
Your love to feel and know;
And when from hence we pass away,
To us your glory show.

Translated by Edward Caswell (1814–1878)

For personal meditation

In the Eastern Orthodox church the same short prayer, known as the Jesus prayer, is sometimes said over and over again as a help to meditation and inward prayer:

Lord Jesus Christ, Son of God , have mercy on me, a sinner.

O Lamb of God, who takest away the sin of the world, look
upon us and have mercy upon us; thou who art thyself both
victim and Priest, thyself both Reward and Redeemer, keep safe
from all evil those whom thou hast redeemed, O Saviour of the
world.

St Irenaeus (1130–1202)

Lord Jesus, think on me,
And purge away my sin;
From earthborn passions set me free,
And make me pure within.

Lord Jesus, think on me,
With care and woe oppressed;
Let me thy loving servant be,
And taste thy promised rest.

Lord Jesus, think on me,
Nor let me go astray;
Through darkness and perplexity
Point thou the heavenly way.

Lord Jesus, think on me,
That when the flood is past,
I may the eternal brightness see,
And share thy joy at last.

Synesius 375–430, translated by
Allen William Chatfield (1808–1896)

Longing for God and Wanting to be Like Him

My spirit has become dry because it forgets to feed on you.

St John of the Cross (1542–1591)

My Lord, I have nothing to do in this world but to seek and serve you; I have nothing to do with a heart and its affections but to breathe after you; I have nothing to do with my tongue and pen but to speak to you and for you and to publish your glory and your will.

Richard Baxter (1615–1691)

O God, our Judge and Saviour, set before us the vision of your purity and let us see our sins in the light of your holiness. Pierce our self-contentment with the shafts of your burning love and let love consume in us all that hinders us from perfect service of your cause; for your holiness is our judgement, so are your wounds our salvation.

William Temple (1881–1944)

O Lord our God, grant us grace to desire you with a whole heart, so that desiring you we may seek you with a whole heart, so that desiring you we may seek and find you; and so finding you, may love you; and loving you, may hate those sins which separate us from you, for the sake of Jesus Christ.

St Anselm (1033–1109)

Our Father, you called us and saved us in order to make us like your Son, our Lord Jesus Christ. Change us, day by day, by the work of your Holy Spirit so that we may grow more like him in all that we think and say and do, to his glory. Amen.

Yes, Lord Jesus Christ, whether we be far off or near, far away from you in the human swarm, in business, in earthly cares, in temporal joys, in merely human highness, or far from all this, forsaken, unappreciated in lowliness, and with this the nearer to you, do you draw us entirely to yourself.

Søren Kierkegaard (1813–1855)

God, the Father of our Lord Jesus Christ, increase in us faith and truth and gentleness and grant us part and lot among the saints.

St Polycarp (69–155)

Glorious God, give me grace to amend my life and to have an eye to mine end without grudge of death, which to them that die in thee, good Lord, is the fate of a wealthy life . . .

Give me, good Lord, a full faith, a firm hope and a fervent charity, a love to thee incomparable above the love to myself.

Give me, good Lord, a longing to be with thee, not for the avoiding of the calamities of this world, nor so much for the attaining of the joys of heaven, as for very love of thee.

Thomas More (1478–1535), from a prayer written a few days before his execution

I am only a spark
Make me a fire.
I am only a string
Make me a lyre.
I am only a drop
Make me a fountain.
I am only an ant hill
Make me a mountain.
I am only a feather
Make me a wing.
I am only a rag
Make me a king!

Prayer from Mexico

Give us, O Lord, a steadfast heart, which no unworthy affection may drag downwards; give us an unconquered heart, which no tribulation can wear out; give us an upright heart, which no unworthy purpose may tempt aside. Bestow upon us also, O Lord our God, understanding to know you, diligence to seek you, wisdom to find you and a faithfulness that may finally embrace you; through Jesus Christ our Lord.

St Thomas Aquinas (1225–1274)

You who are over us,
You who are one of us,
You who are—
Also within us,
May all see you—in me also,
May I prepare the way for you,
May I thank you for all that shall fall to my lot,
May I also not forget the needs of others...
Give me a pure heart—that I may see you,
A humble heart—that I may hear you,
A heart of love—that I may serve you,
A heart of faith—that I may abide in you.

Dag Hammarskjøld (1905–1961)

Father, make us more like Jesus. Help us to bear difficulty, pain, disappointment and sorrow, knowing that in your perfect working and design you can use such bitter experiences to shape our characters and make us more like our Lord. We look with hope for that day when we shall be wholly like Christ, because we shall see him as he is. Amen.

I am God's wheat. May I be ground by the teeth of the wild beasts until I become the fine wheat bread that is Christ's. My passions are crucified, there is no heat in my flesh, a stream flows murmuring inside me; deep down in me it says: Come to the Father.

St Ignatius of Antioch, before his martyrdom in 107

O Christ! who has shown us the beauty of eternal peace and the duty of inseparable love, grant that we may ever think humbly of ourselves, abounding in gentleness and pity towards all, that following the example of your humility and imitating you in all things, we may live in you and never depart from you.

From the Mozarabic Sacramentary

O Saviour Christ, who leads to eternal blessedness those who commit themselves to you: grant that we, being weak, may not presume to trust in ourselves, but may always have you before our eyes to follow as our guide; that you, who alone knows the way, may lead us to our heavenly desires. To you, with the Father and the Holy Ghost, be glory for ever.

Miles Coverdale (1488–1568)

God of your goodness, give me yourself,
for you are sufficient for me . . .
If I were to ask anything less
I should always be in want,
for in you alone do I have all.

Julian of Norwich (?1342–after 1413)

◆ *Telling God's Greatness* ◆

My heart praises the Lord;
my soul is glad because of God my Saviour!

FROM LUKE I

Worship and Praise

*When we speak to God about his greatness and love we forget ourselves,
and fill our minds and thoughts with his worth.*

Worship is the submission of all our nature to God. It is . . . the most selfless emotion of which our nature is capable and therefore the chief remedy of that self-centredness which is our original sin and the source of all actual sin.

William Temple (1881–1944)

Almighty God and Father, help us to be still in your presence, that we may know ourselves to be your people, and you to be our God; through Jesus Christ our Lord. Amen.

From New Every Morning

O God, your immensity fills the earth and the whole universe, but the universe itself cannot contain you, much less the earth, and still less the world of my thoughts.

Yves Raquin

O Father, my hope
O Son, my refuge
O Holy Spirit, my protection,
Holy Trinity, glory to thee.

*St Joannikios, from the service of Compline,
Eastern Orthodox Church*

You are holy, Lord, the only God, and your deeds are wonderful.
You are strong, you are great, you are the most high, you are almighty.
You, Holy Father, are King of heaven and earth.
You are Three and One, Lord God, all good.
You are good, all good, supreme good, Lord God, living and true.
You are love, you are wisdom. You are humility, you are endurance.
You are rest, you are peace.
You are joy and gladness, you are justice and moderation.
You are all our riches, and you suffice for us.
You are beauty, you are gentleness.
You are our protector, you are our guardian and defender.
You are courage, you are our haven and hope.
You are our faith, our great consolation.
You are our eternal life, great and wonderful Lord,
God almighty, merciful Saviour.

St Francis of Assisi (1182–1226)

You are the great God—he who is in heaven.
You are the creator of life, you make the regions above.
You are the hunter who hunts for souls.
You are the leader who goes before us.
You are he whose hands are with wounds.
You are he whose feet are with wounds.
You are he whose blood is a trickling stream,
You are he whose blood was spilled for us.

Prayer of a Xhosa Christian from Africa

May none of God's wonderful works keep silence,
night or morning.
Bright stars, high mountains, the depths of the seas,
sources of rushing rivers:
may all these break into song as we sing
to Father, Son and Holy Spirit.
May all the angels in the heavens reply: Amen! Amen! Amen!
Power, praise, honour, eternal glory to God, the only
Giver of grace.
Amen! Amen! Amen!

Third-century hymn

O God, our true life, to know you is life, to serve you is freedom, to enjoy you is a kingdom, to praise you is the joy and happiness of the soul. I praise and bless and adore you, I worship you, I glorify you. I give thanks to you for your great glory. I humbly beg you to live with me, to reign in me, to make this heart of mine a holy temple, a fit habitation for your divine majesty.

St Augustine (354–430)

O God and Father of all, whom the whole heavens adore : let the whole earth also worship you, all kingdoms obey you, all tongues confess and bless you, and the sons of men love you and serve you in peace; through Jesus Christ our Lord.

Eric Milner-White (died 1963)

May the Lord be blessed for ever for the great gifts
that he has continually heaped upon me,
and may all that he has created praise him. Amen

St Teresa of Avila (1515–1582)

You, my God,
are eternal and all powerful:
through you and in your time
the dew comes down,
the wind blows
and the rain falls.
You feed the living.
You uphold those who waver,
those torn apart by doubt,
those in anguish
and those, indeed, who risk falling into sin.
You restore the sick
and set the prisoners free;
you bring the dead back to life
according to the promise that you gave
to those who lie in darkness
in the earth.

Jewish prayer

All you big things bless the Lord
Mount Kilimanjaro and Lake Victoria
The Rift Valley and the Serengeti Plain
Fat baobabs and shady mango trees
All eucalyptus and tamarind trees
Bless the Lord
Praise and extol him for ever and ever.
All you tiny things bless the Lord
Busy black ants and hopping fleas
Wriggling tadpoles and mosquito larvae
Flying locusts and water drops
Pollen dust and tsetse flies
Millet seeds and dried dagga
Bless the Lord
Praise and extol him for ever and ever.

African canticle

Every living soul shall bless your name, O God.
All created things will give you glory and thanksgiving.
Eternally you are God, and no one can stand before you.
Who but you offers freedom and help,
nourishes and redeems us, sustains and saves us,
and at all times views with unfailing compassion
our sorrow and distress?
There is no one but you.

Jewish prayer

Great is, O King, our happiness
In thy kingdom, thou, our King.
We dance before thee, our King,
By the strength of thy kingdom.
May our feet be made strong;
Let us dance before thee, eternal.
Give you praise, all angels,
To him above who is worthy of praise.

Prayer in sacred dance of the Zulu Nazarite Church

O Lord, whose mercy reaches to the heavens, whose faithfulness knows no end: let the greatness of your love be known to us, that we may worship you with wonder, joy and thanksgiving. Amen.

From New Every Morning

◆ Lord our God, help us to give our minds to you in our worship, so that we may listen to what you have to say to us, and know your will.

Help us to give our hearts to you in our worship, so that we may really want to do what you require from us.

Help us to give our strength to you in our worship, so that through us your will may be done.

In the name of Jesus Christ our Lord. Amen.

From Contemporary Prayers for Church and School

All is silent
In the still and soundless air,
I fervently bow
To my almighty God.

Hsieh Ping-hsin, China

Glory to the Father, who has woven garments of glory
 for the resurrection;
worship to the Son, who was clothed in them at his rising;
thanksgiving to the Spirit, who keeps them for all the saints;
one nature in three, to him be praise.

Syrian Orthodox Church

Glorious Lord, I give you greeting!
Let the church and the chancel praise you,
Let the plain and the hillside praise you,
Let the dark and daylight praise you,
Let the birds and the honeybees praise you,
Let the male and the female praise you,
And I shall praise you, Lord of glory:
Glorious Lord, I give you greeting!

Welsh prayer

O Lord, ruler of the world,
even while the earth was without form you were King
and you will still reign when all things are brought to an end.
You are supreme and you will never be equalled.
You are power and might:
there is neither beginning nor end in you.

Jewish prayer

How great is your goodness, dear Lord!
Blessed are you for ever!
May all created things praise you, O God,
for loving us so much that we can truthfully speak
of your fellowship with mankind, even in this earthly exile;
and however virtuous we may be,
our virtue always depends on your great warmth
and generosity, dear Lord.
Your bounty is infinite.
How wonderful are your works!

St Teresa of Avila (1515–1582)

How great are God's riches! How deep are his wisdom and knowledge! Who can explain his decisions? Who can understand his ways.. . For all things were created by him, and all things exist through him and for him. To God be the glory for ever! Amen.

From Romans 11

Creator of the universe, watch over us and keep us in the light of your presence. May our praise continually blend with that of all creation, until we come together to the eternal joys which you promise in your love, through Jesus Christ our Lord. Amen.

Celtic prayer

We praise, we worship thee, O God,
Thy sovereign power we sound abroad:
All nations bow before thy throne,
And thee, the eternal Father, own.

Glory to thee, O God most high!
Father we praise thy majesty,
The Son, the Spirit we adore:
One Godhead, blest for evermore.

From Gell's Collection (1815)

Holy, holy, holy is the Lord God Almighty,
who is, who was and who is to come.
Let us praise and glorify him for ever.
You are worthy, Lord our God,
to receive praise and glory,
honour and blessing.
Let us praise and glorify him for ever.
Worthy is the Lamb that was slain to receive
divine power, wisdom and strength,
honour, glory and blessing.
Let us praise and glorify him for ever.
Bless the Lord
all you works of the Lord. Let us praise and glorify him for ever.
Praise our God all you his servants,
honour him, you who fear God, small and great.
Let us praise and glorify him for ever.
Let heaven and earth praise your glory:
all creatures in heaven, on earth and under the earth,
the sea and everything in it.
Let us praise and glorify him for ever.

St Francis of Assisi (1182–1226)

Sentences to help us to praise God:

How good is the God we adore,
Our faithful unchangeable Friend!
His love is as great as his power,
and knows neither measure nor end!

Joseph Hart (1712–1768)

Praise the Lord, my soul!
All my being, praise his holy name!

From Psalm 103

Accustom yourself, then, by degrees thus to worship him to beg his grace, to offer him your heart from time to time in the midst of your business, even every moment if you can. Do not always scrupulously confine yourself to certain rules, or particular forms of devotion, but act with a general confidence in God, with love and humility.

Brother Lawrence (1611–1691)

Our Lord and God! You are worthy to receive glory, honour and power. For you created all things, and by your will they were given existence and life.

From Revelation 4

Lord, you are to be blessed and praised;
all good things come from you:
you are in our words and in our thoughts, and in all that we do.
Amen.

St Teresa of Avila (1515–1582)

Let us, with a gladsome mind
Praise the Lord, for he is kind;
For his mercies shall endure,
Ever faithful, ever sure.

John Milton (1608–1674)

Glory to you, O God, Creator and Father,
for the universe in which we live,
and for men made in your own image.
Glory to you, O Christ,
who took a human body
and redeemed our fallen nature.
Glory to you, O Holy Spirit,
who made our bodies
the temple of your presence.
Glory to Father, Son and Holy Spirit,
whose will it is that we should be made whole
in body, mind and spirit.
Glory to God to all eternity.

George Appleton

It is good to sing praise to our God;
it is pleasant and right to praise him.

From Psalm 147

I'll praise my Maker while I've breath;
And when my voice is lost in death,
Praise shall employ my nobler powers:
My days of praise shall ne'er be past
While life, and thought, and being last
Or immortality endures.

Isaac Watts (1674–1748)

Praised be my Lord God for all his creatures, especially for our brother the sun, who brings us the day and who brings us the light; fair is he and shines with a very great splendour; O Lord, he signifies you to us!

Praised be my Lord for our sister the moon, and for the stars which he has set clear and lovely in heaven.

Praise be my Lord for our brother the wind, and for the air and clouds, calms and all weather by which you uphold life in all creatures.

Praised be my Lord for our sister water, who is very serviceable to us and humble and precious and clean.

Praised be my Lord for our brother fire, through whom you give us light in the darkness; and he is bright and pleasant and very mighty and strong;

Praised be my Lord for our mother the earth, who sustains us and keeps us and brings forth various fruits and flowers of many colours and grass.

Praise and bless the Lord, and give thanks to him and serve him with great humility.

St Francis of Assisi (1182–1226)

If my lips could sing as many songs
as there are waves in the sea:
if my tongue could sing as many hymns
as there are ocean billows:
if my mouth filled the whole firmament with praise:
if my face
shone like the sun and moon together:
if my hands
were to hover in the sky like powerful eagles
and my feet
ran across mountains as swiftly as the deer;
all that would not be enough
to pay you fitting tribute,
O Lord my God.

Jewish prayer

O most glorious and exalted Lord,
you are glorified in the heights above by ministers of fire and
spirit in most holy fashion,
yet in your love
you wished to be glorified by mankind on earth as well,
so that you might exalt our mortal race
and make us like supernal beings and brothers in your dominion.
Free us, Lord, in your compassion
from whatever cares hinder the worship of you,
and teach us to seek the kingdom and its righteousness
in accordance with your holy commandments that bring life;
and may we become worthy of that kingdom
along with all the saints who have done your will,
and may we sing your praises.

Maronite Shehimto, from the Syrian Orthodox Daily Office Book

To help me praise God:

Let all the world in every corner sing,
'My God and King!'
The heavens are not too high,
His praise may thither fly:
The earth is not too low,
His praises there may grow,
The church with psalms must shout,
No door can keep them out:
But, above all, the heart
Must bear the longest part.
Let all the world in every corner sing,
'My God and King!'

George Herbert (1593–1633)

O burning mountain, O chosen sun,
O perfect moon, O fathomless well,
O unattainable height, O clearness beyond measure,
O wisdom without end, O mercy without limit,
O strength beyond resistance, O crown of all majesty,
the humblest you created sings your praise.

Mechtild of Magdeburg (1207–1294)

Come, for your name fills our hearts with longing and is ever on
our lips;
yet who you are or what your nature is, we cannot say or know.
Come, Alone to the alone.
Come, for you are yourself the desire that is within me.
Come, my breath and my life.
Come, the consolation of my humble soul.
Come, my joy, my glory, my endless delight.

St Symeon (949–1022)

God's thought in a man's brain,
God's love in a man's heart,
God's pain in a man's body,
I worship.

Margaret Cropper (1886–1980)

We worship you, O Lord God, and give thanks to you for your great glory and power, which you show to your servants in your wonderful world. All the things which we enjoy are from your mighty hand, and you alone are to be praised for all the blessings of the life that now is. Make us thankful to you for all your mercies and more ready to serve you with all our heart; for the sake of Jesus Christ. Amen.

From The Narrow Way (1869)

Lord, we praise you:
you are leading us to life's summit
and giving us the exhilaration of victory
over ourselves,
over sin and death;
victory for ourselves and all mankind

Alan Gaunt

Worthy of praise from every mouth,
of confession from every tongue,
of worship from every creature,
is thy glorious name, O Father, Son, and Holy Ghost:
who didst create the world in thy grace
and by thy compassion didst save the world.
To thy majesty, O God, ten thousand times ten thousand
bow down and adore, singing and praising without ceasing and
saying,
Holy, holy, holy, Lord God of hosts;
Heaven and earth are full of thy praises;
Hosanna in the highest.

From the Nestorian Liturgy (fifth century)

O Lord our God, who has chased the slumber from our eyes, and once more
assembled us to lift up our hands unto you and to praise your just judgments,
accept our prayers and supplications, and give us faith and love. Bless our
coming in and our going out, our thoughts, words and works, and let us begin
this day with the praise of the unspeakable sweetness of your mercy. Hallowed
be your name. Your kingdom come; through Jesus Christ our Lord. Amen.

From the Greek Church Liturgy

O God of Love, we adore you...
You transfigure our disfigured faces,
you strive with our resistant clay,
you bring out of chaos, harmony,
O God of Love, we adore you...

From Prayer at Night

O praise God in his holy place,
praise him in the sky our tent,
praise him in the earth our mother;
Praise him for his mighty works,
praise him for his marvellous power.
Praise him with the beating of great drums,
praise him with the horn and rattle;
Praise him in the rhythm of the dance,
praise him in the clapping of the hands;
Praise him in the stamping of the feet,
praise him in the singing of the chant.
Praise him with the rushing of great rivers,
praise him with the music of the wind;
Praise him with the swaying of tall trees,
praise him with the singing of the sea.
Praise him, the one on whom we lean and do not fall;
Let everything that has breath praise the Lord.

A Psalm for Africa

O God, the Protector of them that hope in thee, grant, we beseech thee, that
we may without ceasing offer praise unto thy majesty; and that we may present
unto thee an abiding service, bestow upon us health of mind and body;
through Jesus Christ our Lord. Amen.

From the Leonine Sacramentary (fifth century)

I am happy because you have accepted me, dear Lord.
Sometimes I do not know what to do with all my happiness.
I swim in your grace like a whale in the ocean.
The saying goes: 'An ocean never dries up',
but we know that your grace also never fails.
Dear Lord, your grace is our happiness. Hallelujah!

Prayer from West Africa

You are God and we praise you,
you are the Lord and we acclaim you;
you are the eternal Father,
all creation worships you.
To you all angels, all the powers of heaven,
cherubim and seraphim sing in endless praise,
Holy, holy, holy, Lord God of power and might,
heaven and earth are full of your glory.
The glorious company of the apostles praise you,
the noble fellowship of prophets praise you,
the white-robed army of martyrs praise you.
Throughout the world the holy Church acclaims you,
Father of majesty unbounded;
your true and only Son, worthy of all worship,
and the Holy Spirit, advocate and guide.

From the Te Deum, Alternative Service Book 1980

Lord, we are humbled as we wonder at your greatness and power, your
gentleness and love. Help us to worship you in our words, in our thoughts and
in our lives. Through Jesus Christ our Lord. Amen.

Father we praise you
for your miracle of love
by which you used the death of Jesus on the cross
to set us free.
The place of defeat
has become the place of victory;
in the humiliation of one man
we are confronted by your glory;
where life was lost
we find eternal life.

Alan Gaunt

Thanksgiving

Thou hast given so much to me,
Give one thing more—a grateful heart;
Not thankful when it pleases me,
As if thy blessings had spare days;
But such a heart whose very pulse may be
Thy praise.

George Herbert (1593–1633)

O God, we thank you for this earth, our home; for the wide sky and the blessed sun, for the salt sea and the running water, for the everlasting hills and the never-resting winds, for trees and the common grass underfoot.

We thank you for our senses by which we hear the songs of birds, and see the splendour of the summer fields, and taste of the autumn fruits, and rejoice in the feel of the snow, and smell the breath of the spring.

Grant us a heart wide open to all this beauty; and save our souls from being so blind that we pass unseeing when even the common thornbush is aflame with your glory, O God our creator, who lives and reigns for ever and ever.

Walter Rauschenbusch (1861–1918)

◆ When I wake up in the morning,
thank you, God, for being there.
When I come to school each day,
thank you, God, for being there.
When I am playing with my friends,
thank you, God, for being there.
And when I go to bed at night,
thank you, God, for being there.

From Infant Prayer

O thou who coverest the high places with waters,
who settest the sand as a bound to the sea and dost uphold
all things:
the sun sings thy praises, the moon gives thee glory,
Every creature offers a hymn to thee, his author and creator
for ever.

Eastern Orthodox Church

Thank you, Lord, for making all things beautiful in their time, and for putting eternity into our hearts.

O most high Almighty, good Lord God, creator of the universe, watch over us and keep us in the light of your presence.

May our praise continually blend with that of all creation, until we come together to the eternal joys which you promise in your love, through Jesus Christ our Lord. Amen.

O God our Father, we would thank you for all the bright things of life. Help us to see them, and to count them, and to remember them, that our lives may flow in ceaseless praise; for the sake of Jesus Christ our Lord.

J.H. Jowett (1841–1923)

Lord God, thank you for loving us
even when we turn away from you.
We are grateful for your constant care
and concern.
Though we feel unworthy of your great love,
we thank you that through our weaknesses
you give us strength;
and in our wanderings you show us the way.

Author unknown

Almighty God, Father of all mercies, we your unworthy servants give you humble and hearty thanks for all your goodness and loving kindness to us and to all men. We bless you for our creation, preservation, and all the blessings of this life; but above all for your immeasurable love in the redemption of the world by our Lord Jesus Christ, for the means of grace and for the hope of glory.

And give us, we pray, such a sense of all your mercies that our hearts may be unfeignedly thankful, and that we show forth your praise, not only with our lips but in our lives, by giving up ourselves to your service, and by walking before you in holiness and righteousness all our days; through Jesus Christ our Lord, to whom, with you and the Holy Spirit, be all honour and glory, for ever and ever. Amen.

Alternative Service Book (1980)

Glory be to God in the highest, the Creator, and Lord of heaven and earth, the Preserver of all things, the Father of mercies, who so loved mankind as to send his only begotten Son into the world, to redeem us from sin and misery, and to obtain for us everlasting life.

Accept, O gracious God, our praises and our thanksgivings for your infinite mercies towards us. And teach us, O Lord, to love you more and serve you better; through Jesus Christ our Lord. Amen.

John Hamilton (1512–1571)

In this hour of this day, fill us, O Lord, with your mercy, that rejoicing throughout the whole day, we may take delight in your praise; through Jesus Christ our Lord. Amen.

From the Sarum Breviary

Lord, as your mercies do surround us, so grant that our return of duty may abound; and let this day manifest our gratitude by doing something well-pleasing unto you; through Jesus Christ our Lord. Amen.

Edward Lake (1641–1704)

We thank you, O Father, for your readiness to hear and to forgive; for your great love to us, in spite of our unworthiness; for the many blessings we enjoy above our deserving, hoping, or asking. You have been so good to us in our ingratitude, thoughtlessness, and forgetfulness of you. For your pity, long-suffering, gentleness and tenderness, we bow our heads in humble thankfulness of heart. We worship you who are infinite love, infinite compassion, infinite power. Accept our praise and gratitude; through Jesus Christ our Lord and Saviour. Amen.

C.J.N. Child

For personal meditation

Using these verses as inspiration, give thanks to God in your own words—or in silence—for all his goodness:

Praise the Lord, my soul!
All my being praise his holy name!
Praise the Lord, my soul, and do not forget how kind he is.
He forgives all my sins and heals all my diseases.
He keeps me from the grave and blesses me with love and mercy.
He fills my life with good things.

From Psalm 103

Thank you, living God, for your undying love,
ever at work for us and the whole world,
made known in every age;
for its triumphant victory
in the cross and resurrection of Jesus Christ,
and for its continuing presence with us,
to be proclaimed to the ends of the earth
through your Holy Spirit.

Alan Gaunt

Honour and praise be unto you, O Lord our God, for all your tender mercies again bestowed upon us throughout another week.

Continual thanks be unto you for creating us in your own likeness; for redeeming us by the precious blood of your dear Son when we were lost; and for sanctifying us with the Holy Spirit.

For your help and succour in our necessities, your protection in many dangers of body and soul; your comfort in our sorrows, and for sparing us in life, and giving us so large a time to repent. For all the benefits, O most merciful Father, that we have received of your goodness alone, we thank you; and we beseech you to grant us always your Holy Spirit, that we may grow in grace, in steadfast faith, and perseverance in all good works, through Jesus Christ our Lord.

John Knox (1505–1572)

I thank you for anything which happened to me which made me feel that life is really and truly worth living.

I thank you for all the laughter which was in today.

I thank you, too, for any moment in which I saw the seriousness and the meaning of life.

I thank you very specially for those I love, and for those who love me, and for all the difference it has made to me to know them, and for all the happiness it brings to me to be with them...

Through Jesus Christ my Lord. Amen.

William Barclay (1907–1978)

We gratefully acknowledge... that you are the Eternal One, our God, and the God of our fathers for evermore; the Rock of our life and the Shield of our salvation. You are he who exists to all ages. We will therefore render thanks unto you, and declare your praise, for our lives, which are delivered into your hand, and for our souls, which are confided to your care; for your goodness, which is displayed to us daily; for your wonders, and your bounty which are at all times given unto us. You are the most gracious, for your mercies never fail; and you are the most compassionate, for your kindnesses never cease. Evermore do we hope in you, O Lord our God. Amen.

From the Jewish Book of Service, Daily Prayers

Thank you, O God, for all the help you have given me today.
Thank you for
Keeping me safe all through today;
Helping me to do my work through today
Giving me strength to conquer my temptations all through
today.
Thank you for
My home and all that it has been to me;
My loved ones and all the circle of those most dear;
My friends and comrades with whom I have worked and talked.
Thank you for
Any kindness I have received;
Any help that was given to me;
Any sympathy that was shown to me.
Help me to lay myself down to sleep tonight, with a glad and
grateful heart.
This I ask through Jesus Christ my Lord. Amen.

William Barclay (1907–1978)

We thank you, O Lord and Master, for teaching us how to pray simply and sincerely to you, and for hearing us when we so call upon you. We thank you for saving us from our sins and sorrows, and for directing all our ways this day. Lead us ever onwards to yourself; for the sake of Jesus Christ our Lord and Saviour. Amen.

Father John of the Russian Church (nineteenth century)

 *Forgiveness*

Forgive us the wrongs we have done, as we forgive the
wrongs that others have done to us.

FROM MATTHEW 6

Asking God for Forgiveness

Forgiving and asking for forgiveness are necessary growing points in a world where we often wrong one another as well as wronging God. The root sin against God is wanting to go my own way instead of obeying him. Sin must be repented of and forgiven by God if we are to know full freedom and come into God's family.

Come, let us to the Lord our God
With contrite hearts return;
Our God is gracious, nor will leave
the desolate to mourn.

John Morison (1750–1798)

Lord, I feel guilty and unclean. It seems as if my constant wrongdoings have made me ashamed to speak to you. I am truly sorry for my sins. Please forgive me, accept me as your child, and renew me, even though I don't deserve it. Thank you for Jesus' blood, which makes me clean. I ask you to forgive me for his sake. Amen.

Almighty and most merciful Father, we have erred and strayed from thy ways like lost sheep, we have followed too much the devices and desires of our own hearts, we have offended against thy holy laws. We have left undone those things which we ought to have done, and we have done those things which we ought not to have done, and there is no health in us. But thou, O Lord, have mercy upon us, miserable offenders; spare thou them, O God, which confess their faults; restore thou them which are penitent, according to thy promises declared unto mankind in Christ Jesus our Lord. And grant, O most merciful Father, for his sake, that we may hereafter live a godly, righteous, and sober life, to the glory of thy holy Name.

From Morning and Evening Prayer (1552)

Lord,
help me to face the truth about myself.
Help me to hear my words as others hear them,
to see my face as others see me;
let me be honest enough to recognize my impatience and conceit;
let me recognize my anger and selfishness;
give me sufficient humility to accept my own weaknesses
for what they are.
Give me the grace—at least in your presence—
to say, 'I was wrong—forgive me.'

Frank Topping

◆ Our Father in heaven:
Please forgive me for the wrongs I have done:
For bad temper and angry words:
For being greedy and wanting the best for myself;
For making other people unhappy:
Forgive me, heavenly Father.

Dick Williams

For personal meditation:

We may want to use our own words to ask God's forgiveness.
Here are some sentences to help us:

Repentance ... is the turning of the mind, and with the mind the
imagination, the affections and the will, away from self and sin
and towards God ... We look towards God in gratitude for his
loving-kindness, towards Jesus in his death for our sins, towards
our own true self in what it is meant to become.

Michael Ramsey

If we confess our sins to God, he will keep his promise and do
what is right: he will forgive us our sins and purify us from all
wrongdoing ... The blood of Jesus, his Son, purifies us
from every sin.

From 1 John

Upon that place stood a Cross, and a little below, in the bottom, a Sepulchre. So I saw in my dream, that just as Christian came up with the Cross, his burden loosed from off his shoulders, and fell from off his back, and began to tumble, and so continued to do, till it came to the mouth of the Sepulchre, where it fell in, and I saw it no more. Then was Christian glad and lightsome.

John Bunyan (1628–1688)

Almighty and everlasting God, who hatest nothing that thou hast made, and dost forgive the sins of all them that are penitent: Create and make in us new and contrite hearts, that we worthily lamenting our sins, and acknowledging our wretchedness, may obtain of thee, the God of all mercy, perfect remission and forgiveness, through Jesus Christ our Lord.

From the Book of Common Prayer Ash Wednesday service

Almighty...
Forgive
My doubt,
My anger,
My pride.
By thy mercy
Abase me,
By thy strictness
Raise me up.

Dag Hammarskjøld (1905–1961)

I am heartily sorry, and beg pardon for my sins, especially for my little respect, and for wandering in my thoughts when in your presence, and for my continual infidelitys to your graces; for all which I beg pardon, by the merits of the Blood you shed for them.

Lady Lucy Herbert (1669–1744)

I have just hung up; why did he telephone?
I don't know ... Oh, I get it ...
I talked a lot and listened very little.
Forgive me, Lord, it was a monologue and not a dialogue.
I explained my idea and did not get his;
Since I didn't listen, I learned nothing,
Since I didn't listen, I didn't help,
Since I didn't listen, we didn't communicate.
Forgive me, Lord, for we were connected,
and now we are cut off.

Michel Quoist

Forgive me my sins, O Lord; forgive me the sins of my youth and the sins of mine age, the sins of my soul and the sins of my body, my secret and my whispering sins, my presumptuous and my crying sins, the sins that I have done to please myself and the sins that I have done to please others. Forgive me those sins that I know and those sins which I know not; forgive them, O Lord, forgive them all of thy great goodness.

From Private Devotions (1560)

Rock of ages, cleft for me,
Let me hide myself in thee:
Let the water and the blood
From thy riven side which flowed,
Be of sin the double cure—
Cleanse me from its guilt and power.

Augustus Toplady (1740–1778)

O most merciful Father, who dost put away the sins of those who truly repent, we come before thy throne in the name of Jesus Christ, that for his sake alone thou wilt have compassion upon us, and let not our sins be a cloud between thee and us.

John Colet (1467–1519)

O Lord our God, you know who we are; men with good consciences and with bad, persons who are content and those who are discontented, the certain and uncertain, Christians by conviction and Christians by convention, those who believe and those who half-believe and those who disbelieve...

But now we all stand before you, in all our differences, yet alike in that we are all in the wrong with you and with one another, that we must all one day die, that we would be lost without your grace, but also in that your grace is promised and made available to us all in your dear Son, Jesus Christ.

Karl Barth (1886–1968)

Great Spirit of the islands and countries, Father of our Lord Jesus Christ, we confess that we have seriously sinned in words, deeds and thoughts. Forgive us, please, and gently guide us in the ways of peace and love. Teach us to be more caring and loving to our families and to others, and to be more responsible in the task committed to us. Amen.

Prayer from Karibati, Micronesia

◆ Forgive me for the angry words
   I didn't mean to say,
   Forgive me for the fit of sulks
   That spoiled a happy day.

   Forgive me for the muddle
   That I left upon the floor,
   The tea I wouldn't eat,
   The hasty way I slammed the door.

   Forgive me for my selfishness
   And all my little sins,
   And help me to be better
   When another day begins.

   Kathleen Partridge

Almighty and merciful God, the fountain of all goodness, who knows the thoughts of our hearts, we confess that we have sinned against you, and done what you see as evil. Wash us, we implore you, from the stains of our past sins, and give us grace and power to put away all hurtful things so that, being delivered from the bondage of sin, we may produce the good fruits of repentance.

Alcuin of York (735–804)

Forgive us, O Christ, for all our wanderings.
Forgive us for not listening to your voice calling us into
right ways.
Forgive us for our complaining and our worrying that have made
us lose our trust in you.
Forgive us for anger and selfishness and for greed.
For all these we are sorry and pray that they may be taken
from us.

A. Murray Smith

O Holy God, whose mercy and pity made thee descend from the high throne down into this world for our salvation: mercifully forgive us all the sins that we have done and thought and said. Send us cleanness of heart and purity of soul; restore us with thy Holy Spirit, that we may henceforth live virtuously and love thee with all our hearts; through Jesus Christ thy Son.

Richard Rolle (1290–1349)

At first light, O Lord, the newspaper and radio remind us that we live in a world of many conflicting interests; we are given the words of world leaders; we learn of accidents and anxieties, of illnesses and poverty; we hesitate to commit little children to the ways of this dangerous world.

O God, who wills not the death of a sinner, but that he should be converted and live: forgive the sins of us who turn to you with all our heart, and grant us the grace of eternal life, through Jesus Christ our Lord.

Scots Celtic prayer

We have not fully learned how to make peace;
we have taken advantage of each other continually;
we have judged each other without true knowledge;
we have set up barriers of pride in possessions;
we have divided people by their skin colour;
we have even shown religious superiority.
Forgive us, merciful God, Father of our bodies,
minds and spirits—
let us commit our whole personalities to You.

Rita Snowden

O almighty God, the searcher of all hearts, who hast declared that all such as shall draw nigh to thee with their lips when their hearts are far from thee are an abomination unto thee: cleanse, we beseech thee, the thoughts of our hearts by the inspiration of thy Holy Spirit, that no wandering, vain, nor idle thoughts may put out of our minds that reverence and godly fear that becomes all those who come into thy presence.

Jonathan Swift (1665–1745)

◆ Dear Lord Jesus, thank you for taking care of me and loving me all through this day. I know that I have not been as good as I should all the time. Sometimes I have been lazy or disobedient and wanted my own way. Sometimes I have been quarrelsome and lost my temper. I have been greedy and selfish, wanting all the best things for myself. Please forgive me and help me to be better tomorrow. Thank you, Lord Jesus, for everything good and lovely today, but most of all, thank you for yourself and your great love for me.

Nina Hinchy

We beseech you, good Lord, that it may please you to give us true repentance; to forgive us all our sins, negligences, and ignorances; and to endue us with the grace of your Holy Spirit, to amend our lives according to your holy Word.

Thomas Cranmer (1489–1556) from The Litany (1544)

Wilt thou forgive that sin where I begun,
Which is my sin, though it were done before?
Wilt thou forgive those sins, through which I run,
And do run still: though still I do deplore?
When thou hast done, thou hast not done,
For I have more.

Wilt thou forgive that sin by which I have won
Others to sin? and made my sin their door?
Wilt thou forgive that sin which I did shun
A year or two: but wallowed in a score?
When thou hast done, thou hast not done,
For I have more.

I have a sin of fear, that when I have spun
My last thread, I shall perish on the shore;
Swear by thyself, that at my death thy Son
Shall shine as he shines now and heretofore;
And, having done that, thou hast done,
I fear no more.

John Donne (1573–1631)

We beseech you, O Lord our God,
be patient with us sinners.
You who know our weakness,
protect the work of your hands
now and in times to come,
deliver us from all temptation
and all danger
and from the powers of darkness of this world,
and bring us
into the kingdom of your only Son and our God.
For to your most holy name
be the glory,
Father, Son and Holy Spirit,
now and for ever, to the ages of ages. Amen.

Eastern Orthodox Church

Forgiving Others and Being Forgiven by Them

*Unless we are ready to let God help us to forgive others, we block the
channel through which God's forgiveness comes to us.
As we think, perhaps with anger, of one who has wronged us, we can tell
God every detail and ask him to let his willingness to forgive
flow into us too.*

Here are some verses to help us: Jesus said:

When you stand and pray, forgive anything you may have
against anyone, so that your Father in heaven will forgive the
wrongs you have done.

From Mark 11

If you forgive others the wrongs they have done to you, your
Father in heaven will also forgive you. But if you do not forgive
others, then your Father will not forgive the wrongs
you have done.

From Matthew 6

Get rid of all bitterness, passion and anger... Instead, be kind
and tender-hearted to one another, and forgive one another, as
God has forgiven you through Christ. Since you are God's dear
children, you must try to be like him.

From Ephesians 4

O Lord Jesus, because, being full of foolishness, we often sin and have to ask
pardon, help us to forgive as we would be forgiven; neither mentioning old
offences committed against us, nor dwelling upon them in thought, nor being
influenced by them in heart; but loving our brother freely, as you freely loved
us. For your name's sake.

Christina Rossetti (1830–1894)

Take away, O Lord, from our hearts all suspiciousness, indignation, anger and contention, and whatever is calculated to wound charity and to lessen brotherly love.

Have mercy, O Lord, have mercy on those who seek your mercy; give grace to the needy; make us to live so that we may be found worthy to enjoy the fruition of your grace and that we may attain to eternal life.

Thomas à Kempis (1380–1471)

Lord Jesus, help us to be kind and tender-hearted to one another, forgiving one another, as God, for your sake, has forgiven us.

As the first martyr prayed to you for his murderers, O Lord, so we fall before you and pray; forgive all who hate and maltreat us and let not one of them perish because of us, but may all be saved by your grace, O God, the all-bountiful.

Eastern Orthodox Church

Dear God, I find it so hard to forgive those who are unkind to me, or who blame me for the things which are not my fault. I go on bearing a grudge against them and even when they try to make it up I feel bitter and hard.

I know this is wrong. When Peter asked Jesus how many times he ought to forgive someone who had wronged him, Jesus said he must go on and on forgiving. Jesus even prayed for forgiveness for those who crucified him. Please help me to be more like him and be willing to forgive.

Nancy Martin

Give us grace, dear Lord, to receive forgiveness from others when we have wronged them. Take away our pride and resentment and give us the humility and courage to accept fully and freely the forgiveness that they offer to us. For Jesus' sake.

I offer also for all those whom I have in any way grieved, vexed, oppressed and scandalized, by word or deed, knowingly or unknowingly; that thou mayest equally forgive us all our sins, and all our offences against each other.

Thomas More (1478–1535)

O Lord, remember not only the men and women of good will, but also those of ill will. But do not remember all the suffering they have inflicted on us; remember the fruits we have bought, thanks to this suffering—our comradeship, our loyalty, our courage, our generosity, the greatness of heart which has grown out of all this, and when they come to judgment let all the fruits which we have borne be their forgiveness.

Prayer written by an unknown prisoner in Ravensbruck concentration camp and left by the body of a dead child

Give us, O Lord, a humble spirit, that we may never presume upon your mercy, but live always as those who have been much forgiven. Make us tender and compassionate towards those who are overtaken by temptation, considering ourselves, how we have fallen in times past and may fall yet again. Make us watchful and sober-minded, looking ever unto you for grace to stand upright, and to persevere unto the end; through your Son, Jesus Christ our Lord.

Dean Vaughan (1816–1907)

Lord,
Why is it so difficult
To make peace with each other?
No wonder there are wars.
Is it pride that holds my mouth tight shut,
A childish feeling
that I am not the one who should apologize?
It wasn't my fault?
In these flare-ups
What does it matter whose fault it is?
The only thing that matters is love and harmony.
Lord, turning my back in anger is weakness,
It reduces me as a human being.
Give me the courage,
The stature
To say, 'I'm sorry.'

Frank Topping

◆ *Asking God* ◆

Don't worry about anything, but in all your prayers ask
God for what you need, always asking him with a
thankful heart.

FROM PHILIPPIANS 4

We ask God for many things, but perhaps our prayers for spiritual help are the most important requests we can make.

Interceding does not mean reminding God of things he has forgotten to do. It is placing ourselves at the heart of a troubled situation.

Anthony Bloom

Prayers for Love

Happy is he who loves you and loves his friend in you and loves his enemy in your name! It is surely he alone who never loses a dear one because all are dear to him through him who is never lost, through our God;

God who created heaven and earth fills them with his presence, just as he created them by filling them with himself...

St Augustine (354–430)

O God, the well of love and Father of all, make us so to love that we know not but to love every man in Jesus Christ your Son our Lord.

Fourteenth-century collect

Grant, most gracious God, that we may love and seek you always and everywhere, above all things, and for your sake, in the life present and at length find you and forever hold you fast in the life to come. Grant this for the sake of Jesus Christ our Lord.

Thomas Bradwardine (1290–1349)

◆ Put love into our hearts, Lord Jesus — love for you; love for those around us; love for those we find it hard to like.

From Talking to God

Lord, lift me up, put me in the palm of your hand and unlock
the sealed chamber of my heart.
Let love come in.
Lord I have been walking,
Been walking in the dark . . .
Lord, hold my hand, I'm tired of stumbling in dark alleys.
Put me in the palm of your hand.
Lord, lift me up.
Show me that love is still around.
Lord, lift me up.
Show me that love is still around . . .

James Matthews

O God, who gives to your children liberally, preserve us from all envy at the
good of our neighbour and from every form of jealousy.

Teach us to rejoice in what others have and we have not, to delight in
what they achieve and we cannot accomplish, to be glad in all that they enjoy
and we do not partake of; and so fill us daily more completely with love,
through our Saviour Jesus Christ.

William Knight (1836–1916)

Verses to help meditation and quiet prayer:

Love is patient and kind; it is not jealous or conceited or proud;
love is not ill-mannered or selfish or irritable; love does not keep
a record of wrongs; love is not happy with evil, but is happy with
the truth. Love never gives up; and its faith, hope, and patience
never fail. Love is eternal.

From 1 Corinthians 13

O Lord, give us more charity, more self-denial, more likeness to you. Teach us to sacrifice our comforts to others and our likings for the sake of doing good. Make us kindly in thought, gentle in word, generous in deed. Teach us that it is better to give than to receive, better to forget ourselves than to put ourselves forward, better to minister than to be ministered unto. And to you, the God of Love, be all glory and praise, now and for ever.

Henry Alford (1810–1871)

Almighty God, and most merciful Father, who has given us a new commandment that we should love one another, give us also grace that we may fulfil it. Make us gentle, courteous and forbearing. Direct our lives so that we may look each to the good of the other in word and deed. And hallow all our friendships by the blessing of your Spirit, for his sake who loved us and gave himself for us, Jesus Christ our Lord.

Bishop Westcott (1825–1901)

Make us ever eager, Lord, to share the good things that we have. Grant us such a measure of your Spirit that we may find more joy in giving than in getting. Make us ready to give cheerfully without grudging, secretly without praise, and in sincerity without looking for gratitude, for Jesus Christ's sake.

John Hunter (1849–1917)

Fill us, we pray, with your light and life that we may show forth your wondrous glory. Grant that your love may so fill our lives that we may count nothing too small to do for you, nothing too much to give and nothing too hard to bear.

St Ignatius Loyola (1491–1556)

O Lord our God, grant us grace to desire you with our whole heart, that so desiring, we may seek and find you; and so finding you we may love you; and loving you we may hate those sins from which you have redeemed us; for the sake of Jesus Christ.

St Anselm (1033–1109)

◆ Lord, I know
   that one of the best ways I can show
   my love for you
   Is by loving other people.
   Sometimes this is easy—when I'm with people I like—
   Please help me when loving is hard,
   when people are unkind,
   when they don't understand,
   when I just don't like them.
   Teach me to love as you loved
   when you were walking about in Palestine—
   Teach me to love as you love now—
   Everyone
   Always.

Brother Kenneth and Sister Geraldine

◆ Lord of the loving heart, may mine be loving too,
   Lord of the gentle hands, may mine be gentle too.
   Lord of the willing feet, may mine be willing too,
   So may I grow more like you
   In all I say or do

From All our Days

Dear Lord, let us start our work in faith, continue in obedience and finish with love.

Prayer found in a church in the English Quantock Hills

Write your blessed name, O Lord, upon my heart, there to remain so indelibly engraved, that no prosperity, no adversity shall ever move me from your love. Be to me a strong tower of defence, a comforter in tribulation, a deliverer in distress, a very present help in trouble and a guide to heaven through the many temptations and dangers of this life.

Thomas à Kempis (1380–1471)

O God, mercifully grant unto us that the fire of your love may burn up in us all things that displease you and make us meet for your heavenly kingdom.

From the Roman Breviary

Thanks be to you, Lord Jesus Christ,
for all the benefits which you have won for us,
for all the pains and insults which you have borne for us.
O most merciful Redeemer, Friend and Brother,
may we know you more clearly,
love you more dearly,
and follow you more nearly,
day by day.

Richard of Chichester (1197–1253)

Let my heart always think of him
Let my head always bow down to him
Let my lips always sing his praise
Let my hands always worship him
Let my body always serve him with love.
O Lord of grace, immense like a mountain peak full of goodness!
Do thou forgive my sins!
When my spirit leaves my body
Let me behold thy divine face, radiant like the lotus
even on the cross on which thy enemies nailed thee,
And let my heart rejoice in thy sacred name.
Grant thou this boon to me, O Lord!

Krishna Pillai, India

Grant unto us your servants
To our God—a heart of flame
To our fellow men—a heart of love
To ourselves—a heart of steel.

St Augustine (354–430) (adapted)

Behold, Lord, an empty vessel that needs to be filled. My Lord, fill it. I am weak in the faith; strengthen me. I am cold in love; warm me and make me fervent that my love may go out to my neighbour. I do not have a strong and firm faith; at times I doubt and am unable to trust you altogether. O Lord, help me. Strengthen my faith and trust in you. In you I have sealed the treasures of all I have. I am poor; you are rich and came to be merciful to the poor. I am a sinner; you are upright. With me there is an abundance of sin, in you is the fulness of righteousness. Therefore I will remain with you of whom I can receive but to whom I may not give. Amen.

Martin Luther (1483–1546)

O God, the God of all goodness and of all grace, who is worthy of a greater love than we can either give or understand, fill our hearts, we beseech you, with such love towards you, that nothing may seem too hard for us to do or suffer in obedience to your will; and grant that thus loving you we may become daily more like unto you and finally obtain the crown of life, which you have promised to those that love you; through Jesus Christ our Lord.

From the Farnham Hostel Manual (nineteenth century)

O Christ, you came so that we might have life and have it
more abundantly,
grant us power in our love,
strength in our humility,
purity in our zeal,
kindness in our laughter,
and your peace in our hearts at all times.

J.L. Cowie

O Almighty God, from whom every good prayer comes, and who pours out on all who desire it the spirit of grace and supplications; deliver us, when we draw near to you, from coldness of heart and wanderings of mind; that with steadfast thoughts and kindled affections we may worship you in spirit and in truth, through Jesus Christ our Lord.

William Bright (1824–1901)

O Lord God, my All in all, Life of my life and Spirit of my spirit, look in mercy upon me and so fill me with your Holy Spirit that my heart shall have no room for love of aught but you...

Sadhu Sundar Singh (1889–?1929)

Grant to me, O Lord, to know what I ought to know, to love what I ought to love, to praise what delights you most, to value what is precious in your sight, to hate what is offensive to you. Do not suffer me to judge according to the sight of my eyes nor to pass sentence according to the hearing of ignorant men; but to discern with true judgement between things visible and spiritual and above all things to enquire what is the good pleasure of your will.

Thomas à Kempis (1380–1471)

Set our hearts on fire with love to you, O Christ our God, that in its flame we may love you with all our heart, with all our mind, with all our soul and with all our strength and our neighbours as ourselves, so that, keeping your commandments, we may glorify you, the giver of all good gifts.

Eastern Orthodox Church

Prayers for Light

Praise God who sends us the light of heaven.

Prayer used in Indian homes at the lighting of the lamps

Almighty God, we invoke you, the fountain of everlasting light and entreat you to send forth your truth into our hearts and to pour upon us the glory of your brightness: through Jesus Christ our Lord. Amen.

From The Book of Worship

O God, who in the work of creation commanded the light to shine out of darkness: we pray that the light of the glorious gospel of Christ may shine into the hearts of men everywhere dispelling the darkness of their ignorance and unbelief and revealing to them the knowledge of your glory in the face of Jesus Christ our Lord. Amen.

Prayer based on 2 Corinthians 4

Eternal Light, shine into our hearts,
Eternal Goodness, deliver us from evil,
Eternal Power, be our support,
Eternal Wisdom, scatter the darkness of our ignorance,
Eternal Pity, have mercy on us;
    that with all our heart and mind and soul and strength we may
seek your face and be brought by your infinite mercy to your
holy presence, through Jesus Christ our Lord.

Alcuin of York (735–804)

O Lord, give us we beseech you in the name of Jesus Christ your Son our
Lord, that love which can never cease, that will kindle our lamps but not
extinguish them, that they may burn in us and enlighten others.

Do you, O Christ, our dearest Saviour, yourself kindle our lamps that
they may evermore shine in your temple and receive unquenchable light from
you that will enlighten our darkness and lessen the darkness of the world.

St Columba (521–597)

As our tropical sun gives forth its light, so let the rays from your face enter
every nook of my being and drive away all darkness within.

Prayer from the Philippines

Shine into our hearts, O loving Master, by the pure light of the knowledge of
yourself and open the eyes of our minds to your teaching: that in all things we
may both think and act according to your good pleasure, and meditating on
those things that are holy, may continually live in your light.

From the Dawn Office of the Eastern and Leonine Churches

Lord, give us weak eyes for things which are of no account and clear eyes for
all your truth.

Søren Kierkegaard (1813–1855)

O Lord our God, in your Son our Lord Jesus Christ you have made us your children. We have heard your call and come now to praise you, to hear your word and to call on you. Be you yourself in our midst, so that this may be an hour of light, in which we see heaven opened and then a little brightness on this dark earth; through Jesus Christ our Lord. Amen.

Karl Barth (1886–1968)

My dearest Lord,
be thou a bright flame before me,
be thou a guiding star above me,
be thou a smooth path beneath me,
be thou a kindly shepherd behind me,
today and for evermore.

St Columba (521–597)

O God, who by your almighty word does enlighten every man that comes into the world, enlighten, we beseech you, the hearts of us, your servants, by the glory of your grace, that we may ever think such things as are worthy and pleasing to your Majesty and love you with a perfect heart, through Jesus Christ our Lord.

Alcuin of York (735–804)

The God and Father of our Lord Jesus Christ open all our eyes, that we may see that blessed hope to which we are called; that we may altogether glorify the only true God and Jesus Christ; whom he has sent down to us from heaven; to whom with the Father and the Holy Spirit be rendered all honour and glory to all eternity.

Bishop Jewell (1522–1571)

O Lord, greatest and most true light, whence the light of the day does spring! O Wisdom of the eternal Father, lighten my mind, that I may see only those things that please you and may be blinded to all other things. Grant that I may walk in your ways and that nothing else may be light and pleasant.

John Bradford (1510–1555)

O thou great Chief, light a candle in my heart, that I may see what is therein and sweep the rubbish from thy dwelling place.

An African schoolgirl's prayer

Dear Jesus, help us to spread your fragrance everywhere we go.

Flood our souls with your spirit and life.

Penetrate and possess our whole being so utterly that our lives may only be a radiance of yours.

Shine through us and be so in us that every soul we come in contact with may feel your presence in our soul.

Let them look up and see no longer us but only Jesus! Stay with us and then we shall begin to shine as you shine; so to share as to be a light to others; the light, O Jesus, will be all from you, none of it will be ours; it will be you shining on others through us . . .

John Henry Newman (1801–1890),
used daily by Mother Teresa's Missionaries of Charity

To you, O Son of God, Lord Jesus Christ, as you pray to the eternal Father, we pray, make us one in him. Lighten our personal distress and that of our society. Receive us into the fellowship of those who believe. Turn our hearts, O Christ, to everlasting truth and healing harmony.

Philip Melanchthon (1497–1560)

◆ Lord Jesus, you are my light
  In the darkness,
  You are my warmth
  In the cold,
  You are my happiness
  In sorrow . . .

Author unknown

Almighty Lord our God, direct our steps into the way of peace and strengthen our hearts to obey your commandments; may the Day-spring visit us from on high and give light to those who sit in darkness and in the shadow of death; that they may adore you for your mercy, follow you for your truth, desire you for your sweetness, who are the blessed Lord God of Israel.

Ancient collect

Eternal God,
the light of the minds that know you,
the life of the souls that love you,
the strength of the wills that serve you;
help us so to know you that we may truly love you,
so to love you that we may fully serve you,
whom to serve is perfect freedom.

From the Gelasian Sacramentary, based on St Augustine's words

Open my eyes that I may see,
Incline my heart that I may desire,
Order my steps that I may follow
The way of your commandments.

Lancelot Andrewes (1555–1626)

Prayers for Guidance

Lead me to do your will;
make your way plain for me to follow.

From Psalm 5

O God, by whom the meek are guided in judgement and light rises up in
darkness for the godly; grant us, in all our doubts and uncertainties, the grace
to ask what you would have us do; that the Spirit of Wisdom may save us
from all false choices and that in your light we may see light and in your
straight path may not stumble; through Jesus Christ our Lord.

William Bright (1824–1901)

Father,
I am seeking:
I am hesitant and uncertain,
but will you, O God,
watch over each step of mine
and guide me.

St Augustine (354–430)

Set free, O Lord, the souls of your servants from all restlessness and anxiety. Give us that peace and power which flow from you. Keep us in all perplexity and distress, that upheld by your strength and stayed on the rock of your faithfulness we may abide in you now and evermore.

Bishop Francis Paget (1851–1911)

Suggested exercise for meditation and private prayer:

Look briefly at the day ahead and beg him [God] to be in it with us in every detail of it. The whole exercise should not take more than fifteen minutes but it is a most valuable fifteen minutes and, if practised daily, we become more sensitive to his action in our lives not only at the time of the exercise, but also in the middle of our activities . . .

Gerard Hughes

Lord,
you understand me,
you know my every thought,
my brain is not a mystery to you.
Enter into my mind, Lord,
guide and direct my thoughts.
Be before me when I speak,
be beside me when I act,
be within me when I listen,
that I might possess
the wisdom born of love,
for you are love,
the love which understands
everything.

Frank Topping

Almighty God, give us wisdom to perceive you, intellect to understand you, diligence to seek you, patience to wait for you, eyes to behold you, a heart to meditate upon you and life to proclaim you, through the power of the Spirit of our Lord Jesus Christ.

Attributed to St Benedict (480–543)

Grant, Lord God, that we may cleave to you without parting,
worship you without wearying,
serve you without failing,
faithfully find you, for ever possess you, the one only God,
blessed for all eternity. Amen.

St Anselm (1033–1109)

Lord, I am blind and helpless, stupid and ignorant,
cause me to hear; cause me to know;
teach me to do; lead me.

Henry Martyn (1781–1812)

Grant me, O Lord, to know what is worth knowing,
to love what is worth loving,
to praise what delights you most,
to value what is precious in your sight,
to hate what is offensive to you.
Do not let me judge by what I see,
nor pass sentence according to what I hear,
but to judge rightly between things that differ
and above all to search out and to do what pleases you,
through Jesus Christ our Lord.

Thomas à Kempis (1380–1471)

O God, grant us the serenity
to accept what cannot be changed,
the courage to change what can be changed
and the wisdom to know the difference.

Reinhold Niebuhr (1892–1971)

Save me, Lord, King of eternal glory, you who have the power to save us all. Grant that I may long for, do and perfect those things which are pleasing to you and profitable for me. Lord, give me counsel in my anxiety, help in time of trial, solace when persecuted and strength against every temptation. Grant me pardon, Lord, for my past wrongdoings and afflictions, correction of my present ones and deign also to protect me against those in the future.

Latin prayer (eleventh century)

You who guided Noah over the flood waves:
Hear us.
You who with your word recalled Jonah from the deep:
Deliver us.
You who stretched forth your hand to Peter as he sank:
Help us, O Christ.
Son of God, who did marvellous things of old:
Be favourable in our day also.

Scots Celtic prayer

Grant, O Lord, that we may
live in your fear,
die in your favour,
rest in your peace.
rise in your power,
reign in your glory;
for your own beloved Son's sake,
Jesus Christ our Lord.

Archbishop Laud (1573–1645)

O God, who knowest us to be set in the midst of so many and great dangers, that by reason of the frailty of our nature we cannot always stand upright; grant to us such strength and protection, as may support us in all dangers and carry us through all temptations; through Jesus Christ our Lord.

From the Book of Common Prayer

O Lord our God,
fill us with hope in the shadow of your wings;
protect and sustain us.
You will uphold us, right from our childhood until our old age,
because our present strength,
if it comes from you, is strength indeed;
but if it is merely our own strength then it is weakness.
When we are close to you we find living goodness,
but at the very moment we turn aside from you
we become corrupt.
So, Lord, make us retrace our steps,
so that we are not defeated.

St Augustine (354–430)

O God our Father, direct and control us in every part of our life:
our tongues, that we speak no false words;
our actions, that we may do nothing to shame ourselves or hurt
others;
our minds, that we may think no evil or bitter thoughts:
our hearts, that they may be set only on pleasing you;
through Christ our Lord.

From the Catholic Prayer Book (1970)

O God,
maker of time and creator of all things,
we your helpless servants
bow our heads before you and so we pray:
send us the blessing of your Spirit
that we may live our lives in all godliness
and in obedience to your commandments.
For you are our God,
the God of salvation and compassion,
and we glorify you,
Father, Son and Holy Spirit,
now and for ever, to the ages of ages. Amen.

Russian Orthodox Church

Save us, O Lord, from the snares of a double mind.
Deliver us from all cowardly neutralities.
Make us to go in the paths of your commandments,
and to trust for our defence in your mighty arm alone,
through Jesus Christ our Lord.

Richard Hurrell Froude (1803–1836)

We humbly beseech thee, O Father, mercifully to look upon our infirmities, and for the glory of thy name turn from us all those evils that we most righteously have deserved; and grant that in all our troubles we may put our whole trust and confidence in thy mercy and evermore serve thee in holiness and pureness of living, to thy honour and glory; through our only Mediator and Advocate, Jesus Christ our Lord.

From the Book of Common Prayer (1549)

Father, you have promised to guide us when we are truly humble and dependent on you. You have promised to give wisdom generously to those who feel their lack of it. We come to you as your children asking for a Father's wise prompting as we wonder what course to take. Lead us in the right path, so that our lives may bring glory and honour to you. Through Jesus Christ our Lord.

Lead us, O Father, in the paths of peace,
Without your guiding hand we go astray,
And doubts appal and sorrows still increase;
Lead us through Christ, the true and living Way.

William Burleigh (1812–1871)

Thank you, Lord Jesus, that you will be our hiding place whatever happens.

Corrie ten Boom

Blessed are you, O Lord, Almighty God,
to whom our inmost thoughts are revealed:
you know our needs much better than we ourselves can ask or
imagine.
Sovereign Lord and ever-loving Redeemer,
in the richness of your mercy give us pure hearts
to call upon your holy name;
lead us not into temptation but deliver us from evil
and order all things for our good.
Because all glory, honour and praise are yours by right,
Father, Son and Holy Spirit, now and for ever, to the ages of
ages. Amen.

Russian Orthodox Church

O God, the author of peace and lover of concord,
to know you is eternal life
to serve you is perfect freedom.
Defend us your servants from all assaults of our enemies;
that we may trust in your defence
and not fear the power of any adversaries;
through Jesus Christ our Lord.

From the Alternative Service Book (1980)

O Lord, this is our desire, to walk along the path of life that you have
appointed us, in steadfastness of faith, in lowliness of heart, in gentleness of
love. Let not the cares or duties of this life press on us too heavily; but lighten
our burdens, that we may follow your way in quietness, filled with thankfulness for your mercy; through Jesus Christ our Lord.

Maria Hare (1798–1870)

Go before us, O Lord, in all our doings with your most gracious favour and
further us with your continual help; that in all our works, begun, continued
and ended in you, we may glorify your holy name and finally by your mercy
obtain everlasting life; through Jesus Christ our Lord. Amen.

Adapted from the Book of Common Prayer (1662)

O thou, from whom to be turned is to fall,
to whom to be turned is to rise,
and in whom to stand is to abide for ever;
Grant us in all our duties thy help,
in all our perplexities thy guidance,
in all our dangers thy protection,
and in all our sorrows thy peace;
through Jesus Christ our Lord.

St Augustine (354–430)

❖ *Learning God's Way* ❖

Teach me, Lord, what you want me to do,
and I will obey you faithfully;
teach me to serve you with complete devotion.

FROM PSALM 86

We all like to have our own way and to be independent. Yet Christians sincerely want to go God's way and to depend on him. But it is often a struggle. Perhaps that is why there have been so many prayers written down the ages about wanting to do God's will and to be wholly his.

Learning God's Way through his Word, the Bible

Lord, here is my Bible,
Here is this quiet room, here is this quiet time, and here am I.
Open my eyes; open my mind; open my heart; and speak.

Dick Williams

Grant, O Lord, that in the written Word, and through the spoken word, we may behold the living Word, our Saviour Jesus Christ.

Simon H. Baynes

Open my eyes so that I may see
the wonderful truths in your law

From Psalm 119

O Lord, heavenly Father, in whom is the fulness of light and wisdom, enlighten our minds by your Holy Spirit, and give us grace to receive your Word with reverence and humility, without which no one can understand your truth. For Christ's sake. Amen.

John Calvin (1509–1564)

Grant unto us, O merciful God, knowledge and true understanding of thy Word, that we may know what thy will is, and also may show forth in our lives those things that we do know; that we be not only knowers of thy Word, but also doers of the same; by our Lord and Saviour Jesus Christ.

Author unknown: from the household of King Henry VIII

Almighty God,
we thank you for the gift of your holy word.
May it be a lantern to our feet, a light to our paths,
and a strength to our lives.
Take us and use us to love and serve all men
in the power of the Holy Spirit,
and in the name of your Son, Jesus Christ our Lord.

From the Alternative Service Book (1980)

Loving Father, as we read the Bible, help us to understand it. Send your Holy Spirit to us to make its message clear. May he also touch our consciences so that we see what you want us to do in obedience to your word. For Jesus Christ's sake. Amen.

Verse for silent prayer and thought before
reading the Bible:

Your word is a lamp to guide me
and a light for my path.

From Psalm 119

Blessed Lord, who caused all Holy Scriptures to be written for our learning: help us so to hear them, to read, mark, learn, and inwardly digest them, that, through patience, and the comfort of your holy word, we may embrace and for ever hold fast the hope of everlasting life, which you have given us in our Saviour Jesus Christ.

Collect for Advent from the Alternative Service Book (1980)

◆ Father, we thank you for all those men and women who toiled and suffered and died in order to give us the Bible in our own language. We pray for all those who are working now to translate the Bible for the first time. Give them patience, skill and wisdom that they may present your Word in all its fulness and power. Through Jesus Christ our Lord. Amen.

O God, speak to us through your Word. Pour out upon us your grace that we may learn your will and obey your call; through Jesus Christ our Lord. Amen.

We are going home to many who cannot read,
so, Lord, make us to be Bibles
so that those who cannot read the Book
can read it in us.

Chinese woman, after learning to read

Learning God's Way through the Holy Spirit's Help

The Spirit comes to help us, weak as we are. For we do not know how we ought to pray; the Spirit himself pleads with God for us ... on behalf of his people and in accordance with his will.

From Romans 8

Holy Spirit, think through me
till your ideas are my ideas.

Amy Carmichael (1868–1951)

Holy Spirit give us faith
Holy Spirit give us hope
Holy Spirit give us love.
Revive your work in this land
beginning with me.

Namirembe, Diocese of Uganda

O Lord Almighty, Father of our Lord Jesus Christ, grant us, we pray thee, to be grounded and settled in thy truth by the coming down of the Holy Spirit into our hearts. That which we know not do thou reveal, that which is wanting in us do thou fill up; that which we know do thou confirm, and keep us blameless in thy service, through the same Jesus Christ our Lord.

Clement of Rome (died 95)

Grant us, we beseech thee, O Lord, the aid of thy Holy Spirit, that whatever by his teaching we know to be our duty, we may by his grace be enabled to perform; through Jesus Christ our Lord. Amen.

J.C. Chute

Holy Spirit of God, source of knowledge
and creator of fellowship;
open our minds to recognize the truth
and our hearts to welcome it,
that in company together we may learn your will
and be strengthened to obey it;
through Jesus Christ our Lord. Amen.

Basil Naylor

◆ Holy Spirit teach us
When your word we read;
Shine upon its pages
With the light we need.

Holy Spirit, prompt us
When we kneel to pray;
Nearer come and teach us
What we ought to say.

Holy Spirit, give us
Each a lowly mind;
Make us more like Jesus,
Gentle, pure and kind.

W.H. Parker (1845–1929)

O heavenly Father, in whom we live and move and have our being, we humbly pray you so to guide and govern us by your Holy Spirit that in all the cares and occupations of our daily life we may never forget you, but remember that we are ever walking in your sight; for your own name's sake.

Ancient collect

Holy Spirit:
As the wind is your symbol, so forward our goings.
As the dove so launch us heavenwards.
As water so purify our spirits.
As a cloud so abate our temptations.
As dew so revive our languor.
As fire so purge out our dross.

Christina Rossetti (1830–1894)

O Spirit of God who speaks to our spirits,
created in your own likeness;
penetrate into the depths of our spirits,
into the storehouse of memories, remembered and forgotten,
into the depths of being, the very springs of personality.
And cleanse and forgive, making us whole and holy,
that we may be yours and live in the new being of Christ
our Lord.

George Appleton

◆ Holy Spirit, give your light
So that I may walk aright;
In your wisdom, love and might
Guide my steps this day.

Make me kind to all around;
In my life let love abound,
All your gracious fruits be found
In your child this day.

Holy Spirit you are one
With the Father and the Son,
May the will divine be done
Now and every day.

Mary Appleby (1874–1929)

Holy Spirit, you make alive;
bless also this our gathering, the speaker and the hearer;
fresh from the heart it shall come, by your aid,
let it also go to the heart.

Søren Kierkegaard (1813–1855)

Lord, Holy Spirit,
You blow like the wind in a thousand paddocks.
Inside and outside the fences,
You blow where you wish to blow.

Lord, Holy Spirit,
You are the sun who shines on the little plant.
You warm him gently, you give him life,
you raise him up to become a tree with many leaves.

Lord, Holy Spirit,
You are the mother eagle with her young,
Holding them in peace under her feathers.
On the highest mountain you have built your nest,
Above the valley, above the storms of the world,
Where no hunter ever comes.

Lord, Holy Spirit,
You are the bright cloud in whom we hide,
In whom we know already that the battle has been won.
You bring us to our Brother Jesus,
To rest our heads upon his shoulder.

Lord, Holy Spirit,
In the love of friends you are building a new house,
Heaven is with us when you are with us.
You are singing your song in the hearts of the poor.
Guide us, wound us, heal us. Bring us to God.

James K. Baxter, Aotearoa, New Zealand

Send out your Spirit in all Creation
and fill the world with your glory.
Fire us with your power
Light us with your Word
And feed us with your living Bread.

Sheffield Diocese

O Holy Ghost, O faithful paraclete,
Love of the Father and the Son ...
You who alone
Are worthily adored
With Father and with Son
To you in heart and word
Be honour, worship, grace,
Here and in every place,
World without end.

Hildebert (1056–1133)

O God, we pray that as the Holy Spirit came in wind and fire to the apostles, so he may come to us, breathing life into our souls and kindling in our hearts the flame of love; through Jesus Christ our Lord. Amen.

J.W.G. Masterton

Grant, O merciful Father, that thy divine Spirit may enlighten, inflame and cleanse our hearts; that he may penetrate us with his heavenly dew and make us fruitful in good works. Through Jesus Christ our Lord.

From The Golden Manual

Giving Ourselves in Obedience to God

Do not be afraid to throw yourself on the Lord!
He will not draw back and let you fall!
Put your worries aside and throw yourself on him;
he will welcome you and heal you.

St Augustine (354–430)

Speak, Lord, for your servant hears.
Grant us ears to hear,
Eyes to see,
Wills to obey,
Hearts to love;
Then declare what you will,
Reveal what you will,
Command what you will,
Demand what you will.

Christina Rossetti (1830–1894)

Here is my heart, O God, here it is with all its secrets;
look into my thoughts, O my hope, and take away all my wrong
feelings;
let my eyes ever be on you and release my feet from the snare.

St Augustine (354–430)

Lord, here I am, do with me as seems best in your own eyes; only give me, I
beseech you, a penitent and patient spirit to expect you. Make my service
acceptable to you while I live, and my soul ready for you when I die.

Archbishop Laud (1573–1645)

Lord, you seized me and I could not resist you.
I ran for a long time but you followed me.
I took by-paths, but you knew them.
You overtook me.
I struggled,
You won.
Here I am, Lord, out of breath, no fight left in me, and I've said
'yes' almost unwillingly.
When I stood there trembling like one defeated before
 his captor,
Your look of love fell on me...
Marked by the fire of your love, I can no longer forget you.
Now I know that you are there, close to me, and I work in peace
beneath your loving gaze.
I no longer make an effort to pray.
I just lift my eyes to you and I meet yours.
And we understand one another. All is light, all is peace.

Michel Quoist

O Lord, let me not henceforth desire health or life except to spend them for
you and with you. You alone know what is good for me; do therefore what
seems best to you. Give to me or take from me; I desire to adore equally all
that comes to me from you, my Lord and God.

Blaise Pascal (1623–1662) (adapted)

You came, Lord Jesus Christ,
to teach us the way of life which God requires:
Make us receptive to your word,
and help us to obey, whatever it may cost,
that our lives may bear much fruit;
to the glory of your name. Amen.

From Collects with the New Lectionary

O Lord, in your great mercy, keep us from forgetting what you have suffered for us in body and soul. May we never be drawn by the cares of this life from Jesus our Friend and Saviour, but daily may we live nearer to his cross.

Hedley Vicars (adapted)

When my whole being is united with you,
then I will feel no more sorrow or pain;
mine will be the true life wholly filled by you.
You raise up all who are filled with your Spirit;
but I am not yet so filled, I am a burden to myself.
The wordly joys that I ought to lament struggle within me
with the sorrows in which I should rejoice,
and I do not know where the victory lies.
Take pity on me, O Lord, for I am not hiding
my wounds from you.
You are the doctor, I am the patient;
you are the giver of mercy—I am in great need of it.

St Augustine (354–430)

O God . . . I acknowledge my utter dependence upon you. I have nothing that I have not received. By you I am sustained in nature and grace, day by day, and moment by moment. Suffer not the work of your hands to perish. Let your Spirit empty me of all that is not yours, that Christ may dwell in me and I in him.

W. Gray Elmslie (1848–1889)

Here I am, Lord;
Here is my body,
Here is my heart,
Here is my soul.
Grant that I may be big enough to reach the world,
Strong enough to carry it,
Pure enough to embrace it without wanting to keep it.
Grant that I may be a meeting-place, but a temporary one,
A road that does not end in itself,
because everything to be gathered there, everything human,
leads towards you.

Michel Quoist

Lord Jesus, I don't know much about you,
But I am willing to learn;
And I am ready to give all that I know of myself
To all that I know of you;
And I am willing to go on learning.

Donald Coggan

Almighty God, whose most dear Son went not up to joy but first he suffered pain, and entered not into glory before he was crucified; mercifully grant that we, walking in the way of the cross, may find it none other than the way of life and peace; through the same, thy Son, Jesus Christ our Lord.

From the American Prayer Book

Teach us, Lord,
to serve you as you deserve,
to give and not to count the cost,
to fight and not to heed the wounds,
to toil and not to seek for rest,
to labour and not to seek for any reward
save that of knowing that we do your will.

St Ignatius Loyola (1491–1556)

Take my life and let it be
Consecrated, Lord, to thee:
Take my moments and my days,
Let them flow in ceaseless praise.

Take my hands and let them move
At the impulse of thy love;
Take my feet and let them be
Swift and beautiful for thee.

Take my voice and let me sing
Always, only, for my King;
Take my lips and let them be
Filled with messages from thee.

Take my silver and my gold,
Not a mite would I withhold;
Take my intellect and use
Every power as thou shalt choose.

Take my will and make it thine;
It shall be no longer mine:
Take my heart, it is thine own;
It shall be thy royal throne.

Take my love; my Lord I pour
At thy feet its treasure store:
Take myself and I will be
Ever, only, all for thee.

Frances Ridley Havergal (1836–1870)

Make us receptive and open
and may we accept your kingdom
like children taking bread from the hands of their father.
Let us live in your peace, at home with you,
all the days of our lives.

Huub Oosterhuis

O Saviour, pour upon me thy spirit of meekness and love, annihilate the selfhood in me, be thou all my life. Guide thou my hand, which trembles exceedingly, upon the rock of ages.

William Blake (1757–1827)

Take, Lord, all my liberty. Receive my memory, my understanding and my whole will. Whatever I have and possess, you have given me; to you I restore it wholly and to your will I surrender it for my direction. Give me the love of you only, with your grace and I am rich enough; nor ask I anything beside.

St Ignatius Loyola (1491–1556)

Lord, when I hear how others praise and pray to you, giving themselves to you without reserve, I am ashamed of my own misgivings and halfheartedness. Fill me with such love for you that I may long to give myself to you too. Let the lesser loves of everyday life take their proper place in my affections, leaving you first. For Jesus' sake.

Here I am, Lord—body, heart and soul. Grant that with your love I may be big enough to reach the world and small enough to be at one with you.

Meditation of Mother Teresa, used by her worldwide Missionaries of Charity

Let us make our way together, Lord;
wherever you go
I must go:
and through whatever you pass,
there too I will pass.

St Teresa of Avila (1515–1582)

O God, who hast so greatly loved us, long sought us, and mercifully redeemed us, give us grace that in everything we may yield ourselves, our wills and our works, a continual thankoffering to you; through Jesus Christ our Lord.

From the Westminster Confession of Faith (1647)

O Lord God, grant us always, whatever the world may say, to content ourselves with what you will say, and to care only for your approval, which will outweigh all worlds; for Jesus Christ's sake.

General Charles Gordon (1833–1885)

Lord, I believe, but would believe more firmly. O Lord, I love, but yet would love more warmly. I offer unto you my thoughts, that they may be towards you; my actions, that they may be according to you; my sufferings, that they may be for you.

From Treasury of Devotion (1869)

Verse for meditation and silent dedication to God:

Because of God's great mercy to us I appeal to you: Offer yourselves as a living sacrifice to God, dedicated to his service and pleasing to him. This is the true worship that you should offer.

From Romans 12

Lord, you have given so much to me, help me to give myself to you.

O Lord Jesu, who art the only health of all men living, and the everlasting life of those who die in thy faith: I give myself wholly unto thy will, being sure that the thing cannot perish which is committed unto thy mercy.

Thomas Cromwell (?1485–1540), part of a prayer he repeated before his execution

With all my heart and soul, O God, I thank you that in all the changes and chances of this mortal life I can look up to you and cheerfully resign my will to yours. I have trusted you, O Father, with myself. My soul is in your hand, which I truly believe you will preserve from all evil—my body and all that belongs to it are of much less value. I do therefore, with as great a sense of security as satisfaction, trust all I have to you.

Thomas Wilson (1663–1755)

Seeking to Know and Do God's Will

In his will is my peace.

Dante Alighieri (1265–1321)

My Father, teach us not only your will, but how to do it. Teach us the best way of doing the best thing, lest we spoil the end by unworthy means.

J.H. Jowett (1846–1923)

O God, grant us in all our doubts and uncertainties the grace to ask what you would have us do; that the spirit of wisdom may save us from all false choices, and that in your light we may see light, and in your straight path may not stumble, through Jesus Christ our Lord.

William Bright (1824–1901)

◆ Lord Jesus, you prayed to your Father, 'do what you want, not what I want.' Help us to follow your example. Help us to want to do the things that please you and to go the way that you have chosen for us, because we love you. Amen.

O Lord, I know not what to ask of thee. Thou alone knowest what are my true needs. Thou lovest me more than I myself know how to love. Help me to see my real needs which are concealed from me. I dare not ask either a cross or consolation. I can only wait on thee. My heart is open to thee. Visit and help me, for thy great mercy's sake. Strike me and heal me, cast me down and raise me up. I worship in silence thy holy will and thine inscrutable ways. I offer myself as a sacrifice to thee. I put all my trust in thee. I have no other desire than to fulfil thy will. Teach me how to pray. Pray thou thyself in me.

Metropolitan Philaret of Moscow (1553–1633)

Batter my heart, three-person'd God, for you
as yet but knock! Breathe, shine and seek to mend;
that I may rise and stand, o'erthrow me, and bend
your force to break, blow, burn and make me new.
I, like an usurp'd town, to another due
labour to admit you, but O, to no end!
Reason, your viceroy in me, me should defend,
but is captiv'd and proves weak or untrue.
Yet dearly I love you, and would be loved fain,
but am betrothed unto your enemy;
divorce me, untie, or break that knot again,
take me to you, imprison me, for I
except you enthral me, never shall be free,
nor ever chaste, except you ravish me.

John Donne (1572–1631)

We beseech you, O Lord, to enlighten our minds and to strengthen our wills, that we may know what we ought to do, and be enabled to do it, through the grace of your most Holy Spirit, and for the merits of your Son, Jesus Christ our Lord.

William Bright (1824–1901)

Govern all by your wisdom, O Lord, so that my soul may always be serving you as you will, and not as I choose.

Do not punish me, I implore you, by granting that which I wish or ask, if it offend your love, which would always live in me.

Let me die to myself, that so I may serve you; let me live to you who in yourself are the true life. Amen.

St Teresa of Avila (1515–1582)

Grant me, I beseech thee, O merciful God,
prudently to study, rightly to understand and perfectly to fulfil
that which is pleasing to thee,
to the praise and glory of thy name. Amen.

St Thomas Aquinas (1225–1274)

O God, the God of all goodness and grace,
who art worthy of a greater love
than we can either give or understand:
Fill our hearts, we beseech thee, with such love towards thee
that nothing may seem too hard for us to do or suffer
in obedience to thy will;
and grant that thus loving thee,
we may become daily more like unto thee,
and finally obtain the crown of life
which thou hast promised to those that love thee;
through Jesus Christ our Lord.

Bishop Westcott (1825–1901)

I find that your will knows no end in me.
And when old words die out on the tongue
New melodies break forth from the heart.

Rabindranath Tagore (1861–1941)

My Father, I abandon myself to you. Do with me as you will. Whatever you
may do with me I thank you. I am prepared for anything. I accept everything,
provided your will is fulfilled in me and in all creatures. I ask for nothing
more, my God. I place my soul in your hands. I give it to you, my God, with all
the love of my heart, because I love you. And for me it is a necessity of love,
this gift of myself, this placing of myself in your hands without reserve in
boundless confidence, because you are my Father.

Charles de Foucauld (1858–1916)

◆ Lord, take our minds and think through them;
take our lips and speak through them;
take our hearts and set them on fire
with the desire to do your holy will;
in the name of Jesus Christ our Lord. Amen.

Student prayer

O Lord our God,
make our hearts obedient to your divine will;
turn our eyes away from vain things,
that, free from the world's attraction,
they may always look on your glorious beauty.
For you are our God,
the God of compassion and salvation,
and we glorify you, Father, Son and Holy Spirit,
now and for ever, to the ages of ages. Amen.

Eastern Orthodox Church

Lord Jesus Christ, who alone art wisdom, thou knowest what is best for us; mercifully grant that it may happen to us only as it is pleasing to thee and as it seems good in thy sight this day. For thy name's sake. Amen.

King Henry VI (1421–1471)

Almighty and eternal God, so draw our hearts to thee, so guide our minds, so fill our imaginations, so control our wills, that we may be wholly thine, utterly dedicated unto thee; and then use us, we pray thee, as thou wilt, but always to thy glory and the welfare of thy people, through our Lord and Saviour, Jesus Christ.

William Temple (1881–1944)

Dear Lord, let thy will be done in my life and give me the wisdom to know, the strength to accept and the courage to do it. In your name. Amen.

Ricky Johnson, prisoner in Westville Correctional Centre, Indiana

O heavenly Father, subdue in me whatever is contrary to your holy will. Grant that I may ever study to know your will, that I may know how to please you.

Grant, O God, that I may never run into those temptations which, in my prayers, I desire to avoid.

Lord, never permit my trials to be above my strength.

Thomas Wilson (1663–1755)

Lord God Almighty, shaper and ruler of all creatures, we pray for your great mercy to guide us to your will, to make our minds steadfast, to strengthen us against temptation, to put far from us all unrighteousness.

Shield us against our foes, seen and unseen, teach us so that we may inwardly love you before all things with a clean mind and clean body, for you are our maker and our redeemer, our trust and our hope.

King Alfred (849–901)

O almighty God, eternal, righteous and merciful, give us poor sinners to do for your sake all that we know of your will, and to will always what pleases you; so that inwardly purified, enlightened and kindled by the fire of your Holy Spirit we may follow in the steps of your well-beloved Son, our Lord Jesus Christ.

St Francis of Assisi (1182–1226)

Inspire and strengthen us by your Holy Spirit, O Lord God,
to seek your will and uphold your honour in all things;
in the purity and joy of our homes,
in the trust and fellowship of our common life,
in daily service of the good;
after the pattern and in the power of your Son
our Lord and Saviour, Jesus Christ.

Jeremy Taylor (1613–1667)

◆ *For Home and Family* ◆

God ... cares for orphans and protects widows.
He gives the lonely a home to live in.

FROM PSALM 68

The most direct way to others is always through prayer.

Dietrich Bonhoeffer (1906–1945)

House and Home

God bless our home.

Often found in Jordan, carved in metal or on wood

Father of all mankind, make the roof of my house wide enough for all opinions, oil the door of my house so it opens easily to friend and stranger and set such a table in my house that my whole family may speak kindly and freely around it. Amen.

Prayer from Hawaii

> Be Christ's cross on your new dwelling,
> Be Christ's cross on your new hearth,
> Be Christ's cross on your new abode,
> Upon your new fire blazing.
> Be Christ's cross on your means and portion,
> Be Christ's cross on your kin and people,
> Be Christ's cross on you each light and darkness,
> Each day and each night of your lives,
> Each day and each night of your lives.

Celtic prayer

> ◆ May the love of God our Father
> Be in all our homes today:
> May the love of the Lord Jesus
> Keep our hearts and minds always:
> May his loving Holy Spirit
> Guide and bless the ones I love,
> Father, mother, brothers, sisters,
> Keep them safely in his love.

From Infant Prayer

Lord, I've discovered it's never a secret
When you live in a home
For you simply cannot be hid.
The neighbours soon know you are there
Even strangers learn of your presence.
When you are the Great First in a home
There is a radiance that speaks of joy
There is gentleness, kindness
Laughter and love.
There is commotion mixed with contentment
There are problems mixed with prayer.
Lord, your own Word says it so vividly:
'It was known that he was in the house.'

Ruth Harms Calkin

Bless our home, Father,
that we cherish the bread before there is none,
discover each other before we leave,
and enjoy each other for what we are,
while we have time.

Prayer from Hawaii

God bless the house
From site to stay,
From beam to wall,
From end to end,
From ridge to basement,
From balk to roof-tree,
From found to summit,
Found and summit.

Celtic prayer

When you sit happy in your own fair house,
Remember all poor men that are abroad,
Eternal dwelling in the house of God.

Alcuin of York (735–804)

◆ Lord, as your friends welcomed you into their homes in your days on earth, may we welcome you into our homes by entertaining friends and strangers. May we give them the welcome that we would give to you, our master, and prepare the meals and make the beds as if we were doing it for you. Amen.

Lord, I'm so glad
We don't have to be creative geniuses
Or serve elegant gourmet meals
To make our guests feel warm and wanted.
We need rather to expose them to love
And introduce them to laughter.
We need to listen and never drown them out.
Above all, we need to remember
That there is no substitute—
None whatever—
For concentrated sharing
And genuine caring.

Ruth Harms Calkin

O God, bless my homestead,
Bless thou all therein.
O God, bless my kindred,
Bless thou my substance.
O God, bless my words,
Bless thou my converse.

Celtic prayer

O God, make the door of this house wide enough
to receive all who need human love and fellowship,
and a heavenly Father's care;
and narrow enough to shut out all envy, pride and hate.
Make its threshold smooth enough
to be no stumbling block to children or to straying feet,
but rugged enough to turn back the tempter's power;
make it a gateway to thine eternal kingdom.

Thomas Ken (1637–1711), written at the door of a Christian hospital

BEATRICE PUBLIC LIBRARY
BEATRICE, NEBR. 68310

The Family Circle

Father, from whom every family receives its true name,
I pray for all the members of my family:
for those who are growing up,
that they may increase in wisdom and love;
for those facing changes,
that they may meet them with hope;
for those who are weak,
that they may find strength;
for those with heavy burdens,
that they may carry them lightly;
for those who are old and frail,
that they may grow in faith.

From More Everyday Prayers

◆ Lord Jesus, help us to be more loving in our homes. Make us thoughtful for others and help us to think of kind things to do. Keep us from grumbling and ill-temper and help us to be cheerful when things go wrong and our plans are upset. May we learn to love and understand each other and think of others before ourselves.

Graham Salmon

O God our heavenly Father, from whom every family in heaven and on earth is named: we trust to your loving care the members of our families, both near and far. Supply their needs; guide their footsteps; keep them in safety of body and soul; and may your peace rest upon our homes and upon our dear ones everywhere; for Jesus Christ our Saviour's sake.

Frank Colquhoun

Lord, behold our family here assembled. We thank thee for this place in which we dwell; for the love that unites us; for the peace accorded us this day; for the hope with which we expect the morrow; for the health, the work, the food, and the bright skies, that make our life delightful; for our friends in all parts of the earth and our friendly helpers in this foreign isle. Let peace abound in our small community. Purge out of every heart the lurking grudge. Give us grace and strength to forbear and to persevere... Give us courage, gaiety and the quiet mind.

Robert Louis Stevenson (1850–1894)

O living bread, that came down from heaven to give life to the world! O loving shepherd of our souls... we commend to you particularly the sick, the unhappy, the poor and all who beg for food and employment, imploring for all and every one the assistance of your providence; we commend to you the families, so that they may be fruitful centres of Christian life. May the abundance of your grace be poured out over all.

Pope John XXIII

We pray for our families, with whom we live day by day.
   May this most searching test of our character not find us
broken and empty.
   By all we do and say help us to build up the faith and confidence
of those we love.
   When we quarrel help us to forgive quickly.
   Help us to welcome new members into our families without reserve and
not to neglect those who in our eyes have become less interesting and
more demanding.

From Contemporary Prayers for Public Worship

Father, how can I express what I owe to my family?
I have shared so much of life with them, old and young.
Even when they are far from me, we are bound closely together.
When I am angry or frustrated, they rescue me from myself;
when I doubt, they rekindle my faith.
My family make demands on my time and energy;
they remind me that I am still wanted.

From More Everyday Prayers

Lord, we commit to your special care those families where there is only one parent. Help the mother or father who is bringing up the children to find in you the resources and wisdom that they need. Put into the hearts and minds of loving friends and neighbours the need to give support and help to provide the benefits that are lacking. Teach us all that you are a loving parent to us, ready to provide when we come to the end of ourselves.

Father, we pray for all who are joined in second marriage. Give them love, perseverance and faith as they try to fill the role of partner and parent. Save them from remorse, jealousy and resentment. Help them to build up a new sense of belonging. May they deal fairly and lovingly with all the situations that crop up in everyday life. Give them faith, hope and love and good success in establishing strong family bonds.

Father, we pray for all children whose lives have been shattered through their family being broken: broken by selfishness, by death, by cruelty, by desertion. Heal the deep wounds that have been made. Give them such a sense of your fatherly love and care that they may grow strong and straight in their emotions, able to form good and loving relationships in their own time.

◆ Please, Lord, bless all the children who don't have a mother or father—and those who may even have no family at all. You know what they are feeling and how much love they need. Father, you love us all. Give more love than ever to these children now. Heal their hurts and ease their pain. In Jesus' name. Amen.

Carol Watson

Lord Jesus Christ,
I praise and thank you for my parents
and my brothers and sisters,
whom you have given me to cherish.
Surround them with your tender loving care,
teach them to love and serve one another in true affection
and to look to you in all their needs.
I place them all in your care,
knowing that your love for them is greater than my own.
Keep us close to one another in this life
and conduct us at last to our true heavenly home.
Blessed be God for ever. Amen.

Michael Buckley

We thank you for the continuing help and support of our parents. We ask your blessing on them as they grow older. May we show them love, kindness and consideration. May we benefit from their wisdom and experience. Help us to give them time in our busy lives and to continue to share with them the little experiences and conversations that mean so much.

Father, we give thanks for the memory of our parents. We thank you for their steadfast love for us, for their generosity and self-sacrifice. Many showed us how to trust and obey you, too.

Forgive us if we failed, while they were still with us, to show them the love that we felt or if we neglected or made little of them. May they know now of our appreciation and love as we build our own lives on the foundation of the example they left to us.

We thank you for our brothers and sisters and for the strong tie of a shared past that binds us together. Help us not to carry the resentments and spite of childhood grudges into our adult relationship. May we support and strengthen and enjoy one another as family members should. For Jesus' sake.

◆ Thanks to you, kind Father
   for my daily bread,
   for my home and playthings,
   For my cosy bed.

   Mother, father, dear ones—
   Bless them while I pray:
   May I try to help them,
   Cheerfully obey.

Charles Healing (1868–1921)

Friends and Neighbours

Pray for me as I will for thee,
that we may merrily meet in heaven.

Thomas More (1478–1535)

Christ who first gave thee for a friend to me,
Christ keep thee well, where'er thou art, for me.
Earth's self shall go and the swift wheel of heaven
Perish and pass, before our love shall cease.
Do but remember me, as I do thee,
And God, who brought us on this earth together,
Bring us together in his house of heaven.

Hrabanus Maurus (788–856) to Grimold, Abbot of St Gall

O blessed Lord, who has commanded us to love one another, grant us grace
that having received your undeserved bounty, we may love everyone in you and
for you. We implore your clemency for all; but especially for the friends
whom your love has given to us. Love them, O fountain of love, and make
them love you with all their heart, that they may will and speak and do those
things only which are pleasing to you.

St Anselm (1033–1109)

Lord, where would we be without our friends?
They give us of themselves unselfishly,
they stand by us in trouble,
in happiness they share our laughter,
they make life more colourful.
Make me a good friend,
ready to help but not to interfere,
loyal but not uncritical,
open rather than exclusive,
dependable at all times.

From More Everyday Prayers

Lord, you taught us that all who come our way are our neighbours. But hear our prayer for those with whom we come in daily contact because they live close to us. Help us to be good neighbours to them. Give us the grace to overlook petty annoyances and to build on all that is positive in our relationship, that we may love them as we love ourselves, with genuine forbearance and kindness. For Jesus' sake. Amen.

Almighty and most merciful God, who has given us a new commandment that we should love one another, give us also grace to fulfil it. Make us gentle, courteous and forbearing. Direct our lives so that we may look to the good of others in word and deed. Hallow all our friendships by the blessing of thy Spirit, for the sake of your Son Jesus Christ our Lord.

Bishop Westcott (1825–1901)

◆ Help me, O God, to be a good and a true friend:
to be always loyal and never to let my friends down:
Never to talk about them behind their backs in a way which I
would not do before their faces;
never to betray a confidence or talk about the things about which
I ought to be silent;
always to be ready to share everything I have;
to be as true to my friends as I would wish them to be to me.
This I ask for the sake of him who is the greatest and truest of all
friends, for Jesus' sake.

William Barclay (1907–1978)

Grant, O God, that we may keep a constant guard upon our thoughts and passions, that they may never lead us into sin; that we may live in perfect charity with all mankind, in affection to those who love us, and in forgiveness to those, if any there are, that hate us. Give us good and virtuous friends. In the name of our blessed Lord and Saviour Jesus Christ.

Warren Hastings (1732–1818)

Lord,
when I have failed friends
I have failed you.
Give me the courage to be a true friend.
In those times when friends are needed,
let me not be afraid of opinion, nor of failure.
Let me not run from sorrow or grief,
but let me stand, with you,
beside my friends
in their hour of need.
Let my friendship be a pledge
of my faith in you.

Frank Topping

O God, who art present to thy faithful people in every place, mercifully hear our prayers for those we love who are now parted from us: watch over them, we beseech thee, and protect them in anxiety, danger and temptation; and assure both them and us that thou art always near and that we are one with thee for ever; through Jesus Christ our Lord.

Bishop Westcott (1825–1901)

Be gracious to all that are near and dear to me and keep us all in thy fear and love. Guide us, good Lord, and govern us by the same Spirit, that we may be so united to thee here as not to be divided when you are pleased to call us hence, but may together enter into thy glory, through Jesus Christ, our blessed Lord and Saviour.

John Wesley (1703–1791)

Holy Father, in your mercy,
Hear our earnest prayer,
Keep our loved ones, now far distant,
'Neath your care.

When in sorrow, when in danger,
When in loneliness,
In your love look down and comfort
Their distress.

May the joy of your salvation
Be their strength and stay;
May they love and may they praise you
Day by day.

Isabel Stevenson (1843–1890)

Marriage

Almighty God, our heavenly Father,
who gave marriage to be a source of blessing to mankind,
we thank you for the joys of family life.
May we know your presence and peace in our homes;
fill them with your love,
and use them for your glory;
through Jesus Christ our Lord. Amen.

From the Alternative Service Book (1980)

Lord, we come to you about our marriage. Help us to begin to put things right. In the quietness show us how to stop thinking of the other's faults and failures and to recognize our own.

Check our negative responses and give us a vision of the partnership that we can create anew with your help. Where we do not yet feel love, give us good intents and wishes for each other's well-being that will bring us closer. Reawaken, in time, we pray, the love we once felt for each other and make us tender-hearted and forgiving because, you, in Christ, freely forgive and receive us.

God,
you are the source of love and you join us together in the miracle
of friendship, marriage and family life.
Let faithfulness, freshness and unselfishness
fill the deep relationships we cherish
and be a sign to the nations that this is the way you love the
world
in Jesus Christ our Lord.

From Further Everyday Prayers

Our loving Father in heaven, we bring to you our deep desire to have a child.
You created the family and we believe that our desire comes from you. You
are the giver of life. Hear our prayer and grant us our request.

Take the stress and anxiety from our lives that we may not become so
obsessive that we forfeit your peace or miss the opportunites of life that the
present offers. Through Jesus Christ our Lord.

Lord, if it is not your plan to give us children, begin to give us the grace to
accept your will. Help us never to feel belittled or lessened by what seems like
failure but to know our worth as your children.

Above all, we pray for those qualities of a father and a mother that will
make us more like you and enable us to love and care for all those you bring
our way.

Lord, teach me to accept, and in accepting
to see all things as part of your plan
in drawing us closer to you.
When things go wrong between us,
let me see there may be some very good reason for it.
May I see clearly my own mistakes and overcome them.
Teach me to make loving and giving
the centre of our every day.

Rosa George

Lord, let the light of your presence bring joy back into our marriage. Burn bright within each of us, to warm us and cheer us so that it breaks down the fog between us.

Dear Lord, shine through me as a person to reach my husband and draw close to him in love and joy, the way you meant us to.

Marjorie Holmes

Through all the years of marriage
We've happily shared with others...
But God, you've given us one priceless gift
That belongs exclusively to us
Not to be shared with another—
The beautiful gift of physical intimacy.
Thank you for its mystery
Its wonder, its delight.
May we never mishandle it.
May we respect and cherish it always.
May our self-giving continue to be
An expression of oneness
A celebration of wholeness.
Keep it alive, fulfilling
And always full of surprises.
O God, what a marvellous expression
Of your own fathomless love!

Ruth Harms Calkin

Parenthood

O Lord God almighty who hast made us out of nothing and redeemed us by the precious blood of thine only Son, preserve, I beseech thee, the work of thy hands and defend both me and the tender fruit of my womb from all perils and evils. I beg thee, for myself, thy grace, protection, and a happy delivery; and for my child, that thou wouldest preserve it for baptism, sanctify it for thyself and make it thine for ever. Through Jesus Christ, thy Son, our Lord.

From The Christian's Guide to Heaven (1794)

God our Father,
maker of all that is living,
we praise you for the wonder and joy of creation.
We thank you from our hearts for the life of this child,
for a safe delivery, and for the privilege of parenthood.
Accept our thanks and praise
through Jesus Christ our Lord. Amen.

From the Alternative Service Book (1980)

Lord, the life we hold in our arms is the life you have given to us in trust. This child is not our property to use for the fulfilment of our own ambitions; this child is yours, whom one day you will call to confess your name and become your disciple. May we be wise in these short years when our influence will be more important than anyone else's. In our love may our child begin to learn the perfect love that casts out fear. In the life that we share as a family, in our talking together, our eating together, our journeying together, and in the disciplines we impose, may our child learn that we are worthy of trust.

From Further Everyday Prayers

Father, we commit to you the child that I am carrying. You know that we had not planned or wanted a baby and we bring to you all our feelings of shock, resentment, worry and inability to cope.

Help us to be accepting, that, even now, this child may never experience rejection or disfavour. Help us to welcome the one that you are sending as a gift from you. Provide where we have no resources and give us the joy of seeing, in the fulness of time, your perfect will fulfilled in the gift of a son or daughter.

Lord Jesus Christ, we come to you with our baby,
we give this new life into your care.
As weakness turns into maturity
may our child grow to love and trust you.
Lord Jesus, draw us together
in deeper love and understanding
so that our child
may grow up in security and peace.

Christian Publicity Organization

Almighty God, look with favour on this child; grant that, being nourished with all goodness, he may grow in discipline and grace until he comes to the fullness of faith, through Jesus Christ our Lord. Amen.

From the Alternative Service Book (1980)   .

Father, may your Holy Spirit
Guide this child into the truth;
Fill with love and light his childhood
Thrill with high ideals his youth.

Show him Jesus Christ, our Saviour,
Prince of peace and King of love.
May he cleave to him for ever.
May he live with him above.

Father, may your Holy Spirit
Guide these parents through the years;
Help them answer children's questions;
Cope with teenage storms and tears.

May their home be rich with laughter;
Peace, in daily worship grow.
Give them grace to train your children,
Make them strong and let them go.

Hymn for a baptism or dedication service.

God our Father,
in giving us this child you have shown us your love.
Help us to be trustworthy parents.
Make us patient and understanding, that our child may always
be sure of our love
and grow up to be happy and responsible;
through Jesus Christ our Lord. Amen.

From the Alternative Service Book (1980), thanksgiving after an adoption

We receive this child into our family with thanksgiving and joy.
Through the love of God we receive her;
with the love of God we will care for her;
by the love of God we will guide her;
and in the love of God may we all abide for ever. Amen.

From the Alternative Service Book (1980), prayer for the whole family after an adoption

God, whose nature is always to have mercy, look down with love on the
natural mother and father of this child: keep them in your good providence,
and give them your peace in their hearts; through Jesus Christ our Lord.

From the Alternative Service Book (1980)

Almighty God and heavenly Father,
we thank you for the children which you have given us:
give us also grace to train them in your faith, fear and love;
that as they advance in years they may grow in grace,
and may hereafter be found in the number of your elect children;
through Jesus Christ our Lord.

Bishop Cosin (1595–1672)

Father, give us wisdom as we care for this child and bring him up for you.
Don't let us be so worried that we lose the happiness of his early days and
draw us closer together as we discover the joy and pains of parenting.

Heavenly Father, from whom all parenthood comes, teach us so to understand
our children that they may grow in your wisdom and love according to your
holy will. Fill us with sensitive respect for the great gift of human life which
you have committed to our care, help us to listen with patience to their worries
and problems and give us tolerance to allow them to develop as individuals, as
your Son did under the loving guidance of Mary and Joseph.

Michael Buckley

Heavenly Father, bless our children with healthful bodies, with good understandings, with the graces and gifts of your Spirit, with sweet dispositions and
holy habits; and sanctify them throughout in their bodies, souls and spirits,
and keep them blameless to the coming of our Lord Jesus Christ.

Jeremy Taylor (1613–1667)

Lord, we give into your care our children who are causing us so much worry. The days are gone when we could correct them and tell them what to do. Now that they are grown up we have to stand by and watch them making mistakes and doing what is foolish or wrong.

Thank you that you have gone on loving and forgiving us, your wayward children, over many years. Help us to be loving and forgiving to our own children. Help us never to stop praying for them. We earnestly ask you to bring them back to yourself and to us.

Ease our own torment and distress and give us peace in trusting you, especially in the dark hours of the night. You are our heavenly Father, who loves our children more than we do and we bring them to you now, in Jesus' name.

> Teach me to let go, Lord:
> to let my child take his own steps into the big world,
> to watch and care but to let him grow,
> as you, Lord, let us all grow, all of us your children.
> You let us make our own choices, our own mistakes,
> although you love us—because you love us.
> He is ours, Lord, yours and mine; upheld by both our loves.
> We both want the best for him.
> Let him be sure of that, now and wherever he goes.
> *From More Everyday Prayers*

Father, we commit to your care our child who is leaving home. We thank you for the years of happiness and shared experience, for the laughter, tears and talking together. We thank you for every sign of your grace in his life. We commit to you the failures and disappointments too.

Now give us the humility to stand aside from his life and choices. Give us wisdom, tact and love that we may support without being intrusive and be at hand without getting in the way.

Take him into your strong keeping for your love is greater than ours.

Give us the grace, Lord, to tell our children
the truth and nothing but the truth.
To issue no idle threats or promises.
To keep our word.
To apologize when we have been wrong.
To be disciplined over time.
To be courteous in all our dealings.
To answer children's questions as honestly and as simply
as we can.
To let them help in all the ways we can devise.
To expect from them no higher standard of honesty,
unselfishness,
politeness than we are prepared to live up to ourselves.

Joan Kendall (adapted)

Lord,
teach me to love my grandchildren as a grandmother should:
not interfering, only understanding;
not pushing myself, just being there when wanted.
Teach me to be the sort of grandmother
my children and my children's children
would want me to be.

Rosa George

❖ *Prayers for Everyday Life* ❖

Everything you do or say, then, should be done in the name
of the Lord Jesus, as you give thanks through him to God
the Father ... Whatever you do, work at it with all your
heart, as though you were working for the Lord and
not for men.

FROM COLOSSIANS 3

God can be present and real in every part of life—daily work and leisure, Sundays and weekdays too.

Think often on God, by day, by night, in your business and even in your diversions. He is always near you and with you; leave him not alone.

Brother Lawrence (1611–1691)

Daily Work

The time of business does not with me differ from the time of prayer, and in the noise and clatter of my kitchen, while several persons are at the same time calling for different things, I possess God in as great tranquillity as if I were upon my knees at the blessed sacrament.

Brother Lawrence (1611–1691)

◆ Lord of all hopefulness, Lord of all joy,
  Whose trust, ever child-like, no cares could destroy,
  Be there at our waking, and give us, we pray,
  Your bliss in our hearts, Lord, at the break of the day.

Lord of all eagerness, Lord of all faith,
  Whose strong hands were skilled at the plane and the lathe,
  Be there at our labours and give us, we pray,
  Your strength in our hearts, Lord, at the noon of the day.

Lord of all kindliness, Lord of all grace,
  Your hands swift to welcome, your arms to embrace,
  Be there at our homing and give us, we pray,
  Your love in our hearts, Lord, at the eve of the day.

Lord of all gentleness, Lord of all calm,
  Whose voice is contentment, whose presence is balm,
  Be there at our sleeping and give us, we pray,
  Your peace in our hearts, Lord, at the end of the day.

Jan Struther

Almighty God, our heavenly Father, without whose help labour is useless, without whose light search is vain, invigorate my studies and direct my enquiries, that I may by due diligence and right discernment establish myself and others in thy holy faith.

Take not, O Lord, thy Holy Spirit from me, let not evil thoughts have dominion in my mind. Let me not linger in ignorance and doubt, but enlighten and support me for the sake of Jesus Christ our Lord. Amen.

Samuel Johnson (1709–1784)

Lift us above the duties and responsibilities of our daily lives so that we may see them in the light of your loving purposes and broaden our imaginations so that now and eternity may be seen as one moment in your time.

From More Everyday Prayers

> Forth in your name, O Lord, I go,
> My daily labour to pursue,
> You, only you, resolved to know
> In all I think, or speak or do.
>
> The task your wisdom has assigned
> O let me cheerfully fulfil,
> In all my works your presence find,
> And prove your good and perfect will.
>
> *Charles Wesley (1707–1788)*

Lord of my commonplace days
Forgive me for foolishly waiting
For 'divine inspiration'
Before moving in on the tasks
Personally assigned to me.
Hopefully I am learning
To face with greater determination
The day-by-day drudgery
The trite, mundane tasks ...
Keep me pushing on and on
With purpose and direction.
Grab my heart and quieten me
When I begin to whine and whimper.
Despite the daily drain
I think I see it more clearly now:
It is only when I begin to do
That you begin to bless.

Ruth Harms Calkin

O Lord, renew our spirits and draw our hearts unto yourself, that our work may not be to us a burden but a delight; and give us such a mighty love to you as may sweeten our obedience. O let us not serve you with the spirit of bondage as slaves, but with cheerfulness and gladness, delighting in you and rejoicing in your work.

Benjamin Jenks (1647–1724)

God give me work
Till my life shall end
And life
Till my work is done.

On the grave of Winifred Holtby, novelist (1898–1935)

O Lord, our heavenly Father, by whose providence the duties of men are variously ordered, grant to us all such a spirit that we may labour heartily to do our work in our several stations, as serving our Master and looking for no reward. Teach us to put to good account whatever talents you have lent us; help us to overcome all sloth and indolence; and enable us to redeem our time by zeal and patience; through your Son, our Saviour.

Bishop Westcott (1825–1901)

Father, give us endurance and cheerfulness as we face the tasks of everyday life. Each of us knows the monotony or difficulty of our own daily work. Help us not to look enviously at others' jobs but to shoulder our own work cheerfully as doing it for you.

God, who has made every calling of man acceptable to yourself, if only your glory be intended in it: Give us day by day the desire to do our work, of what sort so ever it be, for your honour; and the joy of rendering it to you well done; through Jesus Christ our Lord.

From A Cambridge Bede Book

Teach me, my God and King,
In all things thee to see,
And what I do in anything
To do it as for thee.

George Herbert (1593–1633)

O Lord Jesus Christ, only begotten Son of your eternal Father, you have said with your most pure lips: Without me you can do nothing.

Lord, my Lord, with faith I embrace in my heart and soul the words spoken by you; help me, a sinner, to accomplish the task begun for your own sake by me, in the name of the Father and of the Son and of the Holy Ghost.

Prayer before any acts, Eastern Orthodox Church

O Lord God, when thou givest to thy servants to endeavour any great matter, grant us also to know that it is not the beginning but the continuing of the same until it be thoroughly finished which yieldeth the true glory, through him that for the finishing of thy work laid down his life, thy Son Jesus Christ.

Based on words used by Sir Francis Drake (?1540–1596)

Teach me to kneel in spirit before all whom it is my privilege to serve, because they are your children: to look for the family likeness, however homely or unspiritual the appearance of those to whom I am sent; however lowly my sphere of service and their needs may be.

I will be grateful for everything you give me to do ... willing to use very simple things as the instruments of love—the towel and the basin, the cup and plate and loaf, willing to do the most menial duties for the sake of love.

Come Lord! come with me: see with my eyes: hear with my ears: think with my mind: love with my heart—in all the situations of my life. Work with my hands: my strength. Take, cleanse, possess, inhabit, my will, my understanding, my love.

Take me where you will, to do what you will, in your way.

For where you are, there would your servant be.

Evelyn Underhill

What is the work you would have me do, Lord? Please guide me that I may find a job that is worth doing so that I may live full of purpose and joy in serving you, my creator, and helping in this world, whether it be in small ways or with wider responsibilities.

Phyllis Lovelock

O Christ, who being rich, for our sakes was made poor; King of glory, who did will to become the man of sorrows: teach us to serve you in the person of our needy brothers and sisters, weak, suffering and disregarded.

Eugène Bersier (1831–1889)

When many are coming and going and there is little leisure, give us grace, O heavenly Father, to follow the example of our Lord Jesus Christ, who knew neither impatience of spirit nor confusion of work, but in the midst of his labours held communion with you, and even upon earth was still in heaven; where he now reigns with you and the Holy Spirit world without end.

C.J. Vaughan (1816–1897)

Lord Jesus Christ,
alive and at large in the world,
help me to follow and find you there today,
in the places where I work,
meet people,
spend money
and make plans.
Take me as a disciple of your kingdom,
to see through your eyes
and hear the questions you are asking,
to welcome all men with your trust and truth
and to change the things that contradict God's love
by the power of the Cross
and the freedom of your Spirit. Amen.

John Taylor

Father, I share my life with many people
but few are as close as those who work with me.
I praise you for the support they give me,
and for the responsibilities we share.
I thank you for the times when they have saved me from
 serious mistakes
and for the fellowship of common service.
Forgive me for times when I have been stubborn,
refusing to accept the good advice of others
or the new insights of those junior to me.
Forgive me for selfish ambition
and foolish thoughts of my own importance.
Forgive me for careless words when under pressure
and for failing to appreciate the needs of others for
 encouragement and praise.

From More Everyday Prayers

Lord and Saviour, true and kind,
Be the master of my mind:
Bless and guide and strengthen still
All my powers of thought and will.

While I ply the scholar's task,
Jesus Christ, be near I ask:
Help the memory, clear the brain,
Knowledge still to seek and gain.

Bishop Handley Moule (1842–1920)

We pray for all who work within the home, caring for children, for the sick and the elderly. Give them special refreshment and the patience and cheerfulness which they need to do their work without grudging or resentment.

◆O Lord, bless our school;
That, working together and playing together,
We may learn to serve you
And to serve one another.

A.M. Ammon

◆ Thank you, our Father God, for our school, where we learn about the world you made and how to live in it. Thank you for the lessons we learn, the games we play, the stories we hear, the songs we sing. Thank you for hard work done; for difficult things won, and for all our fun.

John Oxenham (1852–1941) and Roderic Dunkerley

Look upon us and hear us, O Lord our God; and assist those endeavours to please you which you yourself have granted to us; as you have given the first act of will, so give the completion of the work; grant that we may be able to finish what you have granted us to wish to begin; through Jesus Christ our Lord.

From the Mozarabic Sacramentary

Lord, we pray for all manner of men and women, boys and girls, in their working lives:

Give courage and cheerfulness to those who work on assembly lines, in supermarkets, and in routine jobs. Give patience and wisdom to those who deal with people: to social workers, teachers, police, nurses and ambulance drivers. Give skill to doctors and surgeons, scientists and researchers. Give integrity and inspiration to skilled workers and creative artists. Give wisdom to all leaders and to judges, magistrates and those who make laws. Give patience and love to those who work in the home. Give motive and inclination to learn to those who study at school, college or university. Let us never despise or envy the work of others but help us to recognize that we are all needed in order to supply the needs of all.

You, who said, 'Come unto me all ye who are weary and heavy-laden and I will give you rest,' I come to you now.

For I am weary indeed. Mentally and physically I am bone-tired. I am all wound up, locked up tight with tension. I am too tired to eat. Too tired to think. Too tired even to sleep, I feel close to the point of exhaustion.

Lord, let your healing love flow through me.

I can feel it easing my tensions. Thank you. I can feel my body relaxing. Thank you. I can feel my mind begin to go calm and quiet and composed.

Thank you for unwinding me, Lord, for unlocking me. I am no longer tight and frozen with tiredness, but flowing freely, softly, gently into your healing rest.

Marjorie Holmes

Lord,
You said so gently,
So persistently
'Give me your weariness
And I'll give you my rest.'
I did—finally.
You did—immediately.
Then, Lord, I marvelled
That I had waited so long.

Ruth Harms Calkin

Money and Possessions

The measure of life is not in the heap of goods or honours nor the length of days one gathers, but in the overcoming of hate and despair, the sharing of burdens, the celebrations of joy and love that each day offers. If you want your measure of life to be filled, pour it out freely.

Beulah Stotter

Lord, show me Poverty
whom you loved so dearly...
I am full of yearning
for my Lady Poverty;
I can find no peace without her...
Jesus, you were very poor,
and I want to call
nothing under heaven mine
but only to live
on what others may give me.

St Francis of Assisi (1182–1226)

Lord, you told us that a person's life does not consist of the things he possesses. Help us not to judge others by what they own. Help us not to want more and more things for ourselves but to spend our lives seeking the true riches that will endure to life everlasting. Amen.

Help me, O God, to spend wisely and to buy fairly, remembering that money and the things of this world are a trust for which I shall have to give an account to you.

Malcolm L. Playfoot

◆Help us to earn money honestly
To spend a little wisely
To save some prudently
And to give generously.

From Prayers for Children and Young People

Be with us, Lord, when we go shopping. If we have very little money, help us to choose wisely and not to hanker after things we can't afford. Make us content, in spite of the voices and pictures all around, inviting us to spend and acquire.

Help us if we are well provided with money. Save us from self-indulgence and extravagance. Help us to contribute to the needs of those who are hungry. Be Lord of all our lives, including our money.

Through Jesus Christ our Lord.

Lord God of earth and heaven, you know better than we that plenty can be as great a spiritual burden as poverty. Forgive us ... who have so many blessings, for taking them so much for granted ... For thinking that they are ours to do with as we please ... For squandering so many of them in such irresponsible and irretrievable ways.

Remind us that your Word is more precious by far than the things we treasure ... more powerful by far than the people and policies we trust ... more promising by far than the schemes we try for gaining the world while giving up our souls.

William Russell

Lord, teach us to value our possessions in the right way. Help us never to think more of them than of people. Make us ready to use them freely for the good of others and to share them generously without grudging. Thank you for the beautiful things that we enjoy possessing. May our enjoyment be wholesome and right and may we hold lightly to all we own. For the sake of Jesus Christ, who became poor that we might be eternally rich. Amen.

Lord, in times of poverty make me perfectly content, and in times of wealth make me generous and liberal.

John Eddison

O Lord our God,
give us by your Holy Spirit
a willing heart and a ready hand
to use all your gifts to your praise and glory;
through Jesus Christ our Lord.

Thomas Cranmer (1489–1556)

Prayers relating to problems with work and money can be found in chapter 9.

Leisure and Holidays

Jesus said to his disciples: 'Let us go off by ourselves to some place where we will be alone and you can rest for a while.'

From Mark 6

> Thank you, God, for holidays
> In the lovely summer days,
> For our picnics, for our fun,
> For our playing in the sun.
> Make us good, with smiling faces,
> So our homes are friendly places,
> And the helpful things we do
> Make all our mothers happy too.

From The Infant Teacher's Prayer Book

Lord of the Sabbath, teach us to enrich our rest and leisure with reverence and with praise.

From All the Glorious Names

> O God, you have preserved me in my journeyings today,
> and I offer thanks for this good day:
> With its cheerful companionship;
> Its pleasant surprises at every turn.
> And now that night has come I look forward to rest and sleep;
> and a new beginning on the morrow.
> I offer thanks for holiday clothes;
> I offer thanks for the new variety of foods.
> Let nothing that I do or say, or leave behind later, spoil this
> lovely spot for others who will come. Amen.

Rita Snowden

God of the seas, to you I pray:
Bless unto me this holiday.

From these wide seas give unto me
A larger heart of charity.

May these strong tides wash out my mind
From all that's bitter and unkind.

With the broad beat of seabird's wings
Lift up my soul to heavenly things.

By the far sight of hills untrod
Call me to undared ventures, God.

Grant that these holidays may be
Your holy days indeed to me.

Lilian Cox

We, who are rich and privileged,
thank you for the gift of leisure,
for time to unwind, reflect and plan,
to exercise or simply sit in quiet.
We thank you for the people who create our holiday
by working in the cockpit and control room,
in garage, signal-box and harbour office;
for those in kitchens, dining rooms and bars,
those guiding tours and running sports and games;
may they too find time for rest and recreation . . .
May we be truly recreated in our recreation,
our lives enlarged with new enthusiasm
and a broader vision of your purpose.

Stephen Orchard

Lord, when you took the disciples away for a rest you were met by large, demanding crowds who needed your help. We pray for all today who can take no holiday and have very little leisure time.

Meet the needs of those who have too much of their own company as well as those who have too much of the company of others. Protect them all from envy and self-pity. Refresh them in the midst of their work. For Jesus' sake.

Thank you, good Lord, for times of leisure: time to read books; time to look at pictures; time to listen to music; time to nurse the cat; time to walk the dog; time to browse round the shops; time to phone a friend; time to chat with a neighbour; time to stand and stare; time to catch up on the little jobs I usually have no time for. Give me time to be quiet with you too. Bless these times of recreation and strengthen me through them to do your will. Amen.

> So much of my time
> is spent in needless hurry;
> in saying, 'Excuse me;
> can't stop, sorry,
> —so much to do; must rush.'
> The joy of casual conversation
> is cut short,
> because somehow
> I think chatting is merely
> wasting time.
> My efficiency robs me of pleasure.
> Lord, teach me
> that time spent talking
> of books, of sport,
> of last night's television,
> is not time lost,
> but time enriched.
>
> *Frank Topping*

What a beautiful relief, dear God,
To sit quietly in my own living room
Soaking up the luxury of aloneness.
No demanding voices
No radio or television
No shouts from the bathroom
Just these few marvellous moments
To kick off my shoes
Shed my confusion
And reclaim myself...
These few marvellous moments
To respond to your persistent plea.

Ruth Harms Calkin

◆ Thank you, Lord, for the pleasures of sport: for the fun and exhilaration of taking part and for the excitement of watching.

May our sport be kept honest and fair, good-natured and friendly. So may the world of sport glorify your name.

◆ I pray, Lord, for all engaged in sporting activity:
in the big events that catch the headlines,
and in the numerous matches and contests
in my own area, in schools, and clubs,
and among families and friends.
Let pleasure and healthy exercise be the motive,
and let the enjoyment and friendly rivalry
contribute to the building up of community life.

From More Everyday Prayers

◆ I thank you, O God, for giving me a body which is specially fit and strong, and for making me able to use it well.

In my training

Help me never to shirk the discipline which I know that I need and ought to accept...

When I compete with others

Help me, win or lose, to play fair. When I win, keep me from boasting; when I lose, keep me from making excuses...

Help me so to live that I will always have a healthy body and a healthy mind.

This I ask for your love's sake. Amen.

William Barclay (1907–1978)

◆ Father, we give you thanks for all who enrich our lives with their creative talents.

We thank you for story-tellers, playwrights and poets.

We thank you for music makers, those who compose and those who play.

We thank you for writers and journalists, programme makers and cameramen who enlarge our understanding and give us new knowledge.

We thank you for those who make us laugh.

Use their gifts in your service; through Jesus Christ our Lord.

From More Everyday Prayers

Celebrations

They sang the Lord's praises, repeating the refrain:
'The Lord is good, and his love for Israel is eternal.'
Everyone shouted with all his might, praising the Lord.

From Ezra 3

BIRTHDAYS AND ANNIVERSARIES

We beseech you, O Lord, open your heavens;
from thence may your gifts descend to her.
Put forth your own hand and touch her head.
May she feel the touch of your hand,
and receive the joy of the Holy Spirit,
that she may remain blessed for evermore.

St Ethelwold (908–984), a birthday blessing

◆ My Father, all last year you took care of me and now you have given me a
birthday. I thank you for all your goodness and kindness to me. You have
given me loving parents, a home, gifts and clothes. Thank you, God. Help me
to be a better child in my new year, to grow strong, to study well, to work
happily.

Prayer from India

Father, you have cared for us since life began. On this birthday, we give you
special thanks for your kindness and protection over the past year. We
commit to you the pain and difficulty encountered and ask that, even now,
you will bring good from evil. Thank you for the times of happiness, laughter
and joy.

Now hear our prayer for the new year that is beginning. May it be filled
with your blessing and bring good success.

Through Jesus Christ our Lord. Amen.

◆ Lord, we thank you for this and every happy birthday; as we grow in age and
strength may we grow also into the knowledge of your love and become more
like you.

From The Lord is My Shepherd

Thank you, Father, for this anniversary, reminding us that another year of your goodness and care has passed. Accept our thanks for all the blessings that we have received during this year. Give us your pardon for our slackness and failure. Grant that as we begin another year we may go in your strength and peace, conscious that you know the way ahead of us and walk with us all the way.

Lord, we give you thanks on our wedding anniversary. We have failed many times to keep the vows we made, but you have never failed us. Thank you that as you forgive us we are able to forgive each other. Today we would make our promises to each other anew. Help us to be faithful, loving, constant and kind. May we seek to meet the other's needs rather than pleasing ourselves. Above all, may our marriage show more self-sacrifice and loving submission, reflecting your union, dear Lord, with your people, the church.

We ask it for your glory. Amen.

We come together to give thanks for your goodness to our two friends on this very special wedding anniversary. Thank you for giving them so many years together. Thank you that you have been with them in all the trials, joys and sorrow that they have shared. Grant them your special joy now and in the days or years that remain. May their marrriage be a blessing to them and to all who come within their influence. Through Jesus Christ our Lord.

WEDDING DAYS

The Lord sanctify and bless you,
the Lord pour the riches of his grace upon you,
that you may please him
and live together in holy love to your lives' end. So be it.
John Knox (1505–1572)

Eternal God, true and loving Father, in holy marriage you make your servants one. May their life together witness to your love in this troubled world; may unity overcome division, forgiveness heal injury, and joy triumph over sorrow; through Jesus Christ our Lord. Amen.

From the Alternative Service Book (1980)

O God, we thank you for our wedding day.
for the ceremony, the reception,
the presents we have received
and the friends and relatives who have shared the day with us.
May the joy and happiness we know today
be something we share
throughout our married life. Amen.

Christian Publicity Organization

Almighty God, giver of life and love, bless N and N, whom you have now joined in Christian marriage. Grant them wisdom and devotion in their life together, that each may be to the other a strength in need, a comfort in sorrow and a companion in joy. So unite their wills in your will and their spirits in your Spirit, that they may live and grow together in love and peace all the days of their life; through Jesus Christ our Lord. Amen

From the Alternative Service Book (1980)

Lord Jesus, we thank you
for all our parents have been able to do for us
for all the sacrifices they were prepared to make.
In our happiness
help us not to forget that they may be feeling a sense of loss.
Help us to be faithful in our concern for them. Amen.

Christian Publicity Organization

Lord, we have made our promises publicly.
Now, privately and sincerely, we confirm what we have done.
Lord Jesus, take our marriage and with it ourselves.
Help us to grow in love for each other and for you. Amen.

Christian Publicity Organization

SUCCESS

Lord, we bring to you all the success we gain in this world. Help us to use it to your glory, not to boast or impress others. If we have money, help us to use it wisely and to lay up treasure in heaven. If we are given responsibility and leadership may we learn to serve as we lead and follow the example of our King and Master, who came to serve others.

Thank you, Father, for giving me good success in these examinations. Thank you for the future that now opens up for me.

Help me not to be conceited or self-satisfied but to recognize your help and fatherly care in all my affairs. Lead me in your way. Amen.

Thank you, Lord, that I have passed my driving test. Thank you for helping me to overcome my nerves and think straight. May I use this new skill to help others and bring glory to you. Help me to drive in a careful and considerate way, that I may serve you well and have respect for others.

We have received the congratulations of others, Lord, but we want to bring our success to you. Thank you for it. Hallow it and use it to bring glory to your name. Amen.

Prayers to celebrate Christian festivals can be found in chapter 21.
General prayers of thanksgiving can be found in chapter 2.

❖ *Journeys* ❖

Two of Jesus' followers were going to a village named
Emmaus ... Jesus himself drew near and walked along with
them.

FROM LUKE 24

*The daily journey to work, to school, to shops; journeys to other towns
and other lands on business or on holiday—travel takes up a good bit of
our everyday lives. But down the ages people have also seen life itself as
a journey, from the cradle to the grave, from this world to the next.*

Travel

God be with you in every pass,
Jesus be with you on every hill,
Spirit be with you on every stream,
Headland and ridge and lawn;
Each sea and land, each moor and meadow,
Each lying down, each rising up,
In the trough of the waves, on the crest of the billows,
Each step of the journey you go.

Celtic prayer

◆ Thank you, God, for the fun of travelling. Thank you for jets and helicopters,
liners and yachts, for rockets and spacecraft, underground trains and
escalators; for cars and trains, scooters and lorries. Please watch over all who
travel today. Give them common sense and politeness. Teach them to guard
against accidents and to obey the rules made for their safety.

Zinnia Bryan

◆ God of all the steamships sailing far away
God of all the railways running every day,
God of all the travellers on bus or car or plane,
Guard and guide them every one and bring them home again.

Joan Gale Thomas

O Lord our God and God of our fathers!
Mercifully direct and guide our steps to our destination
and let us arrive there in health, joy and peace!
Keep us from snares and dangers,
and protect us from any enemies that we might meet along
the way.
Bless and protect our journey!
Let us win favour in your eyes and in the sight of those
around us.
Blessed are you, O Lord,
who hears and grants our prayers!

Jewish prayer

For encouragement on the journey:

I said to the man who stood at the gate of the year: 'Give me a
light that I may tread safely into the unknown.' And he replied:
'Go out into the darkness and put your hand into the hand of
God. That shall be to you better than light and safer than a
known way.'

Minnie Louise Haskins (1875–1957),
quoted by King George VI in his Christmas broadcast, 1939

I pray my God to give me perseverance and to vouchsafe that I bear to him
faithful witness until my passing hence, for his Name's sake.

St Patrick (389–461)

May the road rise to meet you.
May the wind be always at your back.
May the sun shine warm upon your face.
May the rains fall softly upon your fields until we meet again
May God hold you in the hollow of his hand.

Old Gaelic blessing

Eternal God,
you are present in all places,
so that we cannot be in any place
where you cannot be found;
give us the sense of your presence
and the knowledge of your fatherly love.
We commend to your care and keeping
all those who travel by road or rail,
or walk to distant places of our land.
Protect them by your power
and bring them safely to the end of their journey.
In the name of Jesus Christ.

W. Mfulaj, Zambia

God of the nomad and the pilgrim, may we find our security in you and not in
our possessions. May our homes be open to guests and our hearts to one
another so that all our travelling is lighter and together we reach the goal.

Stephen Orchard

Bless to me, O God,
The earth beneath my foot;
Bless to me, O God,
The path whereon I go;
Bless to me, O God,
The thing of my desire;
Thou Evermore of evermore,
Bless thou to me my rest.

Celtic prayer

Lord, I am a countryman
coming from my country to yours.
Teach me the laws of your country,
its way of life, its spirit,
so that I may feel at home there.

William of St Thierry (1085–1148)

Relieve thou, O God, each one
In suffering on land or sea,
In grief or wounded or weeping,
And lead them to the house of thy peace
This night.

Celtic prayer

Grant me a road and a watchful eye,
That none may suffer hurt as I pass by;
Thou givest life—I pray no act of mine
May take away or mar that gift of thine.
Shield those, dear Lord, who bear me company
From fools and fire and all calamity.
Teach me to use my car for others' need,
Nor miss through lack of wit or love of speed
The beauties of thy world, that thus I may,
With joy and courtesy, go on my way.

The motorist's prayer, author unknown

I am weary, weak and cold,
I am weary of travelling land and sea,
I am weary of traversing moorland and billow,
Grant me peace in the nearness of thy repose
This night.

Celtic prayer

O Lord Jesus Christ, who travelled the roads of Palestine and made them serve
the purposes of your kingdom, and who finally took the road to Calvary;
extend your sharp eye, your consideration and your ready compassion to those
of us who travel today's roads at such greater speeds, and so sorely need the
direction and protection you are able to give.

J.B.C.

You have led me through my crowded travels of the day
to my evening's loneliness.
I wait for its meaning through the stillness of the night.

Rabindranath Tagore (1861–1941)

Alone with none but thee, my God,
I journey on my way.
What need I fear, when thou art near
O King of night and day?
More safe am I within thy hand
Than if a host did round me stand.

St Columba (521–597)

Lord, you never slumber or sleep;
Preserve our going out and our coming in
from this time forth and for evermore. Amen.

From Psalm 121

Through the night of doubt and sorrow
Onward goes the pilgrim band,
Singing songs of expectation,
Marching to the promised land

Bernhardt Ingemann (1789–1862),
translated by Sabine Baring-Gould (1834–1924)

Who would true valour see
Let him come hither;
One here will constant be,
Come wind, come weather.
There's no discouragement
Shall make him once relent
His first avowed intent
To be a pilgrim.

Who so beset him round
With dismal stories,
Do but themselves confound;
His strength the more is.
No lion can him fright,
He'll with a giant fight,
But he will have a right
To be a pilgrim.

Hobgoblin, nor foul fiend,
Can daunt his spirit:

He knows he at the end
Shall life inherit.
Then fancies fly away,
He'll fear not what men say,
He'll labour night and day
To be a pilgrim.

John Bunyan (1628–1688)

Lord, you spent your earthly days
travelling on foot.
Your greatest journey was on a donkey.
But you left behind a trail
of hope, and love, and peace.
At least I know
that it is not the distance travelled that matters,
but the quality of the journey.
In all my travels,
Christ be before me,
Christ behind me,
Christ beside me,
Christ at mine end
and at my departing.

Frank Topping

God of all space and time,
and God of stable, fishing boat, market place and cross,
show yourself in today's world
as God of factory and paddy field,
of stock exchange and coffee co-operative,
of university and refugee camp,
as well as of our own hearths and hearts.
May all our journeys be pilgrimages,
and when we reach a goal
may it be the starting point
of positive change and 'another way' of life.

Author unknown

Lord, you have known my downsitting
And my uprising—the come and go
Of life's long littleness,
The moments of departure and arrival,
Waking and lapsing into unconsciousness,
Setting out for the market place
Or back from the fields;
To the longest working day
You saw me go.

You noticed me and knew about
The unimportant times (as I thought of them);
You loved me all the way
As I returned from the far country,
From the land of no-pasture
Back to an inheritance;
Through unseen watchfulness,
When human love forgot,
You welcomed me.

Randle Manwaring

As the banyan spreads her branches to give shelter to the traveller, so be thou
a shelter to me; and when my journey is over, take me home to my native
place—which is with you in heaven.

Prayer from India

In thy journeys to and fro
God direct thee;
In thy happiness and pleasure
God bless thee;
In care, anxiety or trouble
God sustain thee;
In peril and in danger
God protect thee.

Timothy Olufosoye, Nigeria

New Beginnings

Today, Lord,
A new day
Laid open,
And here am I
Waiting to step into it.
And yet there is a feeling of uncertainty,
Even fear,
Of what it holds,
Fear of what it will demand of me.
Have I the resources, Lord,
To meet this day?
Can I enter it
With joy and certainty and contentment?
My child,
This is the day I have made
For you.

Accept it gladly,
Dance into it,
And carry with you
The joy of resurrection,
The peace of self-giving,
The love that forgives and gives.
Delight yourself in this day
As a child delights
In all that is new.
Revel in it,
Absorb it,
For it is *today*, new,
That day that I have made.

Myrtle Hall

Through every minute of this day
Be with me, Lord!
Through every day of this week,
Be with me, Lord!
Through every week of all this year,
Be with me, Lord!
Through all the years of this life,
Be with me, Lord!
So shall the days and weeks and years
Be threaded on a golden cord.
And all draw on with sweet accord
Unto thy fulness, Lord,
That so, when time is past,
By grace I may, at last,
Be with thee, Lord.

John Oxenham (1853–1941)

Lord, may I be wakeful at sunrise to begin a new day for you, cheerful at sunset for having done my work for you; thankful at moonrise and under starshine for the beauty of the universe. And may I add what little may be in me to your great world.

The Abbot of Greve

We thank you, God, for the moments of fulfilment:
the end of a day's work,
the harvest of sugar cane,
the birth of a child,
for in these pauses we feel the rhythm of the eternal. Amen.

Prayer from Hawaii

As the earth keeps turning, hurtling through space, and night falls and day breaks from land to land,

Let us remember people—waking, sleeping, being born and dying—one world, one humanity.

Let us go from here in peace.

Prayer used at the sixth assembly of the World Council of Churches (Vancouver, 1983)

Mysterious new year
So wrapped in reserve and surprise
You have no reason to feel smug
Or even condescending.
After all, the majestic God
Has full knowledge of you
Just as he has of me.
There is not an issue that you can evade.
Furthermore you are powerless
To do anything to me
That God does not permit.
All he allows in his infinite wisdom
Is for my ultimate good
And his greatest glory.
Consequently, new year,
You cannot trick or disillusion me
By your baffling unexplainables
Or your feverish activity.
My times are in the hands
Of my sovereign God
Whose power is limitless
And whose love for me is everlasting.

Ruth Harms Calkin

With every power for good to stay and guide me,
Comforted and inspired beyond all fear,
I'll live these days with you in thought beside me,
And pass, with you, into the coming year.

Dietrich Bonhoeffer (1906–1945)
from prison, New Year 1945

Bless us, O Lord, in this coming year.
May dew and rain be a source of blessing.
Bless to our use the fruits of the earth
and let the earth rejoice in them.
And bless all that we do
and the work of our hands.

Jewish prayer

Father, let me dedicate
All this year to thee,
In whatever worldly state
Thou wilt have me be:
Not from sorrow, pain or care,
Freedom dare I claim;
This alone shall be my prayer,
'Glorify thy name.'

Lawrence Tuttiett (1825–1897)

Eternal God, who makest all things new and abidest for ever the same: grant us
to begin this year in thy faith and to continue it in thy favour; that, being
guided in all our doings and guarded all our days we may spend our lives in
thy service and finally by thy grace attain the glory of everlasting life; through
Jesus Christ our Lord.

William Orchard (1877–1955)

Lord of the years,
we ask your blessing on the year to come.
Give us the resilience to bear its disappointments,
energy to seize its opportunities
and openness to accept the more abundant life
which you have promised to us in Christ Jesus our Lord.

From More Everyday Prayers

◆ Father, at the beginning of this new term we come to you for help and guidance.

Give us courage and energy to take up our work again cheerfully.

Help us to work hard and as well as we can and give us happiness in the things we enjoy doing—music, art, sport and learning.

May our whole school work together well as we all care for one another. Through Jesus Christ our Lord.

Lord, bless your child as he begins this school for the first time. Quieten his fears and give him a spirit of adventure to welcome what is to come. Help him to find his way around. May he make friends and soon become an accepted member of the school.

Lord, hear our prayer for your blessing as your servant begins a new job. May she know your hands on her to protect and bless.

Give her wisdom, courage and the opportunity to use the skills and experience she has gained. May her presence in that workplace bring your light and peace there too.

Thank you, God, for this new home,
for the excitement of moving,
for the challenge of making this place a 'home'.
Thank you
that wherever I go,
whatever I do,
whatever happens,
you are by my side.
Lord Jesus, help me
to put aside those fears, doubts
and any second thoughts I am having
and help
me to enjoy this new home,
to make it a place
where your peace reigns.

Christian Publicity Organization

O God,
thank you for new opportunities
and new beginnings.
I know a new home
does not make new people.
I am sorry if I have brought with me
attitudes and ways
which would have been better
left behind.
But Lord Jesus, I want
to take advantage
of this new start.
Help me to get my priorities right,
to build my life on your promises. Amen.

Christian Publicity Organization

Thank you, Father,
for all homecomings,
all rediscoveries of friendship
which make us realize how important the past is
and how much we need a sense of continuity in our relationships.
You are a thread in all our comings and goings.
Never let us ignore you
or the part others have played in our lives.

From Further Everyday Prayers

Lord, one important part of my life is coming to a close. As I mourn what is passing, help me to remember all that has been happy and worthwhile in the past years. Make me confident in the knowledge that you are always creating new things. May I be certain that as one chapter ends another will begin, filled with your goodness and mercy. Through Jesus Christ my Lord. Amen.

Lord,
when it is time to say 'goodbye'
to friends, family or places we love,
give us courage
to move on to new experiences,
to make new associations
and to allow our children the freedom
to create their own journeys in life.
Where families face division and separation
so that individuals can rediscover their own identity
please be near to sustain and guide.

From Further Everyday Prayers

❖ *Times of Special Need* ❖

Do not be afraid—I will save you.
I have called you by name—you are mine.
When you pass through deep waters,
I will be with you;
your troubles will not overwhelm you.

FROM ISAIAH 43

Fear and Changing Moods

Be patient toward all that is unsolved in your heart.

Dag Hammarskjøld

If thou meet with the cross on thy journey, in what manner soever it be, be not daunted, and say, Alas, what shall I do now? But rather take courage, knowing that by the cross is the way to the kingdom.

John Bunyan (1628–88)

If I had not suffered
I would not have known the love of God.
If many people had not suffered
God's love would not have been passed on.
If Jesus had not suffered
God's love would not have been made visible.

Mizuno Genzo, Japan

When fear comes, pause...
Say what you are afraid of...
Feel the fear...
Take time...
then the barrier to trust will be lower,
the jump to be taken no longer paralyzing,
Have courage...
The Presence is very close and very loving.

From Prayer at Night

Comfort, O merciful Father, by thy Word and Holy Spirit, all who are afflicted or distressed, and so turn their hearts unto thee, that they may serve thee in truth and bring forth fruit to thy glory. Be thou, O Lord, their succour and defence, through Jesus Christ our Lord.

Philip Melanchthon (1497–1560)

Verses to quieten the heart and mind

The Lord is my shepherd;
I shall not want.
He maketh me to lie down in green pastures:
he leadeth me beside the still waters.
He restoreth my soul:
he leadeth me in the paths of righteousness for his name's sake.
Yea, though I walk through the valley of the shadow of death,
I will fear no evil:
for thou art with me; thy rod and thy staff they comfort me.
Thou preparest a table before me in the presence of
mine enemies:
thou anointest my head with oil; my cup runneth over.
Surely goodness and mercy shall follow me all the days
of my life:
and I will dwell in the house of the Lord for ever.

Psalm 23 (King James Version)

Let nothing disturb you, nothing alarm you:
while all things fade away
God is unchanging.
Be patient
and you will gain everything:
for with God in your heart
nothing is lacking,
God meets your every need.

St Teresa of Avila (1515–1582)

◆ Please Lord,
Help me to be brave and strong in you
and take my fear away.

Stephen Matthews (aged 13)

Lord, make possible for me by grace what is impossible to me by nature. You know that I am not able to endure very much, and that I am downcast by the slightest difficulty. Grant that for your sake I may come to love and desire any hardship that puts me to the test, for salvation is brought to my soul when I undergo suffering and trouble for you.

Thomas à Kempis (1379–1471)

Lord, I believe; help with my unbelief
For I believe in your deep love and mercy,
In your forgiving understanding
Of the human heart.
Through lonely watches of the spirit's night
Within the narrow tunnel of my grief,
I know a quiet dawn will come.
Tortured alone in the creeping loathsome dark
And dragged along a labyrinthic maze,
I still believe your healing sun
Will bring the birth of some new day
To break the iron gates of pain,
To bring again life where hopes, broken, lie
Crippled among her ancient battlements;
Lord, I believe that there will surely be
Light, after the midnight burns to death.

Randle Manwaring

O Lord, we beseech you to deliver us from the fear of the unknown future, from fear of failure, from fear of poverty, from fear of sickness and pain, from fear of age, and from fear of death. Help us, O Father, by your grace to love and fear you only. Fill our hearts with cheerful courage and loving trust in you; through our Lord and Master Jesus Christ.

Akanu Ibaim, Nigeria

O Holy Spirit, give me faith that will protect me from despair, from passions and from vice, give me such love for God as will blot out all hatred and bitterness, give me the hope that will deliver me from fear and faint heartedness.

Dietrich Bonhoeffer (1906–1945), from a prayer he used while in prison awaiting trial

Set free, O Lord, my soul from all restlessness and anxiety; give me that peace and power which flow from you; keep me in all perplexities and distresses, in all fears and faithlessness; that so upheld by your power and stayed on the rock of your faithfulness, I may through storm and stress remain in you, through Christ Jesus our Lord.

From New Every Morning

As the rain hides the stars, as the autumn mist hides the hills, as the clouds veil the blue of the sky, so the dark happenings of my lot hide the shining of your face from me. Yet, if I may hold your hand in the darkness, it is enough. Since I know that, though I may stumble in my going, you do not fall.

Gaelic prayer, translated by Alistair MacLean

Most loving Father,
Preserve us from faithless fears and worldly anxieties
and grant that no clouds of this mortal life
May hide from us the light of that love which is immortal
And which you have manifested unto us in your Son
Jesus Christ our Lord.

William Bright (1824–1904)

Ah Lord, my prayers are dead, my affections dead and my heart is dead; but you are a living God and I bear myself upon you.

William Bridge (1600–1670)

Lord, Lord almighty, Father of our Lord Jesus Christ, I am your servant; come to my help. Send me your angel; take my soul and give it peace. That will stop the foul dragon with his reek of blood from blocking my way; no malice of his will then obstruct my soul, none of his stratagems will deceive me.

Give me rest in the company of your martyrs; save your people, too, Lord, from oppression by the godless. For it is fitting that you should have honour, you and your only Son and the Holy Spirit, throughout the ages.

Boniface of Tarsus (died 306)

O God, who has made the heaven and the earth and all that is good and lovely therein, and has shown us through Jesus Christ our Lord that the secret of joy is a heart free from selfish desires, help us to find delight in simple things and ever to rejoice in the riches of your bounty, through Jesus Christ our Lord.

From The Kingdom, the Power and the Glory

O my sweet Saviour Christ, which in thine undeserved love towards mankind so kindly wouldst suffer the painful death of the cross, suffer me not to be cold nor lukewarm in love again towards thee.

Thomas More (1478–1535)

Give me a candle of the Spirit, O God, as I go down into the deeps of my being. Show me the hidden things, the creatures of my dreams, the storehouse of forgotten memories and hurts. Take me down to the spring of my life and tell me my nature and my name. Give me freedom to grow, so that I may become that self, the seed of which you planted in me at my making. Out of the deeps I cry to you, O God.

George Appleton

If I am to complain, let me complain to Jesus fastened on his cross. But in your presence, my Saviour, what have I to complain of? What are my sufferings compared with those you bear without complaining? I might perhaps convince my fellow man that I am unjustly afflicted, but in your presence, Lord, I cannot, for my sins are known to you. You know my sufferings are far less than I deserve. And since all my afflictions proceed from you, to you I come; give me strength and hearten me to suffer in silence; as once you did yourself.

Claude de la Colombière (died 1682)

My strength fails; I feel only weakness, irritation and depression. I am tempted to complain and to despair. What has become of the courage I was so proud of and that gave me so much self-confidence? In addition to my pain, I have to bear the shame of my fretful feebleness. Lord, destroy my pride; leave it no resource. How happy I shall be if you can teach me by these terrible trials that I am nothing, that I can do nothing and that you are all!

François Fénelon (1631–1715)

Who am I? This or the other?
Am I one person today and tomorrow another?
Am I both at once? A hypocrite before others
And before myself a contemptible woebegone weakling?
Or is something within me still like a beaten army,
Fleeing in disorder from victory already achieved?
Who am I? They mock me, these lonely questions of mine,
Whoever I am, thou knowest, O God, I am thine!

Dietrich Bonhoeffer (1906–1945)

Lord, thou art life, though I be dead,
Love's fire thou art, however cold I be;
Nor heaven have I, nor place to lay my head,
Nor home, but thee.

Christina Rossetti (1830–1894)

O Spirit of God,
Set at rest the crowded, hurrying conscious thoughts
within our minds and hearts.
Let the peace and quiet of your presence take possession of us.
Help us to relax, to rest, to become open and receptive to you.
You know our inmost spirits,
the hidden unconscious life within us,
the forgotten memories of hurts and fears,
the frustrated desires,
the unresolved tensions and dilemmas.
Cleanse and sweeten the springs of our being
that freedom, life and love may flow
into both our conscious and hidden life.
Lord, we lie open before you, waiting for your healing,
your peace and your word.

George Appleton

O Lord, calm the waves of this heart; calm its tempest! Calm yourself, O my soul, so that the divine can act in you! Calm yourself, O my soul, so that God is able to repose in you, so that his peace may cover you! Yes, Father in heaven, often have we found that the world cannot give us peace. O but make us feel that you are able to give peace; let us know the truth of your promise; the whole world may not be able to take away your peace.

Søren Kierkegaard (1813–1855)

O God of peace, who has taught us that in returning and in rest we shall be saved and in quietness and in confidence shall be our strength: by the might of your Spirit lift us, we pray you, to your presence, where we may be still and know that you are God; through Jesus Christ our Lord.

J.W. Suter

O my Lord, I am in a dry land, all dried up and cracked by the violence of the north wind and the cold; but as you see, I ask for nothing more; you will send me both dew and warmth when it pleases you.

St Jane de Chantal (1572–1641)

Strengthen, O Lord, our weakness in your compassion, and comfort and help the wants of our soul in your loving kindness. Waken our thoughts from sleep and lighten the weight of our limbs; wash us and cleanse us from all the filth of our sins.

Enlighten the darkness of our minds, stretch forth your helping hand, confirm and give us strength; that we may arise and confess you and glorify you without ceasing all the days of our life, O Lord of all.

From the Nestorian Liturgy

Comfort, we beseech you, most gracious God, all who are cast down and faint of heart amidst the sorrows and difficulties of the world and grant that, by the energy of your Holy Spirit, they may be able to go upon their way rejoicing and give you continual thanks for your sustaining providence, through Jesus Christ our Saviour.

R.M. Benson (1824-1915)

Lord,
in the Garden of Gethsemane
you shared with everyone
who has ever been afraid.
You conquered fear with love
and returned saying,
'Do not be afraid.'
In the light of your love
death has lost its sting
and so has fear.
Lord, may your love
be the key that releases me
from fear.

Frank Topping

O Lord, whose way is perfect, help us, we pray, always to trust in your goodness, that walking with you and following you in all simplicity, we may possess quiet and contented minds and may cast all our care on you, who cares for us. Grant this, O Lord, for your dear Son's sake, Jesus Christ.

Christina Rossetti (1830–1894)

Father, we pray for all lonely people, especially those who coming home to an empty house stand at the door hesitant and afraid to enter. May all who stand on any doorway with fear in their hearts, like the two on the Emmaus road, ask the Living One in. Then, by his grace, may they find that in loneliness they are never alone and that he peoples empty rooms with his presence.

E.M. Farr

O Lord, baptize our hearts into a sense of the needs and conditions of all.

George Fox (1624–1691)

Grant, O God, that amidst all the discouragements, difficulties, dangers, distress and darkness of this mortal life, I may depend upon your mercy and on this build my hopes, as on a sure foundation. Let your infinite mercy in Christ Jesus deliver me from despair, both now and at the hour of death.

Thomas Wilson (1663–1755)

Loving Father, we pray for all whose lives are paralyzed by fear.

Some fears are real, others seem trivial or imaginary, yet all are real to the sufferer.

Set free all who are victims of fear and who put their trust in you. Give them the knowledge of your fatherly care and help them to let go and know release in your strength and your peace. Through Jesus Christ our Lord.

> Banish my fears and increase my love, Lord,
> but convince me again and again
> that in your perfect love fear itself is destroyed
> and that such love is offered to me, fully and freely.
>
> *From More Everyday Prayers*

Lord Jesus Christ, you faced temptation with confidence in God, suffering with serenity, loneliness with the assurance that your Father would not forsake you, and the cross with an inner spirit of peace. You endured all things that we might be saved ... Prepare us for whatever life brings of joy or sorrow so that, being sure of your love, we may be confident of your eternal presence. Amen.

> *From Prayers Before Worship*

> Lord,
> teach me how to still my racing thoughts.
> Help me to come to you
> arguing nothing,
> pleading nothing,
> asking nothing,
> except to be still
> in your presence.
> Give me the faith
> that will enable me
> to lay my burdens at your feet,
> and to leave them there
> in exchange for the peace
> which passes all understanding.
>
> *Frank Topping*

Father in heaven,
we give thanks for life and the experience life brings us.
We thank you for our joys, sorrows, trials, failures and triumphs.
Above all, we thank you for the hope we have in Christ that we
shall find fulfilment in him.

From a prayer of thanksgiving for India

O God, I am lonely.
You know how depressed I get.
You know how time passes so slowly for me.
You know how at times I feel bitter and resentful.
O God, help me
to welcome those who offer friendship,
to look for those who need to be comforted,
so that in giving I might have no time for loneliness.
Thank you for promising
never to leave me alone,
that in quietness and rest
I shall find your strength. Amen.

Christian Publicity Organization

God, give me strength to run this race,
God, give me power to do the right,
And courage lasting through the fight;
God, give me strength to see your face,
And heart to stand till evil cease,
And, at the last, O God, your peace.

Author unknown

◆ Give us a sense of humour, Lord, and also things to laugh about. Give us the
grace to take a joke against ourselves and to see the funny side of the things we
do. Save us from annoyance, bad temper, resentfulness against our friends.
Help us to laugh even in the face of trouble. Fill our minds with the love of
Jesus; for his name's sake.

A.G. Bullivant

No one can put together what has crumbled into dust,
but you can restore a conscience turned to ashes;
you can restore to its former beauty a soul lost and without hope.
With you there is nothing that cannot be redeemed;
you are love, you are Creator and Redeemer;
we praise you, singing: Alleluia!

Gregory Petrov

Testing Times

I asked the Lord
for a bunch of fresh flowers
but instead he gave me an ugly cactus
with many thorns.
I asked the Lord
for some beautiful butterflies
but instead he gave me
many ugly and dreadful worms.
I was threatened,
I was disappointed,
I mourned.
But after many days,
suddenly,
I saw the cactus bloom
with many beautiful flowers,
and those worms became
beautiful butterflies
flying in the spring wind.
God's way is the best way.

Chun-Ming Kao, written from prison

O Lord God,
Great is the misery that has come upon me;
My cares would overwhelm me,
I know not what to do.
O God, be gracious unto me and help me.
Grant me strength to bear what you send
and let not fear rule over me.
As a loving Father, take care of my loved ones...

O merciful God, forgive me all
the sins I have committed against you,
and against my fellow men.
I trust in your grace and commit
my life wholly into your hands.
So do with me as seems best to you and as is best for me.
Whether I live or die, I am with you,
and you are with me, my God.
Lord, I wait for your salvation.

Dietrich Bonhoeffer (1906–1945)

O Blessed Jesu Christ, who bade all who carry heavy burdens to come to you, refresh us with your presence and your power. Quiet our understandings and give ease to our hearts by bringing us close to things infinite and eternal. Open to us the mind of God that in his light we may see light. And crown your choice of us to be your servants by making us springs of strength and joy to all whom we serve.

Evelyn Underhill (1875–1941)

From the depths of my despair I call to you, Lord.
Hear my cry, O Lord: listen to my call for help!

From Psalm 130

Jesus, a great desire have we
To walk earth's troubled path with thee:
Come to us now, in converse stay,
And O walk with us day by day!

Edwin Paxton Hood (1820–1885)

God, how much more can I stand?

Help me, Lord, help me to keep my sanity and my strength. God, please take some of these interminable problems from me. Disperse them, deal with them through some other channel. Surely I have been used enough. Surely I have been pursued and caught and used enough. There is not much left.

Lord, restore me. Give me strength.

But, oh, release me for a little while too. Please give me a respite from these problems.

Marjorie Holmes

I pray today for people faced with difficult decisions: decisions which will seriously affect their lives and the lives of their loved ones: decisions about jobs, about their marriage, about where to live, about money.

I pray for those who can see no way through their problems: for whom it is all too much.

Help them to see that you, who control the universe, are in control of their lives too.

From Further Everyday Prayers

Almighty God,
you know us to be set in the midst of so many
and great dangers,
that, because of the frailty of our nature,
we cannot always stand upright.
Give us such strength and protection
as may support us in all dangers
and carry us through all temptations;
through Jesus Christ our Lord.

From the Alternative Service Book (1980)

Almighty God, the hour of your glory has come; look mercifully upon me and deliver me from this great misfortune. In you I place my hopes, for alone I am helpless and as nothing. Help me, O God, and deliver me from fear.

From a Russian samizdat typewritten collection of prayers

I do not know, O God,
What is there in store for me.
Only let me have your grace
To live with your blessing.

Prayer of Tamil awaiting repatriation to India

We commend to your care all those who find life too much
for them;
those who daily have to face jobs with which they cannot cope;
those who are daunted by the whole business of living;
those whose families make demands on them which they
cannot meet;
those who cannot summon up the strength to do the things they
know have to be done;
those who feel they cannot go on.
Lord, giver of life, give them life.

From Further Everyday Prayers

Particular Situations in the Home and Workplace

Lord, you told us not to worry about tomorrow. You reassured us that our heavenly Father knows about our need for food and clothes. We ask you to meet our need for money to pay the bills.

Help us to be wise and sensible in our use of what money we have. Then free us from the gnawing anxiety of wondering how to make ends meet. We believe that we can trust you to keep your promise and supply our everyday needs.

Father, hear our prayer for our parents and elderly relatives. You have promised to care for your children till the time that their hair is grey. Look down with love and pity on these members of our family and care for them in their frailty and need.

Give us wisdom to know how to do what is best for them. Guide our decision-making. Give us patience and understanding, especially with those who are difficult or obstinate. Supply us with the strength to follow out the course we feel we should follow and give us your love for them.

Lord, we commit to your care all who are strained and stressed in the home; those with poor housing; those with young children; those nursing sick partners, parents or children; those whose marriage is going through difficult times; those with too much to do; those with time on their hands and too little strength to do as they once did. All who are burdened in these and other ways we commit to your fatherly care; through Jesus Christ our Lord.

Father, we pray for all who are under unbearable stress at work; those whose job demands great concentration and skill; those dealing with people in need; those whose seniors or colleagues make life difficult and unpleasant; those with boring or unpleasant jobs; those working long hours; those facing possible unemployment.

Give strength to your servants as they turn to you for help in snatched moments of the day; for Jesus' sake.

O Lord, show me how to decide and give me such trust in you that I may receive your guidance and in calmness may act upon it.

Malcolm Playfoot

Father, we thank you for our daily work. Whatever the difficulties, help us to do it with cheerfulness and courage. For the sake of Jesus Christ, our Lord and our Master. Amen.

Prayers relating to testing times in marriage and parenthood can be found in chapter 6.

Lord, have mercy on all who have been made redundant. Help them as they face the shock and disbelief, then the sadness of loss. Give them help for each day as it comes. May they keep the sense of worth that comes from knowing that they matter to you and to those who love them most. We pray for their parents, partners and children. Help them to bear the sadness and the difficult reactions of the one who has been hurt. Give them all courage for the present and hope for the future.

Father, I pray for those who have no paid employment and who have no colleagues, that they may not despair but may find other ways of working for the well-being of society and may find fellowship in common enterprise. Bless those whose days of retirement have separated them from colleagues and give them a sense of their continuing worth as your children. Enlarge our experience of community life that we may see each other as fellow workers in your wider kingdom, because we all belong to one another in Christ.

From More Everyday Prayers

Hear our prayer for all who bear a heavy load of responsibility at work and whose decisions have far-reaching effects on the life and health of the nation. May they look to you for wisdom. Give them integrity and fairness, justice and kindness. Through Jesus Christ our Lord.

◆ O God, we start exams tomorrow. I've studied hard but I'm sure I haven't learned enough and I cannot always remember what I've learned.

Please help me to keep calm and not be worried, so that I'll remember what I've learned and do my best. Then, if I fail, I need not be ashamed, and if I pass, please help me not to boast but give my thanks to you for helping me to use the gifts which you have given. Thank you, God.

Nancy Martin

General prayers about work, money and possessions can be found in chapter 7

· *In Illness* ·

As a father is kind to his children,
so the Lord is kind to those who honour him.
He knows what we are made of;
he remembers that we are dust.

FROM PSALM 103

When you are sick, do not be negligent,
but pray to the Lord and he will heal you...
And give the physician his place, for the Lord created him.

From Ecclesiasticus 38

Lord, teach me the art of patience when I am well and give me the use of it
when I am sick. In that day either lighten my burden or strengthen my back.
Make me, who so often in my health have discovered my weakness presuming
on my own strength, to be strong in my sickness when I solely rely on your
assistance.

Thomas Fuller (1608–1661)

Lord God,
This illness is making me depressed.
I am irritated by its aches and pains.
I get tired of doing nothing.
I worry about the extra work I am causing others.
O God,
speak to me in the quietness about your majesty,
the wonder and beauty of your creation,
about your love for me.
Speak to me about Jesus Christ my Saviour—
the pain of Calvary, about his resurrection life.
O God, I will worship you.

Christian Publicity Organization

We ask you not, O Lord, to rid us of pain; but grant in your mercy that our
pain may be free from waste, unfretted by rebellion against your will, unsoiled
by thought of ourselves, purified by love of our kind and ennobled by
devotion to your kingdom, through the mercies of your only Son, our Lord.

From the American Prayer Book (1928)

For meditation and quiet prayer:

From the depths of my despair I call to you, Lord.
Hear my cry, O Lord;
listen to my call for help!...
I wait eagerly for the Lord's help
and in his word I trust.

From Psalm 130

Heal us, Lord, and we shall be healed; save us and we shall be saved; for it is you we praise. Send relief and healing for our diseases, our sufferings and our wounds; for you are a merciful and faithful healer. Blessed are you, Lord, who heals the sick.

Jewish prayer

I will rejoice at my tribulations and infirmities
and be strong in the Lord,
at all times giving thanks to God the Father
and to his only Son, our Lord Jesus Christ, and to the
Holy Spirit
for the great grace he has given me
in deigning to assure me, his unworthy servant,
while I am still alive, that his kingdom will be mine.

St Francis of Assisi (1182–1226)

Lord, look down on me in my infirmities
and help me to bear them patiently.

St Francis of Assisi (1182–1226)

Father, I give you thanks for all those times when you have been with me in moments of weakness and suffering. More than ever before, your love seemed all about me and beneath me. I remember with gratitude the encouragement of friends and the care of those who were closest to me. May the remembrance of your goodness fill all the coming days with confidence and with hope.

From More Everyday Prayers

I thank you, Lord God,
for all my pains;
if it please you, Lord,
increase them a hundredfold.
I shall thankfully accept
whatever sorrow you give, not sparing me;
for in the fulfilment of your will
I find my greatest solace.

St Francis of Assisi (1182–1226),
when his illness grew worse.

Lord, we pray for all who are weighed down with the mystery of suffering.
Reveal yourself to them as the God of love who bears all our sufferings. Grant
that they may know that suffering borne in fellowship with you is not waste or
frustration but can be turned to goodness and blessing, something greater than
if they had never suffered, through him who on the cross suffered rejection
and hatred, loneliness and despair, agonizing pain and physical death and rose
victorious from the dead, conquering and to conquer, even Jesus Christ our
Lord.

George Appleton

I thank you for Pain,
the sister of Joy,
I thank you for Sorrow,
the twin of Happiness.
Pain, Joy, Sorrow, Happiness,
Four angels at work on the Well of Love.
Pain and Sorrow dig it deep with aches,
Joy and Happiness fill it up with tears
that come with smiles.
For the seasons of emotion in my heart,
I thank you, Lord.

Chandran Devanasen, India

Holy Lord and Father, almighty and eternal God, who pours into broken human bodies the healing grace of your own blessing and in a thousand ways shows your care for what your hands have made, be good to us and draw near, as we call upon your name. Deliver your servant from his sickness. Give him health anew. Stretch out your hand and set him on his feet again. Put strength into him and keep him safe under your powerful protection. Give him back again to your holy church and may all henceforth be well with him. Through Christ our Lord.

From The Small Ritual

God our Father, whose son, Jesus Christ, loved to bring health and healing to those who were ill, may the Holy Spirit help and teach all doctors so that they try to find out more and more about curing and preventing illness. And help them too always to do their work lovingly and patiently even when they are very tired, just as Jesus did. Father, hear our prayer, for his sake.

Hope Freeman

'The Lord gave and the Lord hath taken away.'
Lord, you made your servant Job say this in the depth of his misfortunes. How kind you are to put these words in the mouth of a sinner like me. You gave me health and I forgot you. You take it away and I come back to you . . . Lord, take away everything that is not you. All is yours. You are the Lord. Dispose everything: comforts, success, health. Take all the things that possess me instead of you that I may be wholly yours.

François Fénelon (1631-1715)

Father, we thank you for all those who bear suffering with courage and patience. We thank you for the way their lives enlighten and inspire our own. Give to them a sense of their high calling. May they find strength in knowing that they are sharing in the sufferings of their Master and following his perfect example. Be close to them and grant them your strength and your peace. Through Jesus Christ our Lord.

Dear Lord, for all in pain
We pray to thee;
O come and smite again
Thine enemy.

Give to thy servants skill
To soothe and bless,
And to the tired and ill
Give quietness.

And, Lord, to those who know
Pain may not cease,
Come near, that even so
They may have peace.

Amy Carmichael (1868–1951)

Your eternal providence has appointed me to watch over the life and health of your creatures. May the love for my art actuate me at all times, may neither avarice nor miserliness nor the thirst for glory or for a great reputation engage my mind ... May I never see in a patient anything but a fellow creature in pain. Grant me strength, time and opportunity always to correct what I have acquired, always to extend its domain, for knowledge is immense and the spirit of man can always extend indefinitely to enrich itself daily with new requirements ...

O God, you have appointed me to watch over the life and death of your creatures. Here I am, ready for my vocation.

Maimonides (1134–1204), the medical oath

Father, we pray for those who are sick in body, mind or spirit. Especially we pray for ... Please bring them your peace in their pain, your strength in their weakness and your comfort in their sadness. Through Jesus Christ our Lord.

In Hospital

The sick and the suffering are the favoured of God. He shows them special love and attention. Be assured that right now you are especially loved, even if in the midst of your pain you are not aware of it.

Basilea Schlink

O God, you understand my feelings at this moment; you know my fears and my nervousness; you know the thoughts that I cannot put into words.

I thank you for all the skill and wisdom of the surgeon, the anaesthetist and the nursing staff. Give them your strength during all their work today and help me to place myself in their hands.

Christian Publicity Organization

◆ Lord, we thank you for the great resources of healing that are available to those who are sick.

> For the skill of surgeons and the technical abilities of support staff in operating theatres,
> thank you.

> For medical knowledge and the healing power of drugs and medicines,
> for chemists and pharmacists,
> thank you.

> For nursing staff, for their professional skill and their capacity for caring and encouraging,
> thank you.

> For support teams of physiotherapists, occupational therapists, radiologists, hospital social workers and hospital chaplains,
> thank you.

> For administrative staff, ward orderlies, hospital porters and ambulance drivers,
> thank you.

From Further Everyday Prayers

◆Father, we commit to your loving care all children in hospital. Comfort them as they miss the familiar surroundings of home. Take away their fear if they face the ordeal of painful treatment. Give gentleness and understanding to all who care for them. Have them now in your safe keeping. For Jesus the Good Shepherd's sake.

My visitors have gone, O God, leaving me flowers, fruit and magazines—and for these I am thankful;
> They have left me, also, fresh things to think about...
> But now I am tired... Save me from self-pity... Establish my faith within serenity, O God; strengthen my memory, that I can hold on to what I know;
> sustain my home-folk and all whose days are now different;
> Give me your sweet gift of sleep this night, refreshing and calm. And bless all who labour to lighten the lot of others in need. In Christ's name. Amen.

Rita Snowden

> Thank you, O God, for all the people who have looked after me today...
> Into your strong hands I place all the patients in this ward;
> the night staff on duty tonight;
> my loved ones whose names I now mention;
> myself, with my fears, my worries and my hopes.
> Help me to sleep, thinking of you and your promises. Amen.

Christian Publicity Organization

O God, these long days of convalescence make demands on my patience that I have not known before. I want to get back to my usual interests—but I get so tired, so soon. It is hard for me to realize that I am still not fit for work. Let me not spoil all that has been done for me by impatience now.

And what I ask for myself I ask for others—at home and still in hospital—whose days seem long... Support all who try their best to lay hold of health and wholeness. For Christ's sake. Amen.

Rita Snowden

Disability

Father, we commend to your loving care those who face lifelong pain or disease. Give them the special courage that such a situation calls for. May they realize how much their patience and cheerfulness can influence others for good. Strengthen them when they are weak and low in spirit and help them to see beyond the pain to the glorious future that you have prepared for those who love you. Through Jesus Christ our Lord.

◆ Dear Father God, today we are remembering in our prayers all those boys and girls who cannot run and play as freely as we can.

We think about children who spend a lot of time in wheelchairs or lying in bed, or perhaps sitting at a window, watching their friends at play.

Help us not to be selfish; to spare time for them; to share our books, our records and our games; to tell our news and write happy letters.

Help boys and girls who are shut in at home, or in hospital, away from the streets and the fields, to know that we think about them and that people care for them.

May they find joy in pictures and in music, in stories and in the friendship of others.

Jean Stevens

O God, we ask your blessing on those who cannot see he beauties of nature or hear the sounds of life. Help them to feel your presence. Guide their hands and feet in safety. Help them to find the gifts which you have given them instead of sight and hearing, so that they may use them to your glory, for the sake of him who healed the blind and the deaf, Jesus Christ our Lord.

B.B.

◆ Lord, we thank you that we can hear the everyday sounds; music and the voices of our friends, radio and television, the fire alarm or the car coming round the corner that warns of danger.

Help us to be considerate to the deaf who often feel alone, cut off from these sounds. Let us talk to them clearly so that they may feel less isolated. And please give patience to those who teach them.

Phyllis Lovelock

Father, we lift up to you all who are disabled —in hearing, in sight, in limb or in mind. Save them from bitterness and frustration and give them joy in the midst of their limitations. May they find peace and fulfilment in knowing you and discovering your will for their lives.

We pray for special grace for those who care for them. Give them your love and kindness and understanding of the real needs of those they look after. For Jesus' sake. Amen.

Lord, we pray for those who nurse a sick parent or partner or child. Where life is threatened by the illness give the carer calmness and wisdom. For those who nurse the chronically sick, knowing that a lifetime of care will be called for, we pray for endurance, patience and gentleness in the face of tiring duties and lost sleep. Care for the carers with your fatherly concern and meet their needs so that they may have strength to persevere with love and kindness. For the sake of Jesus Christ our Lord.

Those Suffering From the AIDS Virus

Dear Lord, you came into the world so that we should know your love and care for us. By your grace help us to share your loving and caring with those whose lives are being changed by the AIDS virus and to bring them help and comfort. Amen.

Bill Kirkpatrick

Almighty God, creator of life, sustainer of every good thing I know, my partner with me in the pain of this earth, hear my prayer as I am in the midst of separation and alienation from everything I know to be supportive and healing and true.

AIDS has caused me to feel separated from you. I say, 'Why me? What did I do to deserve this?' ... Help me to remember that you do not punish your creation by bringing disease, but that you are Emmanuel, God with us. You are as close to me as my next breath.

AIDS has caused a separation between the body I knew and my body now ... Help me to remember that I am more than my body, and while it pains me greatly to see what has happened to it, I am more than my body . . . I am part of you and you me.

AIDS has separated me from my family . . . Oh God, help me and them to realize that I haven't changed, I'm still their child, our love for each other is your love for us . . . Help them to overcome their fear, embarrassment and guilt . . . Their love brought me into this world . . . Help them to share as much as possible with me.

AIDS has caused a separation between me and my friends; my friendships have been so important to me. They are especially important now . . . Help me, oh God, to recognize their fear and my increasing need for them to love in any way they can.

AIDS has separated me from society, my whole world and my community . . . It pains me for them to see me differently now . . . Forgive them for allowing their ignorance of this disease and their fear to blind their judgments . . . Help me deal with my anger towards them.

AIDS has caused a separation between me and my church . . . Help the church restore its ministry to 'the least of these' by reaching out to me and others . . . Help them suspend their judgments and love me as they have before. Help me and them to realize that the church is the body of Christ . . . that separation and alienation wound the body.

God of my birth and God of my death, help me know you have been, you are, and you are to come . . . Amen.

A Litany of Reconciliation, author unknown

Loving God, you show yourself to those who are vulnerable and make your home with the poor and weak of this world;

Warm our hearts with the fire of your Spirit. Help us to accept the challenge of AIDS.

Protect the healthy, calm the frightened, give courage to those in pain, comfort the dying and give to the dead eternal life.

Console the bereaved, strengthen those who care for the sick.

May we, your people, using all our energy and imagination, and trusting in your steadfast love, be united with one another in conquering all disease and fear.

Interfaith Group

◆ *Search for Freedom* ◆

Jesus said to them . . . 'If the Son sets you free, then you will
be really free.'

FROM JOHN 8

Jesus came 'to proclaim liberty to the captives'. Both those behind prison bars and those in the outside world need the freedom he came to bring.

Freedom from Guilt and Fear

Whether we are in a dark cell or a very well-lit prison ward, if we are behind bars we are then in darkness ... There are many prisoners of their own bars in life, but that is also darkness—even if it is self-inflicted. Whether we are behind bars or prisoners of our own making there is only one solution in order not to live in darkness; and that is to have *light*; and that *light* is there if we turn to him to lighten our darkness. Our Lord is the Prisoner's Lantern in the dungeon.

From The Prisoner's Lantern, written by a prisoner in Ethiopia

Who can boast of being free?
Who has not got secret prisons,
invisible chains, all the more constricting
the less they are apparent?

Dom Helder Camara, Brazil

Lord, help me to accept what cannot be changed. If I am guilty, let me learn from my imprisonment; and if not guilty—and being not guilty is harder— then show me why you have put me here. Let me be open enough to see why.

From The Prisoner's Lantern

Lord, thank you for becoming our Brother. I ask that you would free those in prison from the bondage of their shame and disgrace. Let them see prison as a time to share in the sufferings of their brothers—and to know that you share those pains as well.

Charles W. Colson

O Lord Jesus Christ, who for us became a man of sorrows, acquainted with grief, we ask that you will bring hope to those prisoners who despair, peace to those in distress and comfort to those who are fearful. For your name's sake. Amen.

> I lean myself
>   Upon the
> Crucified Lord.
>
> What more can
>   Fall on me
> Than fell on him,
>
> And broke him not?
>   Yet broken bread
> For broken world.
>
> A bruised reed
>   He will not break
> On him I'll lean,
>
> And from the depths
>   Of his great pain
> I'll strength regain.

John McNally, ex-prisoner

Lord, you have come into the world to save sinners—no matter what the world thinks of sin: all have sinned and come short of your glory. You have come to seek and to save the lost sheep like me. I accept your salvation, Lord. I come to be forgiven.

From The Prisoner's Lantern

Lord, there is nothing I can do to alter the situation and there is nothing that you do not know—even the hairs on our head are numbered by you. My anxiety is great and I cannot face thinking about my problems. But you have promised to help. Please give me the necessary faith to unburden my worries on you knowing that you care.

From The Prisoner's Lantern

Lord Jesus Christ,
You were poor and in misery,
a captive and forsaken as I am,
You know all man's distress;
You abide with me
when all others have deserted me;
You do not forget but seek me,
You will that I should know you and turn to you.
Lord, I hear your call and follow you;
Do help me.

Dietrich Bonhoeffer (1906–1945)

Almighty God, we thank and praise you that you are love. We bring to you in sadness the many people in prison who have never received love as children or as adults. Through your Word, your Spirit and your church may they discover your love for them shown in Jesus Christ and experience the joy of the love which you long to give them. Amen.

If ever I was a cluster of grapes,
today I am residue left by the press.
Into the fathomless hunger in me
pour some drop of juice.

On the depth of my hunger
blind deserts open up.
When the last spoonful is eaten
I drop over my bowl and spoon.

O God, you who
out of two fishes and five loaves
made mountains of food
and satisfied thousands of poor.

Repeat the miracle, O Good One,
and satisfy thousands of mouths.
Listen also to my prayer,
Give me the basket of crumbs.

From Hungry by Nichifor Carinic

Lord Jesus,
you experienced in person
torture and death
as a prisoner of conscience.
You were beaten and flogged
and sentenced to an agonizing death
though you had done no wrong.
Be now with prisoners of conscience
throughout the world.
Be with them in their fear and loneliness,
in the agony of physical and mental torture,
and in the face of execution and death.
Stretch out your hands in power
to break their chains.
Be merciful to the oppressor and the torturer
and place a new heart within them.
Forgive all injustice in our lives
and transform us to be
instruments of your peace,
for by your wounds we are healed.

Amnesty International

To help us pray:

As we closed our doors this morning, and walked freely through
the church door, other doors slammed behind other people and
they do not know if or when they will be open again; doors in
prison cells and torture chambers; doors separating families;
doors in labour camp units. Let us ask Christ, who came to set all
men free, to enable us to experience his freedom and to bring
that freedom to others.

Pax Christi, prayer for prisoners of conscience

Lord Jesus, I come to accept your salvation offered to sinners for whom you came. Thank you for that. Before you I can be clean from my guilt of sin even if condemned by man to death or life imprisonment.

From The Prisoner's Lantern

> For so long, dear God
> I stared with dreadful fascination
> At the thick heavy chains
> Binding my burdened life
> When all the while you were waiting
> For my personal consent
> To break the chains and set me free.
> Oh, what liberating joy
> When I finally said Yes!

Ruth Harms Calkin

Dearest Father, please imprint your holy Word in my heart and mind. Protect me from the depths of depression and from forgetting that you will never leave me or forsake me. Amen.

Jane A DiMemmo, prisoner, Pennsylvania

O God our Father, we pray for those in prison who are innocent of charges laid against them. Keep them from bitterness and despair we beseech you. May the truth of their position be established and may your standards of justice prevail in our courts.

Lord, I am waiting for you. I know now that it is not for lesser joys and lesser relief that I wait impatiently. It is you I need above all. Come to me and set me free: from my worries; from my regrets; from my false desires; from my captivity to self-seeking and self-pleasing.

Your service is perfect freedom. Lord, make me your servant that I may be truly free.

I do not know how you can deliver me, Lord, but you are the only just and loving God. Give me the Holy Spirit who will free me from bondage—whatever my bondage, whether behind iron bars or not behind bars.

From The Prisoner's Lantern

I pray for my living and for my dead.
They are all one for me now, friend and foe.
With them I equally frittered away through the years,
my love and my hate I shared with them.

In my evening prayer I gather the dead.
These are they, O Lord, and I too am among the graves.
In them were heights and there were downfalls.
A little in each and in all I was whole.

Of life's storms they now are empty
and of love, of hate, of it all what has remained?
Only a heart-broken prayer for your mercy, O Master,
Forgive them, Lord, I pray you, I too am among the dead.

And gathering my living, to your mercy I turn
when the morning glow crowns the earth.
Give them, O Lord, give them with bounteous hand
the belated wisdom of my dusk.

Nichifor Crainic, evening prayer

Chiefly do I remember all my loved ones,
my fellow prisoners and all who
in this house perform their hard service.
Lord have mercy,
restore me to liberty,
and enable me so to live now,
that I may answer before you and before the world.
Lord, whatever this day may bring,
your name be praised.
Amen.

Dietrich Bonhoeffer (1906–1945)

Freedom To Be What God Wants Us To Be

O God, you have made me free to choose you and love you. Thank you for freeing me from fear! Help me to show your love to each person I meet today and every day. Amen.

Pearline Jones, prisoner, Nebraska

Father, we thank you for your creation; for its beauty, its variety, its magnitude and its order. We pray for all prisoners whose surroundings blot out the changing seasons, prevent them from hearing bird songs, seeing trees and flowers or enjoying the sunshine of a bright spring day. Touch their hearts with what they can experience and reveal your glory to them, we pray. Through Jesus Christ our Lord. Amen.

> We have come after great sorrow,
> Having lost our all in the vain tumult,
> We have not made our nightly prayer
> And at times we have forgotten Christ.
>
> Our long-coarsened hearts have no need
> Of mansions too brightly magnificent,
> No need of the paradise garden's shade.
> We would stay here, beyond the fence,
> And fall at your feet at last.
>
> For that moment alone
> Have we dragged ourselves, scarce breathing, to you.
> We—the generations of the last times,
> The blinded children of earth.
>
> *Vestnik Russkogo Khristianskogo Dvizheniya, USSR*

He that is down needs fear no fall
He that is low, no pride:
He that is humble ever shall
Have God to be his guide.

I am content with what I have,
Little be it or much:
And, Lord, contentment still I crave,
Because thou savest such.

From Pilgrim's Progress, written by John Bunyan in prison

You come through thick stone walls, armed guards and bars: you bring me a starry night and ask about this and that. You are the Redeemer. I recognize you. You are my way, my truth and my life. Even my cellar blooms with stars and peace and light pour forth. You sprinkle beautiful words on me like flowers: 'Son, what are you afraid of? I am with you!'

Viktoras Petkus, Lithuania

Precious Father, help me to trust you in the dark,
for faith is a light and though I may not see the end of the road,
I know you have a plan for me. Amen.

Daniel Quisenberry, prisoner, Indiana

Father, I pray for those who are in prison:
those who are convicted for crime,
those who are awaiting trial,
those who have committed no crime.

I pray too for the families of prisoners, that they may find community and support, for those who administer justice, that they may temper firmness with mercy; for those who serve in prisons, that they may create communities of hope and purpose.

From More Everyday Prayers

Lord, I now see more clearly
Your hand as it moves across my life.
I can see that no instance, no meeting,
Not one word was purposeless or wasted.

I can see clearer your intricate weaving
Tender preparation, endless forgiveness,
A million beginnings all combining
To make the 'me' I am now.

Forgive me for the times when I almost
Demand to see the full picture.
Most of all for that dreadful happening,
A rotten fruit of my then anchorless life.
How profound your grace must be!

What you have revealed astounds me, Lord,
Grant me the wisdom to let you continue
This work in me. Help me
To focus upon your will, my King.

Ricky, HMP Ashwell

Dear Lord, help us to realize that some of our greatest times of devotion to you come when we are the loneliest. Amen.

Darlene Thompson, ex-prisoner

Father, reality is your son dying on the cross, showing us that life is full of pain, distress, sorrow and an uphill climb, with little support or comfort.

And reality is proof that the hill can be climbed.

That a man in all his weariness will find a greater strength through suffering and trial, by letting Christ help him with his burden.

From Meditations of a Lifer, Prison Fellowship

Father, thank you for allowing Jesus to come into my heart, for the forgiveness of sin and for letting me feel your love. Amen.

Sam Casalvera, prisoner, Delaware

Almighty God, we thank you for the men and women in prison who have become your children through faith in Jesus Christ. We pray that when they are released they may find love, acceptance and security within the church and grow to full maturity in Christ. We ask this for your greater glory. Amen.

O Lord, please give me the strength to carry me through my imprisonment.

Let me concentrate, not on feeling sorry for myself, but on what I am doing while I am here.

Let me comfort those left behind, for they are suffering more than I.

Let me not be lonely, for there are many more lonely than I.

I can have friends here . . .

Let me not feel anger or bitterness, for they are negative; instead let me have the strength not to give in to temptation and to make use of my talents.

Above all, Lord, help me to see what I can do best and give me strength to do these things. Amen.

Author unknown

Lord, there is a blessing in suffering however hard it seems behind bars. To change the value of one's life, to be closer to you, to understand and serve others who suffer—teach us what you want us to learn. There are many things to learn.

From The Prisoner's Lantern

Lord, my desire is to be used by you in any way you see fit. Bound or free, I will always serve you. For me to live is Christ and to die is gain—I will be with you. Thank you. Amen.

Tautunu Tanuvasa, prisoner, Honolulu

Lord, make us free:
free to share your new life,
free to be the people you meant us to be;
that, being risen with you,
we may seek the things that are above.

From Further Everyday Prayers

For meditation:

The greatest miracle of all is prayer. I have only to turn my thoughts to God and I suddenly feel a force bursting into me; there is new strength in my soul, in my entire being... The basis of my whole spiritual life is the Orthodox liturgy, so while I was in prison I attended it every day in my imagination... At the central point of the liturgy... I felt myself standing before the face of the Lord, sensing almost physically his wounded, bleeding body. I would begin praying in my own words, remembering all those near to me, those in prison and those who were free, those still alive and those who had died. More and more names welled up from my memory ... the prison walls moved apart and the whole universe became my residence, visible and invisible, the universe for which that wounded, pierced body offered itself as a sacrifice... After this, I experienced an exaltation of spirit all day—I felt purified within. Not only my own prayer helped me, but even more the prayer of many other faithful Christians. I felt it continually, working from a distance, lifting me up as though on wings, giving me living water and the bread of life, peace of soul, rest and love.

Anatoli Levitin, USSR

Believe me, it was often thus
In solitary cells, on winter nights
A sudden sense of joy and warmth
And a resounding note of love.
And then, unsleeping, I would know
A-huddle by an icy wall
Someone is thinking of me now
Petitioning the Lord for me.
My dear ones, thank you all
Who did not falter, who believed in us!
In the most fearful prison hour
We probably would not have passed
Through everything—from start to end—
Our heads held high, unbowed,
Without your valiant hearts
To light our path.

Irina Ratushinskaya, USSR, for those who prayed for her and campaigned for her release and that of fellow prisoners

Thank you, Lord, that those of us who have been behind bars could tell so much of what has been done for us—probably even more than could those who have never known what it means to be in bondage. Praise the Lord for that!

The Prisoner's Lantern

Lead us from death to life,
from falsehood to truth.
Lead us from despair to hope,
from fear to trust.
Lead us from hate to love,
from war to peace.
Let peace fill our hearts,
our world, our universe.
Amen.

Prayer placed on the peace table in Durham Cathedral, during the Gulf War

I would pray for all prisoners this night, because we have to live with so much ignorance, so much false pride, so much hate, so much mistrust, so much fear. All concentrated within a small area of this greatly troubled earth.

Lord, only you have the power to dispel such a cloud of darkness which blights so many lives...

I would like to thank you for today, for my work, for my health, for companions, for friendship, for peace of mind, for my food, for my abilities, for feelings and emotions, for strength, for love, for courage, for hope, for a lot more, but mostly for my life and being able to see goodness.

Lord, bless my family and friends with your grace and peace—may they sleep well this night and awake with a renewed faith and spirit in the morning. I also pray for all Christians everywhere.

Goodnight Lord.

From Meditations of a Lifer

❖ *Death and Bereavement* ❖

[God] will cause the bright dawn of salvation to rise on all
those who live in the dark shadow of death, to guide our
steps into the path of peace.

FROM LUKE I

Death and Dying

[Christ] is the invitation, the challenge
the encouragement to faith, so that through him
the individual is placed before God
to answer to God for his life and death.

Hans Kung (born 1928)

When the day that [Mr Valiant-for-Truth] must go hence was come many
accompanied him to the river side, into which, as he went, he said, 'Death,
where is thy sting?' And as he went down deeper, he said, 'Grave, where is thy
victory?' So he passed over and the trumpets sounded for him on the other
side.

John Bunyan (1628–1688)

Dear Lord Jesus,
you have been through death yourself.
Be near to those who are dying.
Make yourself known to them.
Give them your peace and take away their fears.
Comfort the very old.
May they know your company in their closing years.
Be with those who minister to the dying, who seek to relieve their
pain and to tell them of your love. Amen.

Lord, we thank you for the hospice movement. We pray for your blessing on
the hospices in the cities and towns of our land. Guide all who administer
them; give wisdom to those who counsel patients and their families, and
gentleness and patience to those who nurse the sick and dying.

May all be ready to bring quietness, peace and preparation for the life to
come to those in their care. Through Jesus Christ our Lord.

We bring before you, O Lord Christ, those whose earthly life is almost at an
end. Lessen their fear, encourage them on their journey and give them the
peace that comes from your victory over death.

Author unknown

O God, who has brought us near to an innumerable company of angels and to the spirits of just men made perfect; grant us, during our earthly pilgrimage, to abide in their fellowship, and in our heavenly country to be partakers of their joy; through Jesus Christ our Lord.

William Bright (1824–1904)

Father . . . we thank you for those who die after a good life,
old and full of years.
We pray for those who die young and with promise unfulfilled;
for victims of tragedy and disaster.
We pray for those who die burdened by regrets or resentment.
Give strength to those for whom death is a slow agony.
Give peace to those who die suddenly and without warning.
Comfort those who must watch others die and cannot help them.
Lord Jesus Christ, you have been through everything.
Stay with me through everything.

From Further Everyday Prayers

May God be with me
and with his messenger whom he has sent to greet me
and lead me to heaven.
May the Lord who is great and blessed look upon me,
have pity on me and grant me peace.
May he give me greater strength and courage
that I may not be fearful or afraid.
For the angels of God are about me
and God is with me wherever I may be.

Jewish prayer

Teach me to live that I may dread
The grave as little as my bed;
Teach me to die that so I may
Rise glorious at that awesome day.

Thomas Ken (1637–1711)

O Lord Jesu, our only health and our everlasting life, I give myself wholly unto your will; being sure that the thing cannot perish which is committed unto your mercy.

You, merciful Lord, were born for my sake; you did suffer both hunger and thirst for my sake; you did preach and teach, pray and fast for my sake; and finally you gave your most precious body to die and your blood to be shed on the cross, for my sake. Most merciful Saviour, let all these things profit me which you have freely given me. O Lord, into your hands I commit my soul.

Primer of 1559, repeated by Thomas Cromwell (?1485–1540) on the scaffold

'Jesus has turned our sunsets into sunrises'—or so the saying goes.

Jesus, may this be so not only for me, but for all like me, who are fearful and apprehensive of endings of any kind.

Help us to live and end our days in the faith and fear of your resurrection.

J.B.C.

Lord, if I have to die
Let me die;
But please, take away this fear.

Ken Walsh

O God, be present with me and grant me rest.
Set my soul free from the prison of my body
and it will praise your name
when it receives its just reward among the righteous.
Do not be sad, O my soul,
do not be troubled but take hope,
for your salvation comes from God.

Jewish prayer

As thou wast before
At my life's beginning,
Be thou so again
At my journey's end.

As thou wast beside
At my soul's shaping,
Father, be thou too
At my journey's close

Scots Celtic prayer

O Lord Jesus Christ, who in your last agony did commend your spirit into the
hands of your heavenly Father: have mercy upon all sick and dying persons;
may death be unto them the gate of everlasting life; and give them the
assurance of your presence even in the dark valley; for your name's sake who
are the resurrection and the life and to whom be glory for ever and ever.

From the Sarum Primer (adapted)

Go forth, O Christian soul, from this world in the name of God the Father
almighty, who created thee; in the name of Jesus Christ, the Son of the living
God, who suffered for thee; in the name of the Holy Ghost, who was poured
out upon thee... Today let thy place be in peace and thine abode holy Sion,
though the same Jesus Christ our Lord.

From the commendation of a soul, Western Rite

Hunger and thirst, O Christ, for sight of thee,
Thou sole provision for the unknown way.
Long hunger wasted the world wanderer,
With sight of thee may he be satisfied.

Radbod, Bishop of Utrecht (about 900)

Verses for quiet thought:

The sun will no more be your light by day,
nor will the brightness of the moon shine on you,
for the Lord will be your everlast ing light,
and your God will be your glory.
Your sun will never set again,
and your moon will wane no more;
the Lord will be your everlasting light,
and your days of sorrow will end.

From Isaiah 60

I saw the Holy City, the new Jerusalem ... and I heard a loud voice from the throne saying, 'Now the dwelling of God is with men, and he will live with them. They will be his people and God himself will be with them and be their God. He will wipe every tear from their eyes. There will be no more death or mourning or crying or pain, for the old order of things has passed away.'

From Revelation 21

I beseech thee, good Jesus, that as thou hast graciously granted to me here on earth sweetly to partake of the words of thy wisdom amd knowledge, so thou wilt vouchsafe that I may some time come to thee, the fountain of all wisdom, and always appear before thy face; who livest and reignest, world without end.

Venerable Bede (?673–735)

The shade of death lies upon your face, beloved,
But the Jesus of grace has his hand round about you;
In nearness to the Trinity farewell to your pains,
Christ stands before you and peace is in his mind.

Celtic death dirge

Know that the Lord cometh and that today you shall see his glory, and there shall be in that day a great light ... O Lord, I trust in thee, O Lord in eternity, I shall not be confounded. I believe ... in the life eternal.

The last prayer of Joseph Muller, priest, in the face of death (11 September, 1944)

O God, give me of your wisdom,
O God, give me of your mercy,
O God, give me of your fulness
And of your guidance in face of every strait.

O God, give me of your holiness,
O God, give me of your shielding,
O God, give me of your surrounding,
And of your peace in the knot of my death.
O give me of your surrounding
And of your peace at the hour of my death!

Celtic prayer

Bring us, O Lord our God, at our last awakening into the house and gate of heaven, to enter into that gate and dwell in that house, where there shall be no darkness or dazzling, but one equal light; no noise or silence, but one equal music; no fears or hopes, but one equal possession; no ends or beginnings, but one equal eternity; in the habitations of thy glory and dominion world without end.

John Donne (1572–1631)

Loss and Bereavement

Jesus said: 'Do not let your hearts be troubled. Trust in God; trust also in me. In my Father's house are many rooms ... I am going there to prepare a place for you. And if I go and prepare a place for you, I will come back and take you to be with me that you also may be where I am ... I am the way and the truth and the life.'

From John 14

Lord Jesus Christ, in the darkness of my loss I come to you;
I cannot believe what has happened and yet I know it is true;
sorrow and anxiety fill my life
and it's hard to find rest.
So I come to you, Lord Jesus,
I bring to you the burden in my heart—it is too heavy for me;
please take the weight and bear it with me, Lord.
and give me your peace. Amen.

Christian Publicity Organization

Drink deep of the chalice of grief and sorrow, held out to you
by your dark angel of Gethsemane:
the angel is not your enemy,
the drink, though sharp, is nourishing,
by which you may come to a deeper peace
than if you pass it by...

Stevie Smith

Be open to the night...
Pray with open hand, not with clenched fist...

Lord Dunsany

O Lord God, our heavenly Father, regard, we beseech thee, with thy divine pity the pains of all thy children and grant that the passion of our Lord and his infinite merits may make fruitful for good the miseries of the innocent, the sufferings of the sick and the sorrows of the bereaved; through him who suffered in our flesh and died for our sake, thy Son our Saviour Jesus Christ.

From the Scottish Prayer Book

Father, we pray for all who have suffered deep loss, through desertion by parent, partner, friend or child. Come close to them in their sense of desolation and keep them from bitterness or despair. Bring them a sense of your nearness and your consolation. Through Jesus Christ our Lord.

Lord, we pray for those who have lost friends or family members because they have moved far away. Comfort and strengthen them in their sadness and sense of deprivation. Give them a special share of your peace and love to fill their hearts. Encourage them in the certainty that they can come close to those they love as they bring them to you in prayer.

Almighty God, Father of all mercies and giver of all comfort: Deal graciously, we pray, with those who mourn, that casting all their care on you, they may know the consolation of your love; through Jesus Christ our Lord. Amen.

From the Alternative Service Book (1980)

Jesus,
you wept over Lazarus your friend
and over Jerusalem your city,
and we too are deeply saddened
by personal tragedy and international disaster.
Show us how we can weep with those who weep
so that we can come alongside others in their darkness
rather than judging them for their faults,
as you have done with us and for us
in the Father's name.

From Further Everyday Prayers

◆Dear Lord Jesus, you cried when your friend Lazarus died, so you understand how we are feeling today. Comfort us as we are sad and lonely without the one we loved so much. Help us to be glad that our friend is happy with you and free for ever from sadness and pain. Teach us to trust and love you so that we too may live with you for ever.

But now, this is what the Lord says—
he who created you...
he who formed you...
'Fear not, for I have redeemed you;
I have summoned you by name; you are mine.
When you pass through the waters,
I will be with you;
and when you pass through the rivers,
they will not sweep over you...
I am making a way in the desert
and streams in the wasteland.'

From Isaiah 43

We give back to you, O God, those whom you gave to us. You did not lose them when you gave them to us and we do not lose them by their return to you.

Your dear Son has taught us that life is eternal and love cannot die, so death is only an horizon and an horizon is only the limit of our sight. Open our eyes to see more clearly and draw us close to you that we may know that we are nearer to our loved ones, who are with you. You have told us that you are preparing a place for us; prepare us also for that happy place, that where you are we may also be always, O dear Lord of life and death.

William Penn (1644–1718)

Lord,
where tears fall through tragedy or heartbreak
enter the silence and hold me tight
lest in bitterness I blame you
or those close to me
when I should be trusting you with those I love
and groping my way towards gratitude
for the time I have been privileged to share with them.

From Further Everyday Prayers

Father in heaven, you gave your Son Jesus Christ to suffering and death on the cross, and raised him to life in glory. Grant us a patient faith in time of darkness, and strengthen our hearts with the knowledge of your love; through Jesus Christ our Lord. Amen.

From the Alternative Service Book (1980)

Lord Jesus Christ, I come to you
at the beginning of this day;
in all my loneliness and uncertainty I come.
I thank you for all those who will be sharing the day with me,
for the minister, relatives and friends,
and all those who have been so helpful.
Help me not to worry about the arrangements that have been made,
about the visitors who will be coming,
about my fear of emotion, about the service, about the weather.
I bring this day to you; help me in my weakness to prove your strength.

Christian Publicity Organisation prayer for the funeral day

Loving Father, it is your purpose to bring to completion all that your hands have made. We commend now to your safe keeping this child, born before his time has come. Perfect that which you have begun and take into your care this life that you gave. Give comfort and hope to those whose sorrow is sharp and whose sadness fills their hearts; through the resurrection of Jesus Christ our Lord.

Christian Publicity Organisation prayer after a miscarriage

Almighty God, you make nothing in vain and love all that you have made. Comfort these parents in their sorrow and console them with the knowledge of your unfailing love; through Jesus Christ our Lord.

Heavenly Father, by your mighty power you gave us life, and in your love you have given us new life in Christ Jesus. We entrust this child to your merciful keeping, in the faith of Jesus Christ your Son, our Lord, who died and rose again to save us and is now alive and reigns with you and the Holy Spirit in glory for ever. Amen.

From the Alternative Service Book (1980),
prayer after the birth of a still-born child or the death of a newly-born child

Heavenly Father, whose Son our Saviour
took little children into his arms and blessed them;
receive, we pray, your child (name) in your never-failing care and
love,
comfort all who have loved him on earth,
and bring us all to your everlasting kingdom;
through Jesus Christ our Lord.

Prayer at the funeral of a child

O Lord, the giver of all life,
I thank you for the love I have known,
for joys and sorrows shared.
I accept, Lord, that you have taken the life that you once gave.
Please bring your gentle healing to the hurt that comes with
parting.
Thank you, Lord Jesus, that you care about me. Amen.

Christian Publicity Organization

Lord, support us all the day long of this troublous life, until the shades lengthen and the evening comes and the busy world is hushed, the fever of life is over and our work is done. Then, Lord, in your mercy grant us safe lodging, a holy rest and peace at the last; through Jesus Christ our Lord. Amen.

From the Alternative Service Book (1980)

◆ *The World Around Us* ◆

Every good gift and every perfect present comes from
heaven; it comes down from God, the Creator of the
heavenly lights, who does not change.

From James 1

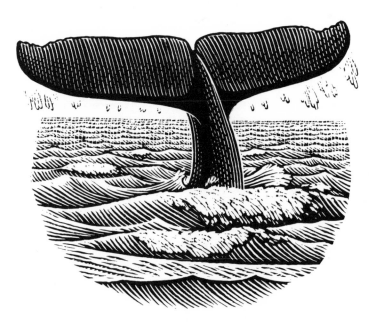

◆All good gifts around us
Are sent from heaven above;
Then thank the Lord, O thank the Lord,
For all his love.

Matthias Claudius (1740–1815),
translated by Jane Montgomery Campbell (1817–1878)

Blessed art thou, O Lord, our God, King of the universe,
who hast such as these in thy world.

Jewish benediction, on seeing a beautiful tree or animal

O Lord, let me feel this world as your love taking form,
then my love will help it.

Rabindranath Tagore (1861–1941)

The Environment

◆ Father, I pray for all who work closely with nature:
for farmers and gardeners who grow our food,
for scientists and technicians who probe the secrets of the earth,
for foresters who plant and harvest the trees,
for those who forecast the weather,
for photographers and artists who capture the beauty for others
to see,
for conservationists and all who guard the precious heritage of
the earth.

From More Everyday Prayers

◆We thank you, Father, for the beauty of all that you have made. We thank you
for the trees, for wild flowers and the flowers we grow in our gardens; for the
mountains and valleys, rivers and lakes, the sea and the delights of the
seashore.

You have made so much for our enjoyment, Lord, and we give you our
thanks. Amen.

Forgive us, Lord, for the damage we have done to the earth.

Forgive us that the rivers and seas have been polluted by the waste of our civilization.

Forgive us that the air has been turned foul by burning fuel and radioactive emissions.

Forgive us that flowers, fauna and wild creatures have become extinct through our relentless invasion of their natural habitat.

Forgive us that we have often valued profit more than the quality of the environment in which people have to live.

From Further Everyday Prayers

Bless, O Lord, the plants, the vegetation, and the herbs of the field, that they may grow and increase to fullness and bear much fruit. And may the fruit of the land remind us of the spiritual fruit we should bear.

From the Coptic Orthodox Liturgy, Egypt

◆ Thank you for the world so sweet,
Thank you for the food we eat,
Thank you for the birds that sing,
Thank you, God, for everything.

E. Rutter Leatham

◆ Bread is a lovely thing to eat—
God bless the barley and the wheat;
A lovely thing to breathe is air—
God bless the sunshine everywhere;
The earth's a lovely place to know—
God bless the folks that come and go!
Alive's a lovely thing to be—
Giver of life—we say—bless thee!

A.W.L. Chitty

Bless this year for us, O our God, and bless every species of its fruits for our benefit. Bestow a blessing upon the face of the earth, and satisfy us with your goodness. O bless our years, and make them good years; for your honour and glory. Amen.

From the Polish Jewish Prayer Book (Jewish calendar 5671)

◆ For the beauty of the earth,
For the beauty of the skies,
For the love which from our birth
Over and around us lies:
Christ, our God, to thee we raise
This our sacrifice of praise.

For the beauty of each hour
Of the day and of the night,
Hill and vale and tree and flower,
Sun and moon and stars of light:
Christ, our God, to thee we raise
This our sacrifice of praise.

Folliot Sandford Pierpoint (1835–1917)

O God, we want to praise and thank you for giving us so much to enjoy in your world. Open our eyes to see all the beauty around us, to appreciate your greatness in giving us the different seasons, each fulfilling our needs. And if we do not understand why nature is sometimes cruel and harsh and why people suffer from earthquakes and other disasters in your world, help us to trust where we cannot see, knowing that you love us all. Help us to do what we can to relieve the sufferings and hardships caused by these disasters and those caused by human errors.

Make us willing and eager to share the many good things you have provided for the benefit of all.

Nancy Martin

◆Dear Father who hast all things made,
And carest for them all,
There's none too great for your great love,
Nor anything too small.
If you can spend such tender care
On things that grow so wild,
How wonderful your love must be
for me, your little child.

G.W. Briggs (1875-1959)

Lord God, we praise you for those riches of your creation which
we shall never see:
for stars whose light will never reach the earth;
for species of living things that were born,
that flourished and perished
before mankind appeared in the world;
for patterns and colours in the flowers,
which only insect eyes are able to see;
for strange, high music
that human ears can never hear.
Lord God, you see everything that you have made, and behold it
is very good.

From Further Everyday Prayers

As the hand is made for holding and the eye for seeing, you have fashioned
me, O Lord, for joy. Share with me the vision to find that joy everywhere: in
the wild violet's beauty, in the lark's melody, in the face of a steadfast man, in a
child's smile, in a mother's love, in the purity of Jesus.

Scots Celtic prayer

Father, we thank you that out of the sea and from the earth we receive
provision you have made for all our needs.
    We thank you for the skills in harvesting the earth's resources that
people have passed on from one generation to another.
    We thank you for those through whose vision and work the products of
our harvesting are channelled into areas of need.

From Further Everyday Prayers

◆ Praise the Lord for all the beauty
Coming with the blossoming spring.
Praise the Lord for summer showers
Praise him for the birds that sing.
Praise the Lord for golden harvest,
Winter frost and white snowfall.
Praise him, praise him when December
Brings his Christmas festival.

Elizabeth Gould

◆ Thank you for the sunshine bright,
Thank you for the morning light.
Thank you for the rain and showers.
Thank you for the fruit and flowers.
Thank you for each tall green tree.
Thank you for the sand and sea.
Thank you for the winds that blow.
Thank you for the frost and snow.

H. Widdows

◆ For all the rich autumnal glories spread—
The flaming pageant of the ripening woods,
The fiery gorse, the heather-purpled hills;
The rustling leaves that fly before the wind
And lie below the hedgerows whispering;
For meadows silver-white with hoary dew;
The first crisp breath of wonder in the air
We thank you, Lord.

From Prayers for Children and Young People

◆ Dear God, who made the world, we thank you for the winter. We thank you
for the cold frosty days when we can jump and run and keep warm; for warm
clothes and good fires and hot dinners. And especially we thank you for the
wonderful time of Christmas when you sent your own Son as a baby to show
us how much you love us all.

From Prayers for Children and Young People

◆ We thank you, Lord, for the brightness of winter sun;
for winter's work and winter's entertainments;
for the warmth of home and all its comforts.
Lord of all times and all seasons,
we thank you that there is no season without its satisfactions,
and that there is no time without its promises.
Lord, when we have no light, show us the treasures of darkness.

From More Everyday Prayers

◆ Dear God,
Thank you for the wind.
For the wind that blows in the trees
And bends their branches to the ground.
The wind that blows the big sailing boats at sea,
And the little ones on the pond.
For the wind that blows the blossom, like snow, in the spring
And blows the leaves to the ground in the autumn.
Thank you for the wind that blows in my hair
And all around me.

Virginia Salmon

◆ Dear God,
Thank you for the snow.
For the snow that falls so softly and quietly;
For the excited feeling we get when we see it on the ground.
For the crunch of our boots through it
And the lovely snowmen we can make.
Thank you for the patterns the snow makes on the leaves
and trees
On roof tops and window ledges.
Dear God, thank you for the snow
And please take care of all old people who don't like it.
Please send someone to help when they are lonely or too tired to
get the coal.

Virginia Salmon

◆ Dear God,
  Thank you for the rain.
  For the rain that runs and trickles down the window
  And makes patterns on the glass.
  For the rain that makes the crops and flowers grow
  And gives us water to drink...
  Thank you for the rain which makes big puddles
  In which we can jump.
  Dear God, thank you for the rain,
  And please take care of people who don't have enough rain and
  water to drink and must go many miles to get it.

Virginia Salmon

We thank thee, Lord, for the glory of the late days and the excellent face of
thy sun. We thank thee for good news received. We thank thee for the
pleasures we have enjoyed and for those we have been able to confer. And
now, when the clouds gather and rain impends over the forest and our house,
permit us not to be cast down; let us not lose the savour of past mercies and
past pleasures; but, like the voice of a bird singing in the rain, let grateful
memory survive in the hour of darkness.

Robert Louis Stevenson (1850–1894)

O God, in whom we live, move and have our being, grant us the rain we need,
so that your answer to our present earthly needs may give us greater
confidence to ask for eternal benefits.

From the Roman Liturgy

We pray, Lord, for the rising of the water of the Nile, this year. May Christ,
our Saviour, bless it and raise it, cheering the earth and sustaining us, his
creatures. And may the rising water remind us of the living water freely given
to all who repent and believe.

From the Coptic Orthodox Liturgy, Egypt

As the rain hides the stars, as the autumn mist hides the hills, as the clouds veil the blue of the sky, so the dark happenings of my lot hide the shining of your face from me. Yet, if I may hold your hand in the darkness, it is enough. Since I know that, though I may stumble in my going, you do not fall.

Gaelic prayer, translated by Alistair MacLean

Animals

I would give nothing for that man's religion whose very dog and cat are not the better for it!

Rowland Hill (1744–1833)

Hear our humble prayer, O God, for our friends the animals, especially for animals who are suffering; for any that are hunted or lost or deserted or frightened or hungry; for all that must be put to death. We entreat for them all thy mercy and pity and for those who deal with them we ask a heart of compassion, gentle hands and kindly words. Make us ourselves to be true friends to animals and so to share the blessing of the merciful.

Albert Schweitzer (1875–1965)

We pray, Lord, for the humble beasts who with us bear the burden and heat of the day, giving their lives for the well-being of their countries ; and for the wild creatures, whom you have made wise, strong and beautiful; we ask for them your great tenderness of heart, for you have promised to save both man and beast, and great is your loving-kindness, O Saviour of the world.

Russian prayer

O Lord Jesus Christ, who has taught us that without our Father in heaven no sparrow falls to the ground, help us to be very kind to all animals and our pets. May we remember that you will one day ask us if we have been good to them. Bless us as we take care of them; for your sake. Amen.

Author unknown

◆ Thank you for the beasts so tall.
Thank you for the creatures small.
Thank you for all things that live.
Thank you, God, for all you give.

H. Widdows

◆Dear Father, hear and bless
Your beasts and singing birds;
And guard with tenderness
Small things that have no words.

From Hymns and Prayers for Children

Father, we have not been good and kindly stewards of the world you have given to us. We confess and repent of the ways in which we have misused your creation. Forgive us for the way in which we have exploited and cruelly treated animals; those given to provide us with food; those who work for us; those we keep as pets.

Teach us to treat them with compassion, care and dignity as the wonderful work of your hands.

◆ Great Father in heaven, thank you for making animals to be our friends. Give us pity for all sick animals, for hunted and caged animals, for animals that are ill-treated and teased and for any that are lost and frightened. Make us brave to defend any animal when we see it being cruelly treated. May we be the friends of all dumb creatures and save us from causing them any suffering through our own thoughtlessness.

Brenda Holloway

We thank you, Father, for all the joy and companionship that we have from animals. We welcome them as part of your varied and bountiful creation. Help us to resist the temptation to treat our pets as fellow humans. May we recognize their proper place in the animal kingdom and honour and love them in the way that is their due.

Our Community

Dear Father God, thank you for the lovely countryside around us. May we do nothing to spoil your wonderful handiwork. Help us to make our village a beautiful place. Show us how to fill it with kind deeds and loving words. Let it be the kind of village that brings you honour and glory.

Dear Lord, thank you for the town in which we live, with all the facilities it offers; for schools, shops, library, sports centre and hospital . Thank you for the well-known residents and the quiet ones, too, who, by their jobs or voluntary work, help to make our town a good place to live in.

Forgive us for those areas where we have all failed; for poor housing, litter-strewn precincts and rough behaviour which brings fear and anger instead of peace and security. Help us to build a better community to your glory. Amen.

Father, thank you for this city in which we are proud to live. We thank you for its history and for all the generations of men and women who created its life and its beauty. Show us how to be worthy successors of those who lived well in past times so that we may hand on our heritage to those who will come after us.

Father, may I not live as if the welfare of this community and the quality of its corporate life were none of my concern. Keep me alert to what is happening around me.

From Further Everyday Prayers

We pray for those who serve as councillors. May they be thoughtful and wise in their decisions and open in their approach to changing conditions.

We pray for council employees. May their skills and experience be respected by elected councillors and their dealings with the public be marked by helpfulness, courtesy and tact.

We remember the services to people for which local government is responsible. May the most vulnerable members of the community be supported and encouraged in their quest for a full and useful life . . .

May our area be one in which people are happy to live.

From Further Everyday Prayers

Lord, increase the sense of community that binds us one to another.
Bless the work of the local church that it may:

> give a sense of identity where now there is none, provide a refuge to
> those who feel threatened by the anonymity of urban living, create a
> place of belonging where people know they are welcomed, remembered
> by name, valued as individuals, celebrate a faith that, in the Word,
> announces that we are forgiven and accepted and, in the Sacrament,
> gathers us again into the life of the Risen Christ. For your Name's sake.

From Further Everyday Prayers

◆ Dear God, our Father, we know how you love everybody all over the world.
Please bless all the people who have come from other countries to live in our
towns and villages. Help them to understand our language and to live happily
with us. Make us willing to be understanding, friendly and helpful to them so
that we may all live peacefully and happily together. We ask this for Jesus'
sake, who taught us to love our neighbours as ourselves.

Nancy Martin

Our Country

We praise you for our country, its beauty, the riches it has for us and the gifts
it showers on us. We thank you for your people, the gift of languages we
speak, the variety of races we have, the cultural heritage we cherish and the
latent possibilities there are for our country to be great. Grant that we accept
these gifts with thankfulness and use them for the good of the human race and
to bring glory to you.

Through Jesus Christ our Lord. Amen.

Prayer of thanksgiving from India

Pour forth, O Christ, your love upon this land today.

Author unknown

O Christ, ruler and Lord of the world, to thee we consecrate this land, its sceptre and its power. Guard thy land, guard it from every foe.

Emperor Constantine (272–337)

Almighty God, by whom alone kings reign and princes decree justice and from whom alone cometh all wisdom and understanding: we thine unworthy servants, here gathered together in thy name, do most humbly beseech thee to send down thy heavenly wisdom from above, to direct and guide us in all our consultations; and grant that, we having thy fear always before our eyes and laying aside all private interests, prejudices and partial affections, the result of all our counsels may be the glory of thy blessed name, the maintenance of true religion and justice, the safety, honour and happiness of the Sovereign, the public welfare, peace and tranquillity of the realm and the uniting and knitting together of the hearts of all persons and estates within the same in true Christian love and charity towards one another;
through Jesus Christ our Lord.

Prayer used at every sitting of the House of Commons,
composed by Sir Christopher Yelverton, about 1578

We remember, O Lord, our land and our nation before you. In shame and humility we confess that we are a hopelessly divided people, ruthlessly selfish, arrogant and conceited... We are prone to despise rather than to love... We are suffocating goodness, beauty and truth and are rushing down the precipice of ruin and destruction.

Lord have mercy on us, miserable offenders, forgive our sins, renew and reclothe us with goodness, beauty and truth... In Christ's name we pray.

Prayer of confession from Calcutta

O God, almighty Father, King of kings and Lord of lords, grant that the hearts and minds of all who go out as leaders before us, the statesmen, the judges, the men of learning and the men of wealth, may be so filled with 'the love of thy laws' and of that which is righteous and life-giving, that they may be worthy stewards of thy good and perfect gifts; through Jesus Christ
our Lord.

Prayer of the Knights of the Garter (fourteenth century)

Lord, we pray for all those who follow a political calling. Strengthen them in the burden of responsibility that we place upon them.

Guide those who shape political programmes that they may plan for the good of all society and not set neighbour against neighbour,

class against class,

region against region.

Encourage those who act as advocates for the oppressed within our society and who seek to channel political power into the cause of justice for everyone ...

From Further Everyday Prayers

O Lord our God, we pray for those who represent us in government. May they be men and women of integrity, who keep their promises. May they be just and compassionate so that we may be led in ways of righteousness and mercy. Through Jesus Christ our Lord.

O God, the king of righteousness, lead us, we pray thee, in the ways of justice and of peace, inspire us to break down all tyranny and oppression, to gain for every man his due service; that each may live for all and all may care for each, in the name of Jesus Christ.

William Temple (1881–1944)

Lord God, we give you thanks for those who have devised the laws upon which our values and security depend...

for those who administer the law with skill and experience to ensure that the law will not be separated from justice:

for the police forces who uphold the law and detect crime.

Deliver us from governments that enact bad laws, from lawyers who have no concern for justice, and from police who abuse the trust placed in them.

From Further Everyday Prayers

Heavenly Father, at whose hand the weak shall suffer no wrong nor the mighty escape just judgment: pour your grace upon your servants our judges and magistrates, that by their true, faithful and diligent execution of justice and equity to all men equally, you may be glorified, the commonwealth daily promoted and increased and we all live in peace and quietness, godliness and virtue; through Jesus Christ our Lord.

Thomas Cranmer (1489–1556)

We pray, O God, for all who work in our prisons. We pray for prison officers, that they may do their work fairly and without prejudice.

Give wisdom to all who have the welfare of prisoners at heart: prison governors; probation officers; prison visitors; prison doctors and teachers.

Forgive us for the shocking conditions in many of our prisons. Give success to those who seek to reform the prison system. May our prisons be places which do good to men and women and encourage honest and law-abiding living for the future.

Lord, we pray for all industrial communities.

For communities built around historic sources of wealth—the coal-mining towns and villages, the ship-building towns; communities that grew around steelworks; those that relied on the railways as their chief source of employment—we pray, remembering especially those that have had to face changes leading to high unemployment and the fragmentation of community life.

For communities built around the new sources of wealth, the new technologies, the computer industries, the car industries and all who contribute to the complex needs of the modern state—we pray, remembering especially those who have never experienced the hardships of the older communities nor known the strength of their solidarity.

Lord, let us remember that we are all members of one another.

From Further Everyday Prayers

Our Father, we pray for those in our land without home or family. We pray for:

> those living in high-rise flats and run-down houses;
> those in hostels or bed and breakfast accommodation;
> those afraid to go out after dark;
> those living in cardboard cities;
> those who are hooked on drugs or alcohol.

> We pray for inspiration and endurance for those who try to help them,
> for those in government who devise laws and benefits;
> for voluntary bodies that provide housing and aid;
> for doctors, clergy, social workers and good neighbours, who come close and listen;
> for Salvation Army and other missioners, who bring good news for body and spirit.

Show us as Christians what we can do to heal these diseases of our nation and give us your love for all in need. For Jesus Christ's sake.

Lord our God, we pray for good industrial relations in our land. We pray that you will help all those who are trying to heal the rifts and lessen the gap between employer and employees, managers and work-force.

Help shop stewards and union leaders to protect those they represent with good-will. Help managers and employees to be fair and just. May workers do their tasks conscientiously and well. We pray that you may be glorified in the industries of our land. Amen.

O Lord Jesus Christ, who was lifted up on the cross to draw all men unto you, look in mercy, we beseech you, upon this nation. Send out your light and your truth that they may lead us into paths of fellowship and peace; break down all barriers of contention and strife and grant that, seeking first your kingdom and righteousness, we may live together in brotherly unity and concord, to your glory and the welfare of this realm.

Hear us, blessed Lord, to whom, with the Father and the Holy Spirit, be all honour and glory, world without end.

Bishop Woods

◆ *The World Today* ◆

The Lord, the Most High, is to be feared;
he is a great king, ruling over all the world.

FROM PSALM 47

Government

Almighty Father,
whose will is to restore all things
in your beloved Son, the king of all:
govern the hearts and minds of those in authority
and bring the families of the nations,
divided and torn apart by the ravages of sin,
to be subject to his just and gentle rule;
who is alive and reigns with you and the Holy Spirit,
one God, now and for ever.

From the Alternative Service Book (1980)

O God, King of kings and Lord of lords,
We pray today for statesmen, leaders and rulers.
May they be quiet in spirit, clear in judgement,
Able to understand the issues that face them.
May they think often of the common people on whose behalf
they must speak and act.
May they remember that in keeping your laws is man's only good
and happiness.
Grant them patience, grant them courage,
Grant them foresight and great faith.
In their anxieties be their security,
In their opportunities be their inspiration,
By their plans and their actions may your kingdom come, your
will be done.

Lilian Cox

Attempt great things for God: expect great things from God.

William Carey (1761–1834)

To those who rule and lead us on the earth, you,
sovereign Master, have given their authority and
kingship —so marvellous that power of yours words
fail to express— that seeing the glory and honour
You have provided for them,
we should be subject to their rule, not resisting your will.
Grant them, Lord, the health, peace, concord and stability to use
aright the sovereignty you have bestowed on them.
For you, King of heaven, you it is that give mortal men
glory, honour and power over what is on earth.
Lord, make their counsels conform to what is good
and pleasing to you, that using with reverence, peacefully, gently,
the power you have given them,
they may find favour with you.

Clement of Rome (died about 100)

For our hope and inspiration:

Jesus shall reign where'er the sun
Does his successive journeys run:
His kingdom stretch from shore to shore
Till moons shall wax and wane no more.

Isaac Watts (1674–1748)

All authority is yours, eternal God. You hold the universe within your hands
and us within your care. You touch the heart of rich and poor alike. You
speak to the powerful and the powerless. The rulers and the ruled are all
within your family. May all in authority recognize afresh that yours is the final
power. Somewhere in the circle of our lives each of us holds influence and
power. As we stand ... in your presence in worship, may pride be reduced,
compassion increased and the good of all become our common aim. Amen.

From Prayers Before Worship

Peace and Unity

You have called us to be one,
to live in unity and harmony,
and yet we are divided:
race from race,
faith from faith,
rich from poor,
old from young,
neighbour from neighbour...
O Lord, by whose cross all enmity is brought to an end,
break down the walls that separate us,
tear down the fences of indifference and hatred;
forgive us the sins that divide us,
free us from pride and self-seeking,
overcome our prejudices and fears,
give us courage to open ourselves to others;
by the power of your Sprit make us one.

*Opening worship of the sixth assembly of the World Council
of Churches (Vancouver, 1983)*

◆ God our Father, Creator of the world,
please help us to love one another.
Make nations friendly with other nations;
make all of us love one another like brothers and sisters.
Help us to do our part to bring peace in the world
and happiness to all people.

Prayer from Japan

O God of many names
Lover of all nations
We pray for peace
in our hearts
in our homes
in our nations
in our world.
The peace of your will
The peace of our need.

George Appleton

O just and holy God, you have brought us peace by making the many peoples into one people, Jew and Gentile, slave and free, male and female, black and white.

We pray for those places where peoples are kept apart because of the colour of their skin. Help us to root out discrimination in our hearts so that we may welcome every stranger in our midst as a fellow citizen, a neighbour and a friend of God.

From Prayer at Night

God of all grace, call to the nations of the earth to cease from strife, that all may join to fight not one another but their common foes of want and ignorance, disease and sin.

Lead back mankind out of the way of death into the way of life; and from destruction to the building up of a new world of righteousness and peace, of liberty and joy.

End the dark night of lies and cruelty; bring in the dawn of mercy and truth.

Prayers for peace, Week of Prayer for World Peace.

Gracious Father,
we pray for peace in our world:
for all national leaders
that they may have wisdom to know and courage to do
what is right;
for all men and women
that their hearts may be turned to yourself
in the search for righteousness and truth;
for those who are working to improve international
relationships,
that they may find the true way of reconciliation;
for those who suffer as a result of war:
the injured and disabled,
the mentally distressed,
the homeless and hungry,
those who mourn for their dead,
and especially for those who are without hope or friend
to sustain them in their grief.

Baptist Peace Fellowship

Make us worthy, Lord,
To serve our fellow men
Throughout the world who live and die
In poverty and hunger.
Give them, through our hands,
This day their daily bread,
And by our understanding love,
Give peace and joy.

Mother Teresa of Calcutta

Trusting in your mercy, Lord, we pray
    that people everywhere may reject the use of nuclear weapons and the threat to use them.
        God of Peace, hear our prayer
    that peace negotiators may discern the ways of peace and meet as fellow human beings rather than as enemies.
        God of Peace, hear our prayer
    that governments may turn from warlike ploys of power to service in the welfare of our common humanity.
        God of peace, hear our prayer
    that the strategists of defence may be free from the fear which produces the arms race.
        God of peace, hear our prayer
    that defence forces may be freed from the passion to punish and take revenge.
        God of peace, hear our prayer
    that we all may learn what it means to love those who are regarded as our enemies.
        God of peace, hear our prayer.

From a Palm Sunday peace service, Sydney, Australia

Lord God, forgive everything that stands in the way of international understanding.
    Forgive our fears of one another that lead us to use our vast resources of power for potential destruction rather than dealing with the areas of human need.
    Forgive our nationalist and racialist posturings that make it difficult for us to work comfortably together.
    Forgive our contempt for imperfect institutions in an imperfect world.
    Lord, deliver us from fear,
    deliver us from arrogance,
    deliver us from the search for perfect solutions.

From Further Everyday Prayers

Father, I am a man of my time and situation,
Around me, the signs and symbols of man's fear, hatred,
alienation;
a bomb exploding in a market square;
... faces on TV twisted in mocking confrontation.
It's not that we haven't tried, Father,
to find ways to peace and reconciliation
but always too little, too late;
the forces of opposition were too great...
I am perplexed, angry, hopeless, sick, I want to turn
my back, wash my hands, save myself, my family, get out.
But every time I turn to go
there stands in my way a cross...

Lord, make me a child of hope, reborn from apathy,
cynicism, and despair, ready to work for that new man
you have made possible by walking the way of the cross yourself.
I do have hope grounded on your victory over powers
of evil, death itself; focused on your kingdom,
breaking on us now as light out of deep darkness.
And I do see signs of hope immediately around me.
I see a wider sign:
I see a sign—flower growing on a bombed-out site.
The sign—an empty cross. The burden, Lord, is yours.
Lord, I am a prisoner of hope! There is a life before death.

Prayer from Northern Ireland

Almighty God, from whom all thoughts of truth and peace proceed:
Kindle, we pray you, in the hearts of all people the true love of peace;
and guide with your pure and peaceable wisdom those who take counsel for
the nations of the earth; that in tranquillity your kingdom may go forward, till
the earth be filled with the knowledge of your love:
through Jesus Christ our Lord.

Francis Paget (1851–1911)

The hatred which divides nation from nation,
race from race, class from class,
Father, forgive.

The covetous desires of men and nations
to possess what is not their own,
Father, forgive.

The greed which exploits the labours of men,
and lays waste the earth,
Father, forgive.

Our envy of the welfare and happiness of others,
Father, forgive.

Our indifference to the plight of the homeless and the refugee,
Father, forgive.

The lust which uses for ignoble ends
the bodies of men and women,
Father, forgive.

The pride which leads to trust in ourselves
and not in God,
Father, forgive.

*Prayer on a plaque on the altar of Coventry Cathedral,
written in 1964, used in the daily lunchtime service*

O God, the source of the whole world's gladness and the bearer of its pain,
may your unconquerable joy rest at the heart of all our trouble and distress.

From Prayer at Night

Give us courage, O Lord, to stand up and be counted,
to stand up for those who cannot stand up for themselves,
to stand up for ourselves when it is needful for us to do so.
Let us fear nothing more than we fear you.
Let us love nothing more than we love you,
for thus we shall fear nothing also.
Let us have no other God before you,
whether nation or party or state or church.
Let us seek no other peace but the peace which is yours,
and make us its instruments,
opening our eyes and our ears and our hearts,
so that we should know always what work of peace
we may do for you.

Alan Paton

Lord, make me an instrument of your peace.
Where there is hatred, let me sow love,
Where there is injury, pardon,
Where there is doubt, faith,
Where there is despair, hope,
Where there is darkness, light,
Where there is sadness, joy.

O Divine Master, grant that I may not so much seek
to be consoled as to console,
not so much to be understood as to understand,
not so much to be loved as to love;
for it is in giving that we receive,
it is in pardoning that we are pardoned,
it is in dying that we awake to eternal life.

A prayer often associated with St Francis of Assisi

Show us, good Lord,
the peace we should seek,
the peace we must give,
the peace we can give,
the peace we must keep,
the peace we must forgo,
and the peace you have given
in Jesus Christ our Lord.

Caryl Micklem

World Poverty and Oppression

Father, we thank you for men and women in every age who have been
prepared to struggle and risk their lives for the rights of others. Thank you for
those whose actions have brought us freedom from slavery, from despotism
and from ignorance and disease. Help forward the work of all who still seek to
bring such freedoms to men and women and children the whole world over.
For your sake. Amen.

We have squandered the gift of life.
The good life of some is built on the pain of many;
the pleasure of a few on the agony of millions.
To you we lift our outspread hands.
We thirst for you in a thirsty land.
We worship death in our quest to possess ever more things;
we worship death in our hankering after our own security,
our own survival, our own peace,
as if life were divisible,
as if love were divisible,
as if Christ had not died for all of us.
To you we lift our outspread hands.

Prayer used at the sixth assembly of the
World Council of Churches (Vancouver, 1983)

O God, our Father,
the fountain of love, power and justice,
the God who cares, particularly for the least,
the most suffering and the poorest among us.
O God, Lord of creation, grant us today your guidance and
wisdom so that we may see the human predicament for what it is.
Give us courage and obedience so that we may follow you
completely.
Help us, Lord, to bear witness to the cross of your Son,
our Lord Jesus Christ, who alone is the reason for hope,
and in whose name we pray. Amen.

Koson Srisang, Thailand

We bring before you, O Lord, the troubles and perils of people and nations,
the sighing of prisoners and captives, the sorrows of the bereaved, the
necessities of strangers, the helplessness of the weak, the despondency of the
weary, the failing powers of the aged. O Lord, draw near to each; for the sake
of Jesus Christ our Lord.

St Anselm (1033–1109)

We beg you, Lord, to help and defend us. Deliver the oppressed, pity the
insignificant, raise the fallen, show yourself to the needy, heal the sick, bring
back those of your people who have gone astray, feed the hungry, lift up the
weak, take off the prisoners' chains. May every nation come to know that you
alone are God, that Jesus Christ is your child, that we are your people, the
sheep of your pasture.

St Clement of Rome (died about 100)

Look in compassion, O heavenly Father, upon this troubled and divided
world. Though we cannot trace your footsteps or understand your working,
give us grace to trust you with an undoubting faith; and when your own time
is come, reveal, O Lord, that new heaven and new earth wherein dwells
righteousness, where the Prince of Peace rules, your Son our Saviour
Jesus Christ.

Charles Vaughan (1816–1897)

Eternal God
We confess to you our sinfulness.
You made the world a paradise
but we have turned our lands into
places of tears and unhappiness.
People are fighting with each other race against race.
The holocaust of chauvinism sweeps through countries,
devouring humanity,
terrorizing us into submission.

Liberating One,
free us from all bondage
so that our faith in you will make us free
to create with courage
a new world—new societies.

Prayer from Sri Lanka

We sincerely thank you, Father God, for your powerful gift of hope in the face of seemingly hopeless situations. We thank you for your peace in the hearts of men and women in this part of Africa who believe you are a living God, quick to save in time of danger. You reign above all, directing the course and destiny of the universe.

Joao Makondekwa

Have mercy, O God, on our distracted and suffering world, on the nations perplexed and divided. Give to us and to all people a new spirit of repentance and amendment; direct the counsels of all who are working for the removal of the causes of strife and for the promotion of goodwill; and hasten the coming of your kingdom of peace and love; through Jesus Christ our Lord.

Charles F. d'Arcy (1859–1938)

O God our Father, in the name of him who gave bread to the hungry we remember all who through our human ignorance, selfishness and sin are condemned to live in want; and we pray that all endeavours for the overcoming of world poverty and hunger may be so prospered that there may be found food sufficient for all; through Jesus Christ our Lord.

Christian Aid prayer

◆ Holy Father, we pray for the people in other lands,
especially for the boys and girls.
Some would learn but have no teacher;
Some are sick and have no doctor;
Some are sad and have no one to comfort them;
Some are hungry and poor and have no helper;
Some are happy and cared for as we are ourselves.
For all we ask your loving care.
Supply their needs and comfort their hearts,
through Jesus Christ our Lord.

From Prayers for Children and Young People

We live in a restless noisy world.
The crash of waves on a small boat.
The noise of gunfire and the explosion of bombs.
The shouts of the market place
and the wail of a hungry child.
The dumb pleading of the addict's needle
and the protests of the oppressed.
The frustrated anger of the unemployed
and the scream of the tortured.
The restless noise of machines.
The clamant knocking of the prisoner
and the noisy silence of unforgiveness.
Out of the depths of our noise
we cry to you, O Lord
the never ceasing prayer of your people,
with your people, for your people,
that the discordant clamour
of your world
may be turned into symphonies of
peace, love and joy.
May the voice of prayer be never silent...
God is not deafened by our noise,
he opens his ears wider when we cry.

Author unknown

◆ In lands of drought and hunger
No more, dear Lord, we pray
Will mothers ask the question
Which child to feed today?

James Carey (aged 10)

◆ Lord Jesus, I pray for those who will be unhappy today:
for parents who have no food to cook for their children;
for those who cannot earn enough money for their families;
for children who are sick or frightened;
and for all who are alone
and without people to love them. Amen.

God of all beauty, whose will it is that all your creatures should enjoy the
world and the life you have given us; we know that many are unable to do this
through hunger, poverty, disease, oppression, ignorance or sin. Let us never
rest content in your joys until we have done everything in our power and by
your grace to help others to share them also . . .

George Appleton

Have mercy, O God, on all who are sorrowful,
those who weep and those in exile.
Have pity on the persecuted and the homeless
who are without hope;
those who are scattered in remote corners of this world;
those who are in prison and ruled by tyrants.
Have mercy on them as is written in your holy law,
where your compassion is exalted!

Jewish prayer

O God, the refuge of the poor, the strength of those who toil and the
comforter of all who sorrow, we commend to your mercy the unfortunate and
needy in whatever land they may be. You alone know the number and extent
of their sufferings and trials. Look down, Father of mercies, at those unhappy
families suffering from war and slaughter, from hunger and disease and other
severe trials. Spare them, O Lord, for it is truly a time for mercy.

Peter Canisius (1521–1597)

Lord, we pray for the victims of oppressors,
We pray for populations who are denied the freedom of
political debate and intellectual enquiry.
We pray for men and women in the prisons and camps of
oppressive regimes:
for those in solitary confinement,
for those who are tortured,
for those who have been imprisoned for many years.
We pray for the families of those who suffer,
for the children of prisoners of conscience,
for wives and husbands whose years of marriage are spent
in waiting
and in praying for the day when the prison doors will be opened.
We pray for all who daily remind us of their plight and whose
vigilance knows no rest.

From Further Everyday Prayers

Lord Jesus, you understand the sufferings of the weak and the oppressed.
Although you are strong, you allowed yourself to be taken prisoner. You were
the victim of bullying and ill-treatment, punishing blows and insulting words.
You suffered an agonizing death for us and for our sins. Be near to those who
suffer innocently as political prisoners and give peace and comfort to them by
your presence.

O God, the father of the forsaken, the help of the weak, the supplier of the
needy; you teach us that love towards the race of man is the bond of
perfectness and the imitation of your blessed self.

   Open and touch our hearts that we may see and do, both for this world
and that which is to come, the things that belong to our peace. Strengthen us
in the work which we have undertaken; give us wisdom, perseverance, faith
and zeal, and in your own time and according to your pleasure prosper the
issue; for the love of your Son, Christ Jesus.

Lord Shaftesbury (1801–1885)

Have mercy, O Lord our God, on those whom war or oppression or famine have robbed of homes and friends and all those who try to help them. We commend also into your care those whose homes are broken by conflict and lack of love; grant that where the love of man has failed, the divine compassion may heal; through Jesus Christ our Lord.

From New Every Morning

Hasten we pray, Lord, the coming of Jesus Christ, the Prince of Peace, who will reign in righteousness, and the new earth in which only goodness will dwell. Cleanse and prepare us for that day and give us hope, faith and love to wait for our Saviour's coming with endurance and joy.

From The Church and the World

◆ *The Church in the World* ◆

I pray that they may all be one. Father! May they be in us,
just as you are in me and I am in you. May they be one, so
that the world will believe that you sent me.

FROM JOHN 17

The Family of the Church

The church is the whole family of God's people—down the ages and across the world—who have become God's children through faith in Jesus Christ. Local churches are branches of the family. When we come to church to worship God and learn from him, we meet as a family.

◆ We thank you, God, that everyone who loves you belongs to your family. You are our Father, we are your children.

Thank you, God, for the worldwide family of your people.
Thank you for our brothers and sisters the whole world over.

Father, bless the family of the church. May we accept one another as brothers and sisters, finding strength and joy in our life together. May we be a family open to all the families of mankind that, in the church, they may overcome all the hostilities and prejudices that might otherwise drive them apart.

From More Everyday Prayers

◆ Father, we have come to church to worship—
to listen and talk, learn and pray.
We've come to meet our friends—young and old.
We've come to hear more about Jesus—and to share with others
what we already know.
Father, that's why we've come to church—and come gladly.
When we go home, help us to be the church—
your people, living in your world.

From Prayers Before Worship

241

Father, we come here to worship you. May our worship be sincere and genuine. May we worship not only because we feel we ought but because we feel we want to. Take from everyone here anything which would come between us and you.

And when we leave, may we take our worship home with us, that the whole of our lives may become acts of worship as we praise you in all we say and do and are; through Jesus Christ, the life of the world. Amen.

From Prayers Before Worship

Christ, from whom all blessings flow,
Perfecting the saints below,
Hear us, who your nature share,
Who your mystic body are.

Move and actuate and guide.
Diverse gifts to all divide;
Placed according to your will,
Let us all our work fulfil.

Sweetly may we all agree,
Touched with loving sympathy;
Kindly for each other care,
Every member feel its share.

Charles Wesley (1707–1788)

O God, we give you thanks that you have promised to be in our midst and to stay with us. You make us aware that we belong together whatever our likes and dislikes may be, whatever we may have achieved and whatever we think of ourselves. Only so can we live together and accept each other fully whoever we may be. We give you thanks that you sojourn with us. Help us to see the different possibilities which you have given us on our way and grant us that throughout our life we may be strengthened by your presence.

Prayer for the Week of Christian Unity, 1991

Lord, we pray for your church in every part of the world, the great family of which we are a part: we pray for those who are denied freedom in their religious beliefs, for those called to the suffering of imprisonment, and for those few who are called to martyrdom itself: may their courage set faith alight in other lives.

We pray for those who struggle against injustice, the men and women who have to establish love's supremacy in violent and oppressive societies: may they be filled with your wisdom in their war against inhumanity.

We pray for our fellow Christians in the developing world, those for whom hunger is a daily reality, those who feel powerless to change the ways of nature or the ways of nations; bring nearer, Lord, the day of their deliverance.

From More Everyday Prayers

Grant unto all your children, the believers, to live in the unity of the Spirit within your fold as one flock belonging to you, O Chief Shepherd. Help us that we may all come to you in one spirit, even though by various ways, all of them leading unto salvation through the blood of the Redeemer. Give us courage that we may kill all disputings and quarrellings among us believers, that we may be united, all of us, in your love and obedience. Amen.

Prayer of Egyptian Christians

Christ our hope,
We give you glory
For the great grace
By which upon the cross
You stretched out your hands in love to us all.
By that same grace
Come, risen Saviour,
Into every gesture of unity and fellowship
We make toward one another.
May the peace we share
Be your peace. Amen.

Jamie Wallace

O God of all power, who has called from death the great pastor of the sheep, our Lord Jesus: comfort and defend the flock which he has redeemed by the blood of the eternal testament.

Increase the number of true preachers; lighten the hearts of the ignorant; relieve the pains of such as be afflicted, especially of those that suffer for the testimony of the truth; by the power of our Lord Jesus Christ.

John Knox (1513–1572)

For meditation and silent worship:

Christ loved the church and gave his life for it. He did this to
dedicate the church to God by his word ... in order to present
the church to himself in all its beauty—pure and faultless,
without spot or wrinkle or any other imperfection.

From Ephesians 5

We thank you, O Lord our God, that the life which we now live in Christ is part of the life which is eternal and the fellowship which we have in him unites us with your whole church on earth and in heaven; and we pray that as we journey through the years we may know joys which are without end, and at last come to that abiding city where you reign for ever more.

From New Every Morning

The Church and the World

Christ has no body now on earth but yours, no hands but yours, no feet but yours; yours are the eyes through which to look at Christ's compassion to the world, yours are the feet with which he is to go about doing good, and yours are the hands with which he is to bless us now.

St Teresa of Avila (1515–1582)

When I see the world from the moon on television, I want to reach out and grab it for God.

*Billy Graham, in the opening address at the
International Congress on World Evangelisation, Lausanne*

God of all the nations of the earth, remember the multitudes who, though created in your image, have not known you, nor the dying of your Son their Saviour Jesus Christ. Grant that by the prayers and work of your holy church they may be delivered from all ignorance and unbelief and brought to worship you; through him whom you have sent to be the resurrection and the life of all people, your Son Jesus Christ our Lord.

St Francis Xavier (1506–1552)

Most merciful Father, we confess that we have done little to forward your kingdom and advance your glory. Pardon our shortcomings and give us greater zeal for your service. Make us more ready and diligent by our prayers, by our alms and by our examples, to spread the knowledge of your truth and to enlarge the boundaries of your kingdom; and may we do it all to your glory.

Bishop How (1823–1897)

God our Father, we pray for those who have never appreciated the riches which you offer them in your Son Jesus; those for whom he has never become a reality;

for those who have never been moved by the story of the cross or felt the need of the forgiveness Jesus won for us;

for those who leave the gospel aside as something that does not concern them; which they feel they can get on well enough without;

for those for whom 'Christ' is only a swear-word.

For all these, and for all who do not pray for themselves, accept our intercessions, through Jesus Christ our Lord.

From Further Everyday Prayers

O Heavenly Father, Lord of the harvest, have respect to these our prayers and send forth labourers into your harvest. Fit and prepare them for the work of their ministry. Give them the spirit of power and of love and of a sound mind. Strengthen them to endure hardness; and grant that both by their life and doctrine they may set forth your glory and set forward the salvation of all men; through Jesus Christ our Lord.

From the Church of Ireland Prayer Book (1878)

Father, we pray for all those who preach the gospel. Thank you for all who tell out your love and grace through lives of holiness and radiant living. Help those who also try to put into words the message of hope and new life to be found in Jesus Christ. Give them the help of your Holy Spirit that their words may go straight to the minds and hearts and wills of those who hear. Through Jesus Christ our Lord. Amen.

O Lord Jesus Christ, great shepherd of the sheep, who seeks those that are gone astray, binds up those that are broken and heals those that are sick: bless, we beseech you, all efforts that are made to convert souls unto you. Open the deaf ears of the wandering, that they may hear the words which belong unto their peace; and grant that those whom you raise to newness of life may through your grace persevere unto the end, of your mercy, blessed Lord, to whom with the Father and the Holy Spirit be all praise and glory.

Richard Meux Benson (1824–1915) (adapted)

O Lord God, we are called to be your witnesses: help us to make our Saviour Jesus known to others—through our words and lives, through our prayers and our gifts; for his sake. Amen.

From Prayers for a Decade

Almighty God, you called us to your service to save us and keep us under your protection. Give your church the love which knows no barriers of race or culture and strengthen us with your trust so that we may accomplish your work in the world.

From the Alternative Service Book (1980)

Lord, we pray for the spread of the gospel.
    Bless those who preach, teach, heal, build, reconcile, bring hope, that their message may be the means of salvation to those who hear;
    and grant that your church may grow and increase in the knowledge of your divine love.

From Further Everyday Prayers

Make us worthy, Lord, to serve our fellow human beings throughout the world who live and die in poverty and hunger.

Through our hands, grant them this day their daily bread; and by our understanding love, give them peace and joy. Amen.

Daily prayer of the co-workers of Mother Teresa of Calcutta

Christ, do not remain here at Corcovado surrounded by divine glory. But go down there into the *favelas*. Come with me into the *favelas* and live with us down there. Don't stay away from us; live among us, and give us new faith in you and in the Father. Amen.

Prayer from Rio de Janeiro, Brazil

Lord God, as we set about this work
we ask that you will lead us step by step.
Help us to see with your eyes.
Help us to listen with your ears.
Help us to think about what we are doing in our world.
Guide us to recognize how great are our resources,
and inspire us to put our plans, your plans, into action.
Lord, for your sake, and not for the sake of those around us
may we not falter nor make empty plans
but work to share your love and grace.

From Mission Pursuit

Almighty God, full of mercy, look down with pity upon all the innkeepers of the world who turn guests away because of their colour or creed or condition. Prepare room in our hearts that those who are hurt or rejected or ignored in the world may find kindness there. In the name of One who had to be born in a stable. Amen.

Prayer from Hawaii

Be merciful, O Father of all mercies, to your church universal dispersed throughout the whole world; and grant that all that confess your holy name may agree in the truth of your holy Word and live in godly concord and unity. And especially be merciful to such as are under persecution for the testimony of their conscience and for the profession of the gospel of your Son, our Saviour Jesus Christ.

From Prayers of 1585

O Lord, we pray for the universal church, for all sections of your church throughout the world, for their truth, unity and stability, that love may abound and truth flourish in them all.

We pray for our own church, that what is lacking in it may be supplied and what is unsound corrected; and unto all men everywhere give your grace and your blessing; for the sake of Jesus Christ, our only Lord and Saviour

Lancelot Andrewes (1555–1626)

May God the Father, and the eternal High Priest Jesus Christ, build us up in faith and truth and love, and grant us our portion among the saints with all those who believe on our Lord Jesus Christ. We pray for all saints, for kings and rulers, for the enemies of the cross of Christ, and for ourselves we pray that our fruit may abound and we be made perfect in Christ Jesus our Lord.

Polycarp (69–155)

O God, the Father of our Lord Jesus Christ, our only Saviour, the Prince of Peace, give us grace seriously to lay to heart the great dangers we are in by our unhappy divisions. Take away all hatred and prejudice and whatsoever else may hinder us from godly union and concord; that as there is but one body and one Spirit and one hope of our calling, one Lord, one faith, one baptism, one God and Father of us all, so we may henceforth be all of one heart and of one soul, united in one holy bond of truth and peace, of faith and charity and may with one mind and one mouth glorify you; through Jesus Christ our Lord. Amen.

Accession Service (1715)

Our Father, your voice has called us,
You have placed your name on our lips
And your work in our hands.
We are your church, your pilgrim people,
We ask you to open up for us
A future that is new.
Make us poor and make us simple,
The better to know your gospel
And to follow Jesus.
We ask your forgiveness for our past faults,
For the pride which has often driven your church
To possess itself of power.
Forgive your church if sometimes
It has not been worthy of your trust.
We are not bringing your peace to this world
Nor your salvation
To men and women divided and distressed
For we ourselves are disunited.
May we who are often divided be able
To be aware of so much that is madness
And always to seek for unity.

From the Vocational Prayer Book of the
seminaries of the Roman Catholic Church in Spain

Your church, Lord, remember,
And thus from all evil deliver her,
Making her perfect in your love.
Bring her united, made holy, from the four corners of the
horizon,
Into your kingdom, which you have prepared for her

From the old Hispanic Litany

O God and Father of our Lord Jesus Christ,
Only Saviour and Prince of Peace,
Banish from us every motive
That can hinder holy union and concord.
And just as there is but one body and one Spirit,
One sole hope of our calling,
One sole Lord, one sole faith, one sole baptism,
One sole God and Father of us all,
So let us from now on all be united
In heart and soul
In a holy bond of truth and peace,
Of faith and love,
That always we may glorify you
In the one Spirit
And with one voice,
Through Christ our Lord. Amen.

Spanish Episcopal Church

Additional prayers for unity and peace can be found in chapter 14

◆ *Prayers for the Day* ◆

Every day I will thank you;
I will praise you for ever and ever.

FROM PSALM 145

Prayers in the Morning

New every morning is the love
Our waking and uprising prove;
Through sleep and darkness safely brought,
Restored to life, and power, and thought.

New mercies, each returning day,
Hover around us while we pray;
New perils past, new sins forgiven,
New thoughts of God, new hopes of heaven.

John Keble (1792–1866)

I rise today with the power of God to guide me, the might of God to uphold
me, the wisdom of God to teach me, the eye of God to watch over me, the ear
of God to hear me, the word of God to give me speech, the hand of God to
protect me, the path of God to lie before me, the shield of God to shelter me,
the host of God to defend me against the snares of the devil and the
temptations of the world, against every man who meditates injury against me,
whether far or near.

The Breastplate of St Patrick (373–462)

My Father, for another night
Of quiet sleep and rest,
For all the joy of morning light,
Your holy name be blest.

Henry William Baker (1821–1877)

O you most holy and ever-loving God, we thank you once more for the quiet
rest of the night that has gone by, for the new promise that has come with this
fresh morning, and for the hope of this day. While we have slept, the world in
which we live has swept on, and we have rested under the shadow of your love.
May we trust you this day for all the needs of the body, the soul, and the spirit.
Give us this day our daily bread. Amen.

Robert Collyer (nineteenth century)

◆ Father, we thank you for the night,
And for the pleasant morning light;
for rest and food and loving care,
And all that makes the day so fair.

Help us to do the things we should,
To be to others kind and good;
In all we do at work or play
To grow more loving every day.

Rebecca J. Weston

You who send forth the light, create the morning, make the sun rise on the good and the evil, enlighten the blindness of our minds with the knowledge of the truth: lift up the light of your countenance upon us, that in your light we may see light, and, at the last, be in the light of grace and in the light of glory.

Lancelot Andrewes (1555–1626)

Thank you, Father, that the longest night ends in dawn and a new day. Thank you that your mercies are new every morning. Clear from my mind now all black thoughts of the night and give me confidence in your loving care as I face today. Give me your strength in my tiredness and the sure hope that your love will guard and keep me. Through Jesus Christ our Lord. Amen.

Prayer after a sleepless night

Sentences to help meditation and quiet
prayer:

The Lord's unfailing love and mercy still continue,
Fresh as the morning, as sure as the sunrise.
The Lord is all I have, and so I put my hope in him.

From Lamentations 3

Rise up, O children of light, and let us give glory to the Lord who alone can save our souls. O Lord, as you withdraw sleep from the eyes of our body, grant us wakefulness of mind so that we may stand before you in awe and sing your praises worthily.

Syrian Orthodox Church

Eternal God,
We say good morning to you.
Hallowed be your name.
Early in the morning, before we begin our work
we praise your glory.
Renew our bodies as fresh as the morning flowers.
Open our inner eyes, as the sun casts new light upon the
darkness which prevailed over the night.
Deliver us from all captivity.
Give us wings of freedom, like the birds in the sky,
to begin a new journey.
Restore justice and freedom as a mighty stream
running continuously as day follows day.
We thank you for the gift of this morning,
and a new day to work with you.

Masao Takenaka, Japan

◆ For this new morning and its light,
For rest and shelter of the night,
for health and food, for love and friends,
for every gift your goodness sends,
We thank you, gracious Lord.

Author unknown

◆ Now another day is breaking,
Sleep was sweet and so is waking.
Dear Lord, I promised you last night
Never again to sulk or fight.
Such vows are easier to keep
When a child is sound asleep.
Today, O Lord, for your dear sake,
I'll try to keep them when awake.

Ogden Nash

We give you hearty thanks, O God, for the rest of the past night and for the gift of a new day with its opportunities of pleasing you. Grant that we so pass its hours in the perfect freedom of your service, that at eventide we may again give thanks to you; through Jesus Christ our Lord. Amen.

Daybreak Office of the Eastern Church

O God, I cannot begin this day without you,
I cannot trust myself.
Help me, that I may know that I am not alone.

H. C. Alleman

Father-Creator, Provider-from-of-old, Ancient-of-days—fresh-born from the womb of night are we. In the first dawning of the new day draw we nigh unto thee. Forlorn are the eyes till they have seen the Chief.

Bushman's prayer, South Africa

O God, who has folded back the mantle of the night to clothe us in the golden glory of the day, chase from our hearts all gloomy thoughts and make us glad with the brightness of hope.

Ancient collect

Open your doors of mercy, Lord:
hear our prayer and have mercy upon our souls.
Lord of the morning and ruler of the seasons:
hear our prayer and have mercy upon our souls.
Shine on us, Lord, and make us light like the day:
let your light shine in our minds and drive away
the shadows of error and night.
The creation is full of light, give your light also to our hearts:
that we may praise you all the day long.
The morning and the evening praise you, Lord:
they bring you the praise of your church.
Light which gives light to all creatures:
give light to our minds that we may thank you, Lord.

Syrian Orthodox Church

Thanks to thee, ever, O gentle Christ, that thou hast raised me freely from the black and from the darkness of last night, to the kindly light of this day.

Celtic prayer

O God, it is good to know that I am not alone. You have given me human companionship at every turn; you have given me, above all, the assurance of your own presence, dependable at all times, and available whatever my need.

In this morning hour
I want a fresh chance
to start again.
I don't want to waste the minutes and hours
That have been given to me.
I want to be alive
To every experience,
In conversation,
In the mundane tasks of this day.
In moments of relaxation
I want to find joy in living.
Lord of the morning, help me.

Frank Topping

I accept this new day as your gift,
and I enter it now with eagerness;
I open my senses to perceive you;
I lend my energies to things of goodness and joy.
Amen.

Rita Snowden

Prayers for the Whole Day

Do not say 'It is morning' and dismiss it with a name of yesterday. See it for the first time as a new-born child that has no name.

Rabindranath Tagore

All through this day, O Lord,
by the power of thy quickening Spirit,
let me touch the lives of others for good,
whether through the word I speak, the prayer I speak
or the life I live.

Author unknown

Dear Lord Jesus, we shall have this day only once; before it is gone, help us to do all the good we can, so that today is not a wasted day.

Stephen Grellet (1773–1855)

Lord, we offer you ourselves this day
for the work you want accomplished,
for the people you want us to meet,
for the word you want to be uttered,
for the silence you want to be kept,
for the places you want us to enter,
for the new ways you want pioneered.
Go with us along the way, Lord,
and enable us to realize your presence
at all times and in all places,
our loving Lord Jesus Christ.

Morris Maddocks

O Lord, lift up the light of your countenance upon us; let your peace rule in our hearts, and may it be our strength and our song in the house of our pilgrimage. We commit ourselves to your care and keeping; let your grace be mighty in us, and sufficient in us, for all the duties of the day. Keep us from sin. Give us the rule over our own spirits, and guard us from speaking unadvisedly with our lips. May we live together in holy love and peace, and do you command your blessing upon us, even life for evermore.

Matthew Henry (1662–1714)

In the evening and the morning and at noon
we praise and bless you,
we pray to you in thanksgiving and supplication.
Father of all,
may our prayers be set before you like incense
and may our hearts not yield
to the words of the wicked;
deliver us from all
who seek to take possession of our souls.
For our eyes are fixed on you, O Lord,
our refuge is in you and you are our hope;
do not abandon us, O Lord our God.
For to you belong all glory
honour and worship,
Father, Son and Holy Spirit,
now and for ever, to the ages of ages. Amen.

Prayer of the Eastern Orthodox Church

Help us this day, O Lord, to serve thee devoutly, and the world busily. May we do our work wisely, give succour secretly, go to our meat appetitely, sit thereat discreetly, arise temperately, please our friends duly, go to our beds merrily, and sleep surely; for the joy of our Lord Jesus Christ.

Medieval prayer, author unknown

O Lord, whose way is perfect: help us, we pray, always to trust in your goodness; that walking with you in faith, and following you in all simplicity, we may possess quiet and contented minds, and cast all our care on you, because you care for us; for the sake of Jesus Christ our Lord.

Christina Rossetti (1830–1894)

May my mouth praise the love of God this morning.
O God, may I do your will this day.
May my ears hear the words of God and obey them.
O God, may I do your will this day.
May my feet follow the footsteps of God this day.
O God, may I do your will this day.

Prayer from Japan

Bless me, and all I am to go about and do this day, with the blessing of thy love and mercy. Continue thy grace and love in Jesus Christ upon me, and give me a mind cheerfully to follow thy leadings and execute thine appointment. Let thy Holy Spirit guide me in my beginning, and my progress, on to my last end.

Jacob Boehme (1575–1624)

Lord, help me to enjoy the common things of my everyday life.
I often find myself saying that nothing happened today,
when in fact the ordinary events of my life make a rich pattern,
but they are so familiar I hardly notice them:
things like cups of tea and coffee
and meals shared with friends and colleagues;
or listening to favourite family stories
that we have heard and told so often.
Lord of Life, help me to recognize the joy of simple things.

Frank Topping

Make me remember, O God, that every day is your gift and ought to be used according to your command, through Jesus Christ our Lord.

Samuel Johnson (1709–1786)

O Lord, grant me to greet the coming day in peace. Help me in all things to rely upon your holy will. In every hour of the day reveal your will to me. Bless my dealings with all who surround me. Teach me to treat all that comes to me throughout the day with peace of soul and with firm conviction that your will governs all. In all my deeds and words guide my thoughts and feelings. In unforeseen events let me not forget that all are sent by you. Teach me to act firmly and wisely without embittering or embarrassing others. Give me strength to bear the fatigue of the coming day with all that it shall bring. Direct my will, teach me to pray, pray yourself in me.

Metropolitan Philaret of Moscow (died 1867)

Grant to us, O God, this day, to do whatever duty lies before us with cheerfulness and sincerity of heart. Help us in all things fearlessly to do what we know to be right; save us from hypocrisy and pretence. Make us truthful, unselfish and strong. And so bring us to the ending of the day unashamed and with a quiet mind. We ask this through Jesus Christ our Lord.

From Prayers For Use in Hospitals

> Lord, I have time,
> I have plenty of time,
> All the time that you give me,
> The years of my life,
> The days of my years,
> The hours of my days,
> They are all mine.
> Mine to fill, quietly, calmly,
> But to fill completely, up to the brim,
> To offer them to you, that of their insipid water
> You may make a rich wine such as you made once in Cana of
> Galilee.

Michel Quoist

You know, O Lord, all that lies before us this day, of duty and of danger and of temptation. Keep us, we beseech you, in all things true to you, that nothing may come between us and your holy presence; through Jesus Christ our Lord.

John Hunter (1849–1917)

To you, O Master, who loves all people, I hasten on rising from sleep; by your mercy I go forth to do your work, and I make my prayer to you, help me at all times and in all things; deliver me from every evil thing of this world and from pursuit by the devil; save me and bring me to your eternal kingdom. For you are my Creator, you inspire all good thoughts in me; in you is all my hope and to you I ascribe glory, now and for ever and unto the ages of ages.

St Macarius the Great

Lord, help me to remember that nothing is going to happen today that you and I cannot handle together.

Saidie Patterson, prayer for a difficult day ahead

O make your way plain before my face. Support me this day under all the difficulties I shall meet with. I offer myself to you, O God, this day, to do in me, and with me, as to you seems most meet.

Thomas Wilson (1663–1755)

Lord, you know the fears and anxieties that fill our hearts at what today will bring. Free us from panic and worry. Anchor our thoughts and minds in your great power and love. Send us into this day with your peace in our hearts and sure confidence in your fatherly care. Through Jesus Christ our Lord.

Grant us, O Lord, to pass this day in gladness and in peace, without stumbling and without stain; that, reaching the eventide victorious over all temptation, we may praise thee, the eternal God, who art blessed, and dost govern all things, world without end.

From the Mozarabic Sacramentary

O God,
Early in the morning I cry unto you.
Help me to pray
And to think only of you.
I cannot pray alone.
In me there is darkness
But with you there is light.
I am lonely but you leave me not.
I am feeble in heart but you leave me not.
I am restless but with you there is peace.
In me there is bitterness, but with you there is patience;
Your ways are past understanding, but
You know the way for me.
O heavenly Father,
I praise and thank you
For the peace of the night.
I praise and thank you for this new day.
I praise and thank you for all your goodness
and faithfulness throughout my life.
You have granted me many blessings:
Now let me accept tribulation from your hand.
You will not lay on me more than I can bear.
You make all things work together for good
For your children.

Dietrich Bonhoeffer (1906–1945),
written Christmas 1943 for his fellow prisoners

❖ *Prayers for the Night* ❖

I lie down and sleep, and all night long
the Lord protects me.

FROM PSALM 3

Be off, Satan, from this door and from these four walls. This is no place for you; there is nothing for you to do here. This is the place for Peter and Paul and the holy gospel; and this is where I mean to sleep, now that my worship is done, in the name of the Father and of the Holy Spirit.

One of the earliest Christian prayers recorded

At Night

Day is done
Gone the sun
From the lake, from the hills, from the sky.
Safely rest,
All is well!
God is nigh.

Author unknown

Blessed are you, O Lord our God,
King of the universe!
At your word night falls.
In your wisdom you open heaven's gates,
you control the elements and rotate the seasons.
You set the stars in the vault of heaven.
You created night and day.
You cause the light to fade when darkness comes
and the darkness to melt away in the light of the new day.
O ever-living and eternal God,
you will always watch over us, your creatures.
Blessed are you, O Lord,
at whose word night falls.

Jewish prayer

Lord, keep us safe this night,
Secure from all our fears;
May angels guard us while we sleep,
Till morning light appears.

John Leland (1754–1841)

O Lord our God, what sins I have this day committed in word, deed, or thought, forgive me, for you are gracious and you love all people. Grant me peaceful and undisturbed sleep, send me your guardian angel to protect and guard me from every evil, for you are the guardian of our souls and bodies and to you we ascribe glory, to the Father and the Son and the Holy Ghost, now and for ever and unto the ages of ages.

Russian Orthodox Church

Maker of all things made, to you
We come before the last of light,
That your dear mercy which we know
Enfold us through the coming night.

Cleansed and secure we lay us down
To take from you the gift of sleep;
And, if we wake, in quietness
With you a trusting watch to keep.

This night is yours, and we are yours;
You are our Father, Brother, Friend.
Your love enfolds your children now,
This night, tomorrow, without end.

Lilian Cox

O Lord Jesus Christ, our watchman and keeper, take us into thy care, and grant that, our bodies sleeping, our minds may watch in thee and be made merry by some sight of that celestial and heavenly life wherein thou art the King and Prince, together with the Father and the Holy Ghost, where the angels and holy souls be most happy citizens. O purify our souls, keep clean our bodies, that in both we may please thee, sleeping and waking, for ever.

From Christian Prayers (1566)

O God, I am glad that I need not pretend during prayer:
I am tired now and my words do not come easily;
I have not kept all my bright promises of the morning;
I have smudged the clear truth of some of my words;
I have been a little short in some of my replies;
I have overlooked others' needs, absorbed in my own;
I have failed in cheerfulness at times.

You know, O God my Father, what troubles me now, on recollection, as I come to my rest. I seek your forgiveness. Without your forgiving, sustaining, renewing love I cannot fully rest.

I commit myself to you anew—in the name of Jesus my Master. Amen.

Rita Snowden

◆We thank you, loving Father, for all the happiness of today, for food and games and friends and family. Now that the night has come, help us to go to bed without grumbling or fussing. Thank you for your angels who take care of us while we sleep. Thank you, Father, that you are always awake and ready to hear whenever we talk to you. Please keep us all in this home safe through the night. For Jesus' sake. Amen.

We pray thee, O Creator of everything, at this hour preceding night, that thou be clement and watch over us.

Let dreams and phantoms of the night be scattered. Keep us safe from our enemy and make us pure!

Attributed to St Ambrose of Milan (340–397)

Lord, this night
Help me to die to self,
So that I might awake
To live more fully
For others and in you.
Help me to trust
That as you have led me this far
Your guidance will continue.

Frank Topping

Abide with me, fast falls the eventide;
The darkness deepens, Lord, with me abide;
When other helpers fail and comforts flee,
Help of the helpless, O abide with me.

Reveal yourself before my closing eyes,
Shine through the gloom and point me to the skies;
Heaven's morning breaks and earth's vain shadows flee—
In life, in death, O Lord, abide with me.

Henry Lyte (1793–1847)

The sun has disappeared.
I have switched off the light,
and my wife and children are asleep.
The animals in the forest are full of fear,
and so are the people on their mats.
They prefer the day with your sun
to the night.
But I still know that your moon is there,
and your eyes and also your hands.
Thus I am not afraid.
This day again
you led us wonderfully.
Everybody went to his mat
satisfied and full.
Renew us during our sleep,
that in the morning we may come afresh to our daily jobs.
Be with our brothers far away in Asia
who may be getting up now. Amen.

Prayer of a young Ghanaian Christian

Sentence for meditation and quiet prayer:

When I lie down, I go to sleep in peace;
you alone, O Lord, keep me perfectly safe.

From Psalm 4

Visit, we beseech you, O Lord, our homes and drive far away from them all the snares of the enemy: let your holy angels dwell therein to preserve us in peace; and may your blessing be upon us evermore; through Jesus Christ our Lord.

From the Office of Compline

O Lord my God, I thank you that you have brought this day to a close;
I thank you that you have given me peace in body and in soul.
Your hand has been over me and has protected and preserved me.
Forgive my puny faith, the ill that I this day have done,
and help me to forgive all who have wronged me.
Grant me a quiet night's sleep beneath your tender care.
And defend me from all the temptations of darkness.
Into your hands I commend my loved ones
and all who dwell in this house;
I commend my body and soul.
O God, your holy name be praised. Amen.

Dietrich Bonhoeffer, from prison

Abide with us, O Lord, for it is towards evening and the day is far spent; abide with us and with your whole church.

Abide with us in the evening of the day, in the evening of life, in the evening of the world.

Abide with us and with all your faithful ones, O Lord, in time and eternity.

From the Lutheran Manual of Prayer

Into your hands, O Lord and Father, we commend our souls and our bodies, our parents and our homes, friends and servants, neighbours and kindred, our benefactors and departed brethren, all your people faithfully believing and all who need your pity and protection. Enlighten us with your holy grace and suffer us never more to be separated from you, one God in Trinity, God everlasting.

Edmund of Abingdon (?1175–1240)

Glory to thee, my God, this night
For all the blessings of the light;
Keep me, O keep me, King of kings,
Beneath thine own almighty wings.

Forgive me, Lord, for thy dear Son,
The ill that I this day have done,
That with the world, myself and thee
I, ere I sleep, at peace may be.

O may my soul on thee repose,
And with sweet sleep mine eyelids close,
Sleep that may me more vigorous make
To serve my God when I awake.

Thomas Ken (1637–1711)

Save us, Lord, while we are awake; guard us while we are asleep; that awake we may watch with Christ, and asleep may rest in his peace.

Look down, Lord, from your throne in heaven,
    let the light of your presence dispel the shadows of the night; and from the children of light banish the deeds of darkness;
    through Jesus Christ our Lord. Amen.

From the Office of Compline

Merciful Father, you know that this has been a busy day—but you have brought me through it safely.
    Jesus also knew tiredness and fell asleep in the boat;
    he discovered how exhausting people can prove.
    Renew in sleep, I pray, any who know special tiredness now—keep us through the hours of night;
    and guard all those on night-duty—doctors, nurses, night-watchmen of buildings, policemen, firemen;
    train-drivers, captains and crews of planes and ships.
    Watch over little children, support the sick, comfort the grieved, guide the harassed among us, for the sake of Christ. Amen.

Rita Snowden

O Lord our God,
who lives in unapproachable light,
in your great mercy you have been our constant guide
throughout this day
and have called us together to give you glory at eventide:
Hear the prayers of your unworthy servants
and keep us safe from the darkness of sin.
Give light to our souls
that being ever in awe of you and going forward in your light
we may glorify you in all things
who in your unfailing love for all mankind
are the one true God.
For yours is the greatness, the majesty, the power and the glory,
Father, Son and Holy Spirit,
now and for ever, to the ages of ages. Amen.

Be with us, merciful God, and protect us through the silent hours of this night;
that we, who are wearied by the changes and chances of this fleeting world,
may rest upon your eternal changelessness; through Jesus Christ our Lord.
Amen.

From the Office of Compline

In thy name, O Jesu who wast crucified,
I lie down to rest;
Watch thou me in sleep remote
Hold thou me in thy one hand.
Bless me, O my Christ,
Be thou my shield protecting me,
Aid my steps in the pitiful swamp,
Lead thou me to the life eternal.
Keep thou me in the presence of God,
O good and gracious Son of the Virgin,
And fervently I pray thy strong protection
From my lying down at dusk to my rising at day.

Celtic prayer

◆ Dear Jesus, as a hen covers her chicks with her wings to keep them safe, do you this night protect us under your golden wings.

Prayer from India

Send your peace into my heart, O Lord, that I may be contented with the mercies of this day and confident of your protection for this night; and having forgiven others, even as you forgive me, may I go to rest in tranquillity and trust; through Jesus Christ our Lord. Amen.

St Francis of Assisi (1182–1226)

O God, our Father, utterly loving, utterly wise, hold me this night within your safe-keeping:
    at night men and women have long turned towards you;
    I come with my own faults, my own small faith, seeking more;
    I bow before you in humility and wonder.
    Let no experience of this day hinder my true service, I pray;
let your Kingdom come among men and women, your will be done.

Rita Snowden

Into your hands, O Lord, we commend our souls and bodies, beseeching you to keep us this night under your protection and to strengthen us for our service on the morrow, for Christ's sake. Amen.

Archbishop Laud (1573–1645)

God, who by making the evening to succeed the day has bestowed the gift of sleep on human weakness, grant, we beseech you, that while we enjoy your blessings we may acknowledge him from whom they came, through Jesus Christ.

From the Mozarabic Sacramentary

Show your loving-kindness tonight, O Lord, to all who stand in need of your help. Be with the weak to make them strong, and with the strong to make them gentle. Cheer the lonely with your company and the worried with your peace. Prosper your church in the fulfilment of her mighty task and grant your blessing to all who have toiled today in Christ's name.

John Baillie

◆Jesus, tender Shepherd, hear me,
Bless your little lamb tonight;
Through the darkness please be near me,
Watch my sleep till morning light.

All this day your hand has led me,
And I thank you for your care;
You have clothed me, warmed and fed me,
Listen to my evening prayer.

Let my sins be all forgiven;
Bless the friends I love so well;
Take me, when I die, to heaven,
Happy there with you to dwell.

Mary L. Duncan (1814–1840)

O living God, in Jesus Christ you were laid in the tomb at this evening hour
and so sanctified the grave to be a bed of hope to your people. Grant us
courage and faith to die daily to our sin and pride, that even as this flesh and
blood decays, our lives still may grow in you, that at our last day our dying
may be done so well that we live in you for ever.

From Prayer at Night

Lord of the night,
Be with me through the hours of darkness,
Let all my questions,
Problems, decisions,
Be enveloped in sleep
That through the mystery
Of the sleeping mind
The difficulties of this day
Will be seen to be easier
In the morning light.
Into your hands, O Lord,
I commit my spirit.

Frank Topping

God of the busy daytime;
God of the quiet night;
Whose peace pervades the darkness
And greets us with the light.
Safe with thy presence near us
Wherever we may be,
Thou, God, our great protector
We love and worship thee.

John Oxenham (1852–1941)

O Lord our God,
we come to you now with open hearts
to call upon your holy name and to give you thanks
for keeping us safe during this day
and for bringing us to the light of evening.
We pray that this evening and the approaching night
and all the days of our earthly life may be free from sin:
clothe us with the armour of your Holy Spirit
to fight against the forces of evil and the passions of the flesh;
put far from us all sin
and make us worthy of your eternal kingdom.
For to you belong all glory, honour and praise,
Father, Son and Holy Spirit,
now and for ever, to the ages of ages. Amen.

Eastern Orthodox Church

Go with each of us to rest; if any awake, temper to them the dark hours of watching; and when the day returns, return to us, our sun and comforter, and call us up with morning faces and with morning hearts, eager to labour, eager to be happy, if happiness should be our portion, and if the day be marked for sorrow, strong to endure it.

Robert Louis Stevenson (1850–1894),
written and read the night before he died

273

Prayers for the Night Watches

When we lie awake, in pain, in anxiety or because we are poor sleepers , it is good to pray
and direct our thoughts to God, who never slumbers or sleeps.

O Lord, my heart is all a prayer,
But it is silent unto thee;
I am too tired to look for words,
I rest upon thy sympathy
to understand when I am dumb;
And well I know thou hearest me.

I know thou hearest me because
A quiet peace comes down to me,
And fills the places where before
Weak thoughts were wandering wearily;
And deep within me it is calm,
Though waves are tossing outwardly.

Amy Carmichael (1868–1951)

Watch, dear Lord, with those who wake, or watch,
or weep tonight,
and give your angels charge over those who sleep;
Tend your sick ones, O Lord Christ, rest your weary ones,
bless your dying ones, soothe your suffering ones,
pity your afflicted ones, shield your joyous ones,
and all for your love's sake. Amen.

St Augustine (354–430)

O Lord our God,
in your great goodness
and in the richness of your mercy
you have protected us this night from the test of evil;
you who are the creator of all things
bring us safely to the time
when we offer you our prayers at daybreak,
and together with your gift of true light
pour out in our hearts the treasure of knowing you
that enables us to do your will.
For you, O God,
are good and loving to all mankind
and we give you the glory,
Father, Son and Holy Spirit,
now and for ever, to the ages of ages. Amen.

From the Night Office of the Eastern Orthodox Church

For meditation or personal prayer

Sometimes, when we lie awake, prayer can take the form of repeating, in God's presence, some much-loved and comforting Bible verses:

My help will come from the Lord, who made heaven and earth.
The protector of Israel never dozes or sleeps.
The Lord will protect you from all danger; he will keep you safe.

From Psalm 121

He will cover you with his wings;
you will be safe in his care;
you need not fear any dangers at night
or sudden attacks during the day.

From Psalm 91

Jesus said: 'Do not be worried and upset. Believe in God and
believe also in me.'

From John 14

St Paul said: 'Don't worry about anything, but in all your prayers
ask God for what you need, always asking him with a thankful
heart. And God's peace, which is far beyond human understanding, will keep your hearts and minds safe in union with
Christ Jesus.'

From Philippians 4

God before me, God behind me,
God above me, God below me;
I on the path of God,
God upon my track.
Who is there on land?
Who is there on wave?
Who is there on billow?
Who is there by door-post?
Who is there along with us?
God and Lord.
I am here abroad,
I am here in need,
I am here in pain,
I am here in straits,
I am here alone,
O God, aid me.

Celtic prayer

O God, my guardian, stay always with me.
In the morning, in the evening, by day or by night,
always be my helper.

Prayer from Poland

The angels of God guard us through the night,
and quieten the powers of darkness.
The Spirit of God be our guide
to lead us to peace and to glory.

From Prayer at Night

Three in the morning, Lord, it's so quiet;
it's almost as though the world has died.
The baby woke me with her teething cries
and I can't get back to sleep.
All around there's a silent expectation,
Soon light will come and there will be the dawn chorus
and your gift of a new day.
It's rather like your Son's dying and rising.
Each day is a new opportunity to rise up to serve you afresh—
Please help me to do that every day of my life.

Tony Castle

For meditation and personal prayer

When we feel well enough, a wakeful period is an opportunity to pray for others. Mention the names of those you love and those in need, silently holding them up to God for his blessing.

I will lie down in peace and take my rest,
for it is in God alone that I dwell unafraid.
Let us bless the Life-Giver, the Pain-Bearer, the Love-Maker,
let us praise and exalt God above all for ever.
May God's name be praised above the furthest star,
glorified and exalted above all for ever.

From Prayer at Night

Be present, O merciful God, and protect us through the silent hours of the night, that we who are wearied by the changes and chances of this fleeting world may repose upon your eternal changelessness, through the everlasting Christ our Lord.

From the Roman Breviary

May the Light of lights come
To my dark heart from thy place;
May the Spirit's wisdom come
To my heart's tablet from my Saviour.
Be the peace of the Spirit mine this night,
Be the peace of the Son mine this night,
Be the peace of the Father mine this night,
The peace of all peace be mine this night,
Each morning and evening of my life.

Celtic prayer

Lighten our darkness, we beseech thee, O Lord; and by your great mercy defend us from all perils and dangers of this night; for the love of your only Son, our Saviour, Jesus Christ. Amen.

From the Gelasian Sacramentary

◆ *All Times of Life* ◆

[God] has set the right time for everything.

FROM ECCLESIASTES 3

Through all the changing scenes of life,
In trouble and in joy,
The praises of my God shall still
My heart and tongue employ.

Nahum Tate (1652–1715) and Nicholas Brady (1659–1726)

Children and Young People

Give, I pray thee, to all children grace reverently to love their parents, and lovingly obey them. Teach us all that filial duty never ends or lessens; and bless all parents in their children, and all children in their parents.

Christina Rossetti (1830–1894)

Father, whose Son called children to him,
we pray for boys and girls everywhere,
that their childhood may
be filled with laughter and happiness.
As they learn so many facts
and enter into so many new experiences,
may they learn of your love,
and how to serve Jesus as Master and Lord.

Bernard Thorogood

O God, the Father of all, we commend to your ceaseless compassion all homeless children and orphans and those whose lives are overshadowed by violence or thwarted by disease or cruelty. Awaken in us your living charity that we may not rest while children cry for bread or go uncomforted for lack of love.

From The Mother's Union Service Book (1980)

Father, we pray for all children who have been abused and cruelly treated. Give them your healing and a sense of worth that comes from knowing that each one of them is loved and valued in your eyes. Amen.

Lord Jesus, you welcomed children and spoke sternly to those who wanted to send them away. Help us to take time with children for your sake and not to resent their presence but make them welcome.

Dear Lord, please bless this child and give him understanding.

Break down the barriers that are keeping him from grasping these skills, this knowledge. Stir and awaken his now dreaming mind.

Bless his books. Let your power and love work through them to excite and delight him so that their message is clear and strong.

Bless his tools—his paper and pencils and crayons, so that they become lovely and sure, a source of joy to his hands.

Bless his teacher. Give her patience. Give her understanding. Give her the ability to guide him out of dark confusion into the light of comprehension and command...

For in you is all wisdom. And that wisdom is a part of this child.

Marjorie Holmes (adapted)

Lord, as I teach others may I remember the ways through which I learned. May I feel the excitement of my pupils as they encounter new ideas and may I understand their difficulties in grasping those things they find obscure. Remind me of my responsibilities. May I not try to force children into my way of thinking but help them to learn how to think for themselves. May I create a learning environment sufficiently open for children not to feel intimidated, sufficiently disciplined for every child to have the freedom to learn.

A teacher's prayer from Further Everyday Prayers

We pray for all who teach children about you, O God, in church or in school. Give them honesty, sincerity and a love for you and for their pupils which will convey the good news of Jesus as strongly as the lessons they teach.

Lord, we pray for all young people who are trying to serve you in an alien world. Give them courage, wisdom and tact and the knowledge that you are round about them keeping them from evil.

O God our Father, we pray for our young people growing up in an unstable and confusing world. Show them that your ways give more meaning to life than the ways of the world and that following you is better than chasing after selfish goals. Help them to take failure not as a measure of their worth but as a chance for a new start. Give them strength to hold their faith in you and to keep alive their joy in your creation; through Jesus Christ our Lord.

Episcopal Church, USA

Father, we pray for young people growing up in a difficult and dangerous world.

We pray for those who are unemployed, who have not worked since they left school and have never earned their own money.

We pray for those who are taking their first steps in their skill, trade or profession.

We pray for those who feel they have no support from the adults around them and who grow resentful at what they see to be their indifference.

We pray for those who are caught up in violence either giving it or receiving it.

We pray for those who are morally confused and uncertain of what is right or wrong.

We pray for young Christians as they strive to live out their faith in an unsympathetic world.

Father, you are head of all the family. Hear our prayers in Jesus' name.

From Further Everyday Prayers

Children's prayers and prayers by children can be found in chapter 19

The Middle Years

Now thank we all our God,
With heart and hand and voices,
Who wondrous things has done,
In whom his world rejoices;
Who from our mother's arms
Has blessed us on our way
With countless gifts of love
And still is ours today.

O may this bounteous God
Through all our life be near us,
With ever joyful hearts
And blessed peace to cheer us;
And keep us in his grace,
And guide us when perplexed,
And free us from all ills
In this world and the next.

Martin Rinkart (1586–1649) translated by Catherine Winkworth (1829–1878)

Lord, we pray for all those who are struggling with the pressures and busyness of adult life.

Give wisdom to those whose professions call for accurate skill and critical decision-making.

Give courage and endurance to those whose daily work is hard or monotonous.

Strengthen and reassure all those who are bringing up families: struggling with broken nights and childhood illnesses; dealing with teenage rebellion and self-will.

Give patience and love to those endeavouring to make their marriage good and enduring.

For all we ask your peace and encouragement. Through Jesus Christ our Lord. Amen.

You gave us, O God,
understanding, reason and intellect.
O my God, grant that we may use them
to discern good from evil
and to do good.

Jewish prayer

Father, we pray for those who are facing change in their lives. Some are coming to terms with loneliness, others with lack of employment or ill-health. Give fresh reserves of strength to meet the demanding challenges that life brings. Through Jesus Christ our Lord.

Sentences to aid quiet prayer and meditation:

We need to find God and he cannot be found in noise and
restlessness. God is the friend of silence ... the more we receive
in silent prayer, the more we can give in our active life.

Mother Teresa

Lord, you have examined me and you know me.
You know everything I do;
from far away you understand all my thoughts.
You see me, whether I am working or resting;
you know all my actions.
Even before I speak,
you already know what I will say.
You are all round me on every side;
you protect me with your power ...
Examine me, O God, and know my mind;
test me, and discover my thoughts.
Find out if there is any evil in me
and guide me in the everlasting way.

From Psalm 139

O Lord God Almighty, who gives power to the faint and increases strength to those who have no might; without you we can do nothing... Lord of power and love, we come, trusting in your almighty strength, and your infinite goodness, to ask from you what is wanting in ourselves; even that grace which shall help us such to be and such to do as you would have us. O our God, let your grace be sufficient for us... We will trust in you.

Benjamin Jenks (1646–1724)

Lord, if you will make
The autumn of my life
As lovely as this golden autumn morning,
I will not look back to grieve the passing days of summer.
Of all the regal seasons autumn is most brilliant.
Make my life brilliant, too!

Ruth Harms Calkin

Lord, on the way to goodness, when we stumble, hold us, when we fall, lift us up, when we are hard pressed by evil, deliver us, when we turn from what is good, turn us back, and bring us at last to your glory.

Growing Old

Grow old along with me!
The best is yet to be,
The last of life, for which the first was made:
Our times are in his hand
Who saith 'A whole I planned,
Youth shows but half; trust God: see all nor be afraid!'

Robert Browning (1812–1889)

Don't let me be so afraid of ageing, God. Let me rejoice and reach out to be replenished; I know that each day I can be reborn into strength and beauty through you.

Marjorie Holmes

Dear God, Holy Spirit,
    the things of the spirit are the only realities that age cannot weary.
And the spirit that reaches out to Spirit is, in time, set free from the flush and
quiver of ambition, the fleeting joys of status and possessions, and the physical
indignities of age.
    Lord,
    as I grow older, may I be blessed with faith enough
    to make the journey
    from ageing body to ageless life.

Frank Topping

Words to help meditation and private prayer:

We fix our attention, not on things that are seen, but on things
that are unseen ... so we are always full of courage.

From 2 Corinthians

God is our shelter and strength,
always ready to help in times of trouble.
So we will not be afraid, even if the earth is shaken ...
even if the seas roar and rage,
and the hills are shaken by the violence ...
The Lord almighty is with us.

From Psalm 46

Lord, you know better than I know myself that I am getting older and will
some day be old. Keep me from the fatal habit of thinking I must say
something on every subject and on every occasion. Release me from craving to
straighten out everybody's affairs. Make me thoughtful but not moody:
helpful but not bossy. With my vast store of wisdom it seems a pity not to use
it all, but you know, Lord, that I want a few friends at the end.

    Keep my mind free from the recital of endless details, give me wings to
get to the point. Seal my lips on my aches and pains. They are increasing and
love of rehearsing them is becoming sweeter as the years go by. I dare not ask
for grace enough to enjoy the tales of others' pains, but help me to endure
them with patience.

    I dare not ask for improved memory, but for a growing humility and a

286

lessening cocksureness when my memory seems to clash with the memories of others. Teach me the glorious lesson that occasionally I may be mistaken.

Keep me reasonably sweet; I do not want to be a saint—some of them are so hard to live with—but a sour old person is one of the crowning works of the devil.

Give me the ability to see good things in unexpected places, and talents in unexpected people. And give me, Lord, the grace to tell them so. Amen.

Attributed to a seventeenth-century nun

For personal prayer and meditation

As you contemplate your own increasing age or the old age of those you love, think, in the words of this hymn, of God's goodness in the past and his promises for the future:

How good is the God we adore,
Our faithful, unchangeable Friend!
His love is as great as his power,
And knows neither measure nor end!
'Tis Jesus, the First and the Last,
Whose Spirit shall guide us safe home:
We'll praise him for all that is past,
We'll trust him for all that's to come.

Joseph Hart (1712–1768)

May all in whom the light of faith shines dimly, see at last.

St Thérèse of Lisieux

O Lord Jesus Christ, who didst hear the prayer of thy two disciples and didst abide with them at eventide: Abide, we pray thee, with all thy people in the evening of life. Make thyself known to them, and let thy light shine upon their path; and whenever they shall pass through the valley of the shadow of death, be with them unto the end; through Jesus Christ our Lord.

George Appleton

O Lord Jesus Christ, King of kings, you have power over life and death, you know even what is uncertain and obscure, our thoughts and feelings are no secret from you. Cleanse me from my hidden faults, for I have done evil and you have seen it.

Day by day as my life draws nearer to its end my sins increase in number. O Lord, God of spirit and of all composed creatures, you know how frail I am, in soul and in body. Give me strength, Lord, in my weakness and uphold me in my sufferings.

Knowing that I have come to be regarded by many people as an oddity, you strengthen and support me. Give me prudent judgment, good Lord, and let me always remember your blessings. Do not think of my many sins; put my faults out of your mind . . .

I am unworthy and sinful, Lord. But still I bless and praise you, for you have poured out your mercies lavishly over me; you have been my Helper and Protector; your great name deserves eternal glory.

Glory to you, O Lord, our God.

Ephraem (died 373)

When the signs of age begin to mark my body and still more when they touch my mind; when the illness that is to diminish me or carry me off strikes from without or is born within me; when the painful moment comes in which I suddenly awaken to the fact that I am ill or growing old; in all those dark moments, O God, grant that I may understand that it is you, provided only my faith is strong enough, who are painfully parting the fibres of my being in order to penetrate to the very marrow of my substance and bear me away within yourself.

Teilhard de Chardin (1881–1955)

May the right hand of the Lord
Keep us ever in old age,
The grace of Christ continually defend us from the enemy,
O Lord, direct our heart in the way of peace;
Through Jesus Christ our Lord.

Aedalwald, The Book of Cerne (ninth century)

◆ Children's Prayers ◆

Jesus called a child, made him stand in front of them, and said, 'I assure you that unless you change and become like children, you wil never enter the Kingdom of heaven... Whoever welcomes in my name one such child as this, welcomes me.'

FROM MATTHEW 18

Prayers for Children

Dear Father, whom I cannot see,
I know that you are near to me.
Quite quietly I speak to you:
Please show me what you'd have me do.
Please help me plan kind things to do
For other people and for you.
Thank you for always helping me,
Dear Father, whom I cannot see.

Lilian Cox

Jesus, friend of little children,
Be a friend to me;
Take my hand and ever keep me
Close to thee.

W.J. Mathaus

Thank you, Lord, that you are close to me all the time, even though I cannot see you. You know how I am feeling and what I am thinking even when I do not tell you out loud. Thank you for listening to me and being ready to forgive and help me. Stay with me always.

O Father of goodness,
We thank you each one
For happiness, healthiness,
Friendship and fun,
For good things we think of
And good things we do,
And all that is beautiful,
Loving and true.

Prayer from France

Dear God, you are so very wonderful: more wonderful than the flowers, more wonderful than the sky, more wonderful than the sun. We praise you: we bless you: we worship you.

From Infant Prayer

We thank you, Lord, that we can freely worship you. Help us, we pray, to continue our worship through the coming week by living lives which are filled with love, both for you and for all mankind.

From Prayers for Today's Church

> For these and all your gifts, Lord,
> We thank you.
> For health and strength and life itself,
> We thank you.
> For our friends, our homes, our families,
> We thank you.
> For our church and our worship,
> We thank you.
> For every chance to serve you,
> We thank you.
> For Jesus Christ our Lord,
> We thank you.
> And now we pray for all who govern our land.

> Loving Father, we praise you for the wonderful things
> which you have given to us:
> For the beautiful sun,
> For the rain which makes things grow,
> For the woods and the fields,
> For the sea and the sky,
> for the flowers and the birds
> And for all your gifts to us.
> Everything around us rejoices.
> Make us also to rejoice and give us thankful hearts.

From Prayers and Hymns for Junior Schools

Thank you, Lord Jesus, for coming
Into the world for me,
For taking a human mother,
Silently.

Thank you, Lord Jesus, for growing
As a boy for me,
Learning the ways of home life,
Obediently.

Thank you, Lord Jesus, for being
A perfect man for me,
Working hard for Joseph,
So willingly.

Thank you, Lord Jesus, for saying
Wonderful things for me,
Written down in the Bible
Truthfully.

Thank you, Lord Jesus, for taking
The cruel cross for me,
Allowing rough men to kill you,
Most brutally.

Thank you, Lord Jesus, for rising
In resurrection for me;
Now you are alive for ever
Triumphantly.

Randle Manwaring

God, our loving Father, thank you that you never change. You are as strong
and wise and loving as the day you made the world. Thank you that nothing
can ever happen that will make you alter. You are the one true God and Maker
of all. We worship you in Jesus' name.

Zinnia Bryan

Dear Father God, thank you for loving and caring for us every day of our lives. Help us to remember your love, and to love you in return.

From The Infant Teacher's Prayer Book

We ask you to bless them.
For all who minister in our church,
We ask you to bless them.
For all who provide our daily needs,
We ask you to bless them.
For all who do not yet know you,
We ask you to bless them.
For all who are tired, or ill, or lonely,
We ask you to bless them.
Hear these prayers, Lord our God, for Jesus' sake.

Christopher Idle

Loving Father, on this day
Make us happy in our play,
Kind and helpful, playing fair,
Letting others have a share.

From The Infant Teacher's Prayer Book

O God our Father, may we work and play together well. Help us not to be jealous or spiteful, not to argue or quarrel, but to find happiness in helping one another. For Jesus' sake. Amen.

Lord, through this day,
In work and play,
Please bless each thing I do.
May I be honest, loving, kind,
Obedient unto you.

From The Infant Teacher's Prayer Book

Dear Lord Jesus, please help me with the tests that I have to do at school today. Help me not to be nervous but to keep calm and do my best, knowing that you are close beside me. Amen.

> Lord, we need your help.
> We need a calm mind; grant us your peace.
> We need a clear head; grant us your wisdom.
> We need to be careful; grant us your patience.
> We need to be inspired; grant us your enthusiasm.
> Keep us from all panic as we put our trust in your power
> to keep us this day.
>
> *K.A. Clegg*

Dear Lord Jesus, help us to enjoy the jobs we do to help today: at home, when we clear away our toys or wash the dishes; at school, when we give out books and tidy our classroom. May we do everything cheerfully and well, because we love you.

> Then let us praise the Father, who shows us, of his grace,
> The secret paths of science, the mastery of space,
> The wonder of the wireless, of TV, cars and trains,
> For man made these, but God made man,
> And God gave man his brains.
>
> *Lesbia Scott*

> Our Father, maker of this wonderful world,
> thank you for Saturday, for holiday time
> and freedom and the open air.
> Come into all I am going to do today
> at home, out of doors, with my friends.
> Help me to enjoy everything you have made for me.
> For Jesus' sake.
>
> *From Sunday, Monday...*

For all the men and women, boys and girls, who love
and serve you,
We thank you, God.
For everybody who makes Jesus real to other people,
We thank you, God.
For everyone who has taught about you by the way they think,
the way they act and by what they say,
We thank you, God.
For everyone who helps those who are sick or sad, and for all
those who are brave and patient when things are going wrong,
We thank you, God.
Dear God, may we know you better and better so that we may
love you more and more and serve you with all our hearts.
Please God hear us.
May we help those in need; may they know that God is real and
that God is love.
Please God hear us.
May we be friends with you, friends with all your children,
friends with one another.
Please God hear us.

Dick Williams

God, this is your world,
You made us,
You love us;
Teach us how to live
In the world that you have made.

Hope Freeman

Space counts for nothing, Lord, with thee;
Your love enfolds each family
Across the ocean, far away,
And here at home, where now we pray,
And praise you for your care this day.

From Missionary Prayers and Praises

Dear Father of the world family,
please take care of all children everywhere.
Keep them safe from danger,
and help them grow up strong and good.

From The Infant Teacher's Prayer Book

Let us think of all the people who work for us:
The men and women in factories, shops, and offices,
Bless them and help them, O Lord.
The farm workers, gardeners, builders, and all who help to
provide our homes and food and clothing:
Bless them and help them, O God.
Those who carry people and goods, by road, railway, sea or air,
Bless them and help them, O Lord.
The police, firemen, soldiers, sailors and airmen, who protect us:
Bless them and help them, O Lord.
The scientists, doctors, nurses, and hospital workers, who care
for our bodies:
Bless them and help them, O Lord.
The artists, entertainers, musicians and writers, who delight and
instruct our minds:
Bless them and help them, O Lord.
Those who teach, govern, and guide us:
Bless them and help them, O Lord.
Those who can find no work to do:
Bless them and help them, O Lord.
Blessed Lord, who worked as a carpenter at Nazareth, teach all
people to work together for the good of the world and the glory
of God.

A Brownie Guide prayer

Dear Lord Jesus, who did not fear the sea, guard all fishermen and sea-going people. If danger comes, help them to be calm and courageous, and be with the people who answer their call for help.

Give clear vision to coastguards and lighthouse keepers that they may quickly heed all calls from people in difficulty or danger.

Give courage and strength to the brave men who man the lifeboats in response to calls for rescue.

Help them to feel the power of your presence and calm the fears of relatives and friends of those in danger on the sea.

Nancy Martin

God of the coalmine away under ground,
God of all workshops and wheels that go round,
God of all industry teach me to be
One of the many that labour for thee.

Joan Gale Thomas

Loving heavenly Father, who takes care of us all,
please bless all the people on the roads today:
please bless the people driving buses, cars and lorries,
please bless the people riding bicycles and scooters,
please bless the people walking and crossing busy roads,
please help them to be careful on the roads today
and help us to be careful when we cross the roads.

From Infant Prayer

Thank you, dear Lord, for good health and good spirits.
Please Father God,
Bless those who do not have good health.
Strengthen them and give them patience.
Let them know that your love is always there
when they are feeling low. Amen.

Carol Watson

Lord Jesus, I am ill.
Please make me well.
Help me to be brave
and thankful to the people looking after me.
Thank you for being here with me.

Zinnia Bryan

Lord Jesus, who for our sakes became a man, and who showed your love of children by taking them up in your arms and blessing them: we ask you to bless those who are ill. Your love for them is greater than ours can ever be; therefore we trust them to your care and keeping.

From Prayers and Hymns for Junior Schools

Lord Jesus Christ, we confess to you now
the wrong things we have done,
the wrong things we have said,
the wrong in our hearts: please forgive us
and help us to live as you want us to.

Christopher Idle

Lord Jesus, you taught us to forgive others, just as you forgave those who treated you badly. Help us to remember how much you have forgiven us and to be willing to forgive those who hurt us. For your sake. Amen.

Dear Father,
When we are tempted to be unkind,
When we are tempted to be unfair,
When to others' troubles we are blind,
Remind us how we would feel, and make us care.

Jack and Edna Young

Thank you, Father, for all the animals, birds and fish that you have made. Thank you especially for our pets, and for those belonging to our friends that we can enjoy too. Teach us to be gentle with all your creatures and to show them kindness and patience. May we make their lives happy and full of fun. For Jesus' sake.

Dear Lord Jesus, our little dog has died. We cried because she was so loving and good. She made everyone happy. We're glad it's you who've got her now.

Please take care of her, but of course you will.

You love all animals, you made them all.

Thank you for letting us have her first and for all the happy times we've had with her.

Nina Hinchy

Let us give thanks
For friends and home,
For work and play,
For hands to make, and eyes to see, and lips to speak,
For strength to do our daily task
And, at the end, the gift of quiet sleep.

A. M. Ammon

Be near me, Lord Jesus, I ask thee to stay
Close by me for ever, and love me, I pray.
Bless all the dear children in thy tender care;
And fit us for heaven to live with thee there.

John MacFarland

Lord, when we have not any light,
And mothers are asleep,
Then through the stillness of the night
Your little children keep.

When shadows haunt the quiet room,
Help us to understand
That you are with us through the gloom,
To hold us by the hand.

Anne Matheson (1853–1924)

Loving Shepherd of your sheep
Keep your lamb in safety, keep;
Nothing can your power withstand,
None can pluck me from your hand.

Jane Eliza Leeson (1807–1882)

Prayers By Children

*These prayers were written for the Hammick's/Lion Publishing
children's prayers competition*

dear Lord

thank you for football thank
you for the sea thank you for
the world and thank you for me.

Mark Fennelly

Dear father god,
Thankyou for the gift of nature
For trees, flowers, fish, birds and
animals.
But, god, let us think about extinc
creatures like the Great Auk, the
Pliosaur, the Dodo and the Passenger

Pigeon.
And let us think about endagered
species, like the Tiger, the Giant Panda
the Golden Eagle and the Elephant.

Oh god,
please stop man destroying the
home you made for us.

Amen

Toby Keeley

Dear god
   Thank you for all the wonderful things
you've given me: a family, a happy home
lots of love, friends, food and clothes
I'm sorry I don't always get things
right, and some times quarrel with my
brother.

   Thank you for Easter and the love
you show us.

   please let the Easter Bunny come.

      Amen,

Elaine Round

E is for Easter, coming again soon,

A is for angels near the tomb,

S is for stone which was rolled away

T is for Tomb found empty that day,

E is for early morning, the women are glad,

R is for the Risen Lord, no need to be sad

Rachel Hartley

Thank - you God for the joys of spring,
For blooming flowers . and colourful blossom,
For fresh, new leaves,
For sun and rain,
For fun times out-doors.
    We thank you, Heavenly Father.

Thank-you God for the joys of Summer,
Thank- you God for long, warm Summer days,
For picnies and holidays,
For singing birds and buzzing insects,
And butterflies that flutter by.
    We thank yo Heavenly Father.

Thank - you god for the joys of Autumn,
For falling leaves,
For Plums, Pears, blackberries and apples,
For potatoes, carrots, beans and sprouts,
And for all the colours of nature.
　　We thank - you Heavenly Father,

Thank - you God. for the joys of winter,
For skidding ice and frost,
For snow and winter sports,
For warm houses and families,
For pets to keep us joyful.
　　We thank - you Heavenly Father.
　　　　　　　　Amen.

Rachel Bunting

Dear God.
I am sorry for being naughty to-day.
Please make me a better boy to-morrow
Bless all my family and friends.

Amen

James Kennedy

Dear Lord,

Before I go on up to bed,
And on my pillow rest my head,
I thank you, Lord, for the day I've had,
All the good times and the bad,
Thank you for the things I've seen,
And all the places that I have been,
Thank you for my friends and relations
And the people in the different nations;
And as I come to the last verse,
I thank you for the universe.

Amen.

Fiona Braddock

Dear God

Thank you for a lovely day and my
friends and family.
Sorry for the wrong thing I have done
you have given us a beautiful world to
live in and trusted us to take care of it,
Sometimes we don't treat it very well
Please show us how.
Please guard me for ever and please
give me sweet dreams
                    Amen.

John Livesley

---

*Prayers suitable for children and young people can be found throughout
the collection: they are marked with* ◆

◆ *Grace Before Meals* ◆

Jesus took the five loaves and the two fish, looked up to
heaven, and gave thanks to God.

FROM MARK 6

Each time we eat,
may we remember God's love.

Prayer from China

Be present at our table, Lord,
Be here and everywhere adored:
Thy creatures bless, and grant that we
May feast in paradise with thee.

John Cennick (1718–1755) (sometimes attributed to John Wesley)

Blessed be thou, Lord God,
who bringest forth bread from the earth
and makest glad the hearts of thy people.

Ancient Hebrew prayer

For health and strength and daily food,
We praise your name, O Lord.

Author unknown

Heavenly Father, make us thankful to thee and mindful of others as we receive these blessings, in Jesus' name.

From The Book of Common Worship

◆ For food in a world where many walk in hunger;
For faith in a world where many walk in fear;
For friends in a world where many walk alone,
We give you humble thanks, O Lord.

A Girl Guide world hunger grace

O Lord who fed the multitudes with five barley loaves, bless what we are about to eat.

Arabic grace from Egypt

Some ha'e meat, and canna eat,
And some would eat that want it;
But we ha'e meat, and we can eat,
And sae the Lord be thankit.

Robert Burns (1759–1796)

Great God and giver of all good,
Accept our praise and bless our food.
Grace, health and strength to us afford
Through Jesus Christ, our risen Lord.

Jeremiah Clarke

◆ We thank thee, Father, for thy care
For all thy children everywhere.
As thou dost feed us all our days
May all our lives be filled with praise.

A. C. Osborn Hann

Here a little child I stand,
Heaving up my either hand:
Cold as paddocks though they be,
Here I lift them up to thee,
For a benison to fall
On our meat and on our all.

Robert Herrick (1591–1674)

You who give food to all flesh,
who feeds the young ravens that cry unto you
and has nourished us from our youth up:
fill our hearts with good and gladness
and establish our hearts with your grace.

Lancelot Andrewes (1555–1626)

Come, Lord Jesus, be our guest,
And may our meal by you be blest. Amen.

Attributed to Martin Luther (1483–1546)

The eyes of all things do look up and trust in thee; O Lord, thou givest them their meat in due season, thou dost open thy hand and fillest with thy blessing everything living. Good Lord, bless us and all thy goods which we receive of thy bountiful liberality; through Jesus Christ our Lord.

Queen Elizabeth I (1533–1603)

To God who gives our daily bread
A thankful song we raise,
And pray that he who sends us food
May fill our hearts with praise.

Thomas Tallis (?1505–1585)

Bless me, O Lord, and let my food strengthen me to serve thee, for Jesus Christ's sake.

Isaac Watts (1674–1748)

◆Heavenly Father, bless this food, bless those who have prepared it and give food to those who at this time go hungry in our world.

Michael Buckley

No ordinary meal—a sacrament awaits us
On our table spread.
For men are risking lives on sea and land
That we may dwell in safety and be fed.

Grace from Scotland

Bless, O Lord, this food to our use and ourselves to your service, through Jesus Christ our Lord

Author unknown

◆Bless, dear Lord, my daily food,
Make me strong and make me good.

A. C. Osborn Hann

Bless us, O Lord, and these your gifts which we are about to receive from your bounty, through Jesus Christ our Lord. Amen.

Tony Castle

May the food which we bless in your name, O Lord, give us the strength to serve you through Jesus Christ our Lord.

Tony Castle

Give me a good digestion, Lord,
And also something to digest;
But when and how that something comes
I leave to thee, who knowest best.

Part of a refectory grace, Chester Cathedral

◆ For every cup and plateful
Lord, make us truly grateful.

◆ Lord, bless this bunch
As they munch
Their lunch.

Graces for Special Occasions

AT CHRISTMAS

◆ Father, we thank you for all your wonderful gifts to us. Thank you for this special food. Give us happiness as we celebrate and share it together. Thank you for your best gift of all—Jesus—who came at this Christmas season to bring us back to you.

FOR MOTHERS' DAY

◆ Thank you, Lord, for this good food. Today we thank you too for mothers who spend so much time preparing our meals. Bless them on this special day. Help us to look after one another every day and so to serve you. Through Jesus Christ our Lord.

AT EASTER

Be present at our meal, risen, living Lord. Renew us in body and spirit and help us to live in newness of life, to glorify you. Amen.

AT HARVEST

At this harvest supper we give you thanks for your generous gifts to us, dear Father. Thank you for this good food. Help us to remember the needs of those who are without. Through Jesus Christ our Lord.

AT A WEDDING

We join in the happiness of bride and bridegroom, O Lord, and share in this wedding breakfast with thankfulness to you. May this meal be a communion, celebrating the pledges they have made to each other and blessing their marriage. Through Jesus Christ our Lord.

AT A BIRTHDAY OR ANNIVERSARY

Thank you, Lord, for this special celebration meal. As we eat it we remember another year that has past and we thank you for your goodness and mercy throughout it. We look forward to the new year ahead and pray for your help and continuing grace in the days to come. Amen.

◆ *Christian Festivals* ◆

Open to me the gates of the Temple;
I will go in and give thanks to the Lord!
This is the day of the Lord's victory;
let us be happy, let us celebrate!

FROM PSALM 118

Sunday

The Lord is risen indeed!
From Luke 24

Father, we rejoice that you have given us Sunday:
the day when we remember that you created the world
and all that is within it,
the day when Jesus was raised from the dead and death
and hell laid waste,
the day in which all things were made and re-made.
Father, may we approach Sunday with longing and expectation;
as the hungry seek for bread,
so may we yearn for word and sacrament;
save our worship from all that is trivial;
rooted in the reality of the world in which we live,
may it yet glimpse the glory of your presence,
and stand in awe at the light of your holiness;
may we sense the presence of all who have gone before us,
hearing in our own songs the echo of unseen heaven's praise.
From More Everyday Prayers

Sweet is the work, my God my King,
To praise your name, give thanks and sing;
To show your love by morning light,
And talk of all your truth at night.

Sweet is the day of sacred rest,
No mortal cares disturb my breast;
O may my heart in tune be found,
Like David's harp of solemn sound.
Isaac Watts (1674–1748)

Shout joyfully to God, all the earth,
sing praise to his name,
proclaim his glorious praise.

Say to God: How tremendous your deeds are!
On account of your great strength
your enemies woo your favour.

Let the whole earth worship you,
singing praises, singing praises to your name.
Come and listen,
all you who fear God,
while I tell you what great things
he has done for me.

To him I cried aloud,
high praise was on my tongue.

From his holy temple
he heard my voice,
my entreaty reached his ears.

Bless our God, you peoples,
loudly proclaim his praise.

In him every race
in the world be blessed;
all nations shall proclaim his glory.

Blessed be the Lord, the God of Israel
who alone does wondrous deeds.

St Francis of Assisi (1182–1226),
prayer for nine o'clock in the morning (Terce)
on Sundays and major feastdays

Lord Jesus, we see you, in the Gospel stories, going to synagogue on the
Sabbath, spending time in the home of your friends and doing good, healing
and helping others. May we follow your example and spend Sunday, the day
of your glorious resurrection, as you did, to please and glorify our Father in
heaven. For your sake. Amen.

Almighty God our heavenly Father, at your call we come reverently to worship you. May your Holy Spirit be with us, teaching us to recognize your goodness and truth, and helping us to praise you, not only with words, but with lives which are obedient to you; through your Son, Jesus Christ. Amen.

From Together in Church

O most great and mighty God, whose glory is above all our thoughts and whose mercy is over all thy works: Let the inspiration of the Holy Spirit assist us in all the duties of this sacred day; let us join in the praise of thy church with ardent affection; let us hear thy Word with earnest attention and let the prayers and sacrifices of thy holy church, offered unto thee this day, be graciously accepted.

Being created by thee, let us ever act for thy glory and being redeemed by thee, let us render unto thee what is thine;

through Jesus Christ our Lord. Amen.

John Wesley (1703–1791)

O God, who makes us glad with the weekly remembrance of the glorious resurrection of your Son our Lord; vouchsafe us this day such a blessing through your worship, that the days which follow it may be spent in your favour; through the same Jesus Christ our Lord. Amen.

William Bright (1824–1901)

O loving Lord, be near us in this time of worship. Open our ears to hear your voice; open our eyes to behold your glory; open our hearts to receive your grace; open our lips to show forth your praise; for the sake of Jesus Christ our Saviour. Amen.

Lord, teach us to pray.
Help us to come with boldness to the throne of grace.
Make us conscious of your presence in our midst.
Give us the freedom of the Holy Spirit.
Enlarge our vision and increase our faith.
And may our words and thoughts be now acceptable in your sight,
O God, our rock and our redeemer. Amen.

Eric Milner-White (died 1963)

For a Sunday meditation:

They went to Capernaum, and when the Sabbath came, Jesus
went into the synagogue and began to teach. The people were
amazed at his teaching, because he taught them as one who had
authority, not as the teachers of the law. Just then a man in their
synagogue who was possessed with an evil spirit cried out,
'What do you want with us, Jesus of Nazareth? Have you come
to destroy us? I know who you are—the Holy One of God!'
'Be quiet!' said Jesus sternly. 'Come out of him!' The evil spirit
shook the man violently and came out of him with a shriek.
The people were all so amazed that they asked each other, 'What
is this? A new teaching—and with authority! He even gives
orders to evil spirits and they obey him.' News about him spread
quickly over the whole region of Galilee.

As soon as they left the synagogue, they went with James and
John to the home of Simon and Andrew. Simon's mother-in-law
was in bed with a fever, and they told Jesus about her. So he went
to her, took her hand and helped her up. The fever left her and
she began to wait on them.

That evening after sunset the people brought to Jesus all the sick
and demon-possessed. The whole town gathered at the door, and
Jesus healed many who had various diseases. He also drove out
many demons, but he would not let the demons speak because
they knew who he was.

Very early the next morning, while it was still dark, Jesus got up,
left the house and went off to a solitary place, where he prayed.

From Mark 1

Advent

At Advent we should try the key to our heart's door. It may have gathered rust. If so, this is the time to oil it, in order that the heart's door may open more easily when the Lord Jesus wants to enter at Christmas time!

Lord, oil the hinges of our hearts' doors that they may swing gently and easily to welcome your coming.

Prayer of a New Guinea Christian

And now we give you thanks because in his coming as man the day of our deliverance has dawned; and through him you will make all things new, as he comes in power and triumph to judge the world.

From the Alternative Service Book (1980)

Almighty God,
give us grace to cast away the works of darkness
and to put on the armour of light,
now in the time of this mortal life,
in which your Son Jesus Christ came to us
in great humility;
so that on the last day,
when he shall come again in his glorious majesty
to judge the living and the dead,
we may rise to the life immortal,
through him who is alive and reigns with you
and the Holy Spirit, now and ever. Amen.

From the Alternative Service Book (1980)

Here I wait in quiet hope
That you will come
To water my barren fields,
To make blossom the flower and fruit
that wither in merciless heat.
Do not forsake me.

Frank Topping

O thou, who hast foretold that thou wilt return to judgement in an hour that we are not aware of: grant us grace to watch and pray always; that whether thou shalt come at even, or at midnight, or in the morning, we may be found among the number of those servants who shall be blessed in watching for their Lord; to whom be all glory, now and for evermore.

From the Non-jurors Prayer Book (1734)

◆Father God, this is the day when the church begins to think about Christmas. The very word makes us feel excited. You want us to be excited about Christmas, Father, and you want us to enjoy it. But you also want us to understand it. In these Sundays of Advent teach us, Father, what Christmas means... Through Jesus Christ our Lord.

For the first Sunday in Advent

◆Our Father, we thank you for the Bible which tells us the Christmas story. Thank you, too, for the writings, centuries before, which tell of the coming Saviour and King. Thank you for those who toiled and gave their lives so that we could have the Bible in our own language. Help us to understand your Word and to treasure it as you speak to us from it, preparing our hearts for Christmas.

For the second Sunday in Advent

Father, through John the Baptist you tried to prepare your people for the coming of Jesus. Will you try to prepare us too? Prepare our hearts and minds that we may know what to look for in the coming of Jesus Christ into our world... May we show the joy of the Advent message in our lives day by day. Through him who came at Christmas time. Amen.

For the third Sunday in Advent, from Prayers Before Worship

Lord, as you dispelled
the fears of a maiden mother
by whispering the promise of your presence,
so banish the world's misconceptions
about you and your ways.
Come to each of us.
Roll back the clouds of doubt and pessimism.
Fill our individual lives with servant love
and direct the nations to humble awareness;
for you are God,
rich in mercy,
strong in righteousness,
ready to make your home with us
now and for ever.

For the fourth Sunday in Advent,
from Further Everyday Prayers

Christ the Sun of Righteousness shine upon you and scatter the
darkness from before your path.

From the Alternative Service Book (1980)

Christmas

The Child of glory,
The Child of Mary,
Born in the stable
The King of all,
Who came to the wilderness
And in our stead suffered;
Happy they are counted
Who to him are near.

Celtic prayer

Almighty God,
you make us glad with the yearly remembrance
of the birth of your Son Jesus Christ.
Grant that as we joyfully receive him for our redeemer,
we may with sure confidence behold him
when he shall come to be our judge;
who is alive and reigns with you and the Holy Spirit
one God, now and for ever.

From the Alternative Service Book (1980)

Lord Jesus Christ, come and dwell in our hearts this Christmastide, so that our home may have you in it and be full of joy and peace. May no ill-temper, impatience, envy or jealousy spoil the gladness of your birthday, but may love shine in our midst, bringing light to all our hearts and minds.

J. McDougall Ferguson

Ah, dearest Jesus, holy Child,
Make thee a bed, soft, undefiled,
Within my heart, that it may be
A quiet chamber kept for thee

Martin Luther (1483–1546)

Compassionate and holy God,
we celebrate with joy your coming into our midst;
we celebrate with hope your coming into our midst;
we celebrate with peace your coming into our midst;
for you have come to save us.
By your grace we recognize your presence in men and women
in all parts of your world...
through your strength our lives can proclaim joy and hope;
through your love we can work for peace and justice.
You are the source of our being;
you are the light of our lives.

Based on lines from a Latin American prayer

Lord Jesus Christ,
Child of Bethlehem and Son of God:
help us this night to join our songs of glory
to those of the heavenly host,
that the joy of the church on earth
may be heard in the praise of heaven. Amen.

C. N. R. Wallwork

Jesus, new-born child of all time,
We greet your birth with wide-eyed delight.
You are precious beyond words
for our world needs your presence more than ever.
Let the angels' promise of your good news
offering joy and peace to all the world
be heard by those who lead and guide.
Let kings bow down and all creation greet this holy moment
as we seek to grasp its magnitude.
For you are God's gift
silently delivered to every human heart.

From Further Everyday Prayers

As we gather for worship today, Father, there is excitement in the air, a song on our lips and joy in our hearts. Help us to remember why we celebrate Christmas. May the Word which was made flesh be heard in our worship. May Christ be born again in this congregation and in the life of each person here. May the love of Christmas fill the church and the peace of Christmas fill our hearts; through Jesus Christ our Lord. Amen.

From Prayers Before Worship

O God who has made this most hallowed night resplendent with the glory of the true Light; grant that we who have known the mysteries of that Light on earth, may enter into the fulness of his joys in heaven.

Christmas midnight, Western Rite

Almighty God, who has poured upon us the new light of your incarnate Word; grant that the same light enkindled in our hearts may shine forth in our lives; through Jesus Christ our Lord.

Mass of Christmas at dawn, Sarum Rite

Almighty God, Mary gave birth to a Son who offers salvation to the whole world. May we, like Mary, both treasure him in our hearts and bring him to all men, through the same Christ our Lord. Amen.

From A Christian's Prayer Book

Loving Father, help us remember the birth of Jesus, that we may share in the song of the angels, the gladness of the shepherds and the wisdom of the wise men.

Close the door of hate and open the door of love all over the world.

Let kindness come with every gift and good desires with every greeting.

Deliver us from evil by the blessing which Christ brings and teach us to be merry with clean hearts.

May the Christmas morning make us happy to be your children and the Christmas evening bring us to our beds with grateful thoughts, forgiving and forgiven, for Jesus' sake. Amen.

Robert Louis Stevenson (1850–1894)

Christ is born, give glory. Christ comes from heaven, meet him. Christ is on earth, be exalted. O all the earth, sing unto the Lord and sing praises in gladness, O all you people, for he has been glorified.

Wisdom and Word and Power, Christ our God is the Son and the Brightness of the Father; and unknown to the powers both above and upon the earth, he was made man and so has won us back again: for he has been glorified.

Eastern Orthodox Church

For thanksgiving:

When the time had fully come, God sent his Son, born of a woman, born under law, to redeem those under law, that we might receive the full rights of sons.

From Galatians 4

O sweet Child of Bethlehem, grant that we may share with all our hearts in this profound mystery of Christmas. Put into the hearts of men this peace for which they sometimes seek so desperately and which you alone can give them. Help them to know one another better and to live as brothers, children of the same Father.

Reveal to them also your beauty, holiness and purity. Awaken in their hearts love and gratitude for your infinite goodness. Join them all together in your love. And give us your heavenly peace.

Pope John XXIII (1881–1963)

Sacred infant, all divine,
What a tender love was thine,
Thus to come from highest bliss
Down to such a world as this!

Teach, O teach us, holy child,
By thy face so meek and mild,
Teach us to resemble thee
In thy sweet humility.

Edward Caswall (1814–1878)

O God our Father, who by the bright shining of a star
led the wise men to the city of David:
guide us by the light of your Spirit,
that we too may come into the presence of Jesus
and offer our gifts and our worship to him,
our Saviour and our Lord. Amen.

Alan Warren

Heavenly Father, please comfort the people who won't be happy this Christmas: those who won't get any presents, or even any Christmas cards: those who won't have the money to buy the presents they would love to give their friends; those who won't have a Christmas dinner, or won't get the things they are longing for; and those who will be sad because someone they love will not be with them.

Zinnia Bryan

O Lord, there sit apart in lonely places,
On this, the gladdest night of all the year,
Some stricken ones, with sad and weary faces
To whom the thought of Christmas brings no cheer:
For these, O Father, our petition hear,
And send the pitying Christ Child very near.

Author unknown

Christ, the Son of God, born of Mary, fill you with his grace to trust his promises and obey his will.

From the Alternative Service Book (1980)

Lent

O Lord and heavenly Father, who has given unto us your people the true bread that comes down from heaven, even your Son, Jesus Christ, grant that throughout this Lent our souls may so be fed by him that we may continually live in him and he in us; and that day by day we may be renewed in spirit by the power of his endless life, who gave himself for us and now lives and reigns with you and the Holy Spirit, one God, for ever and ever.

Frederick B. Macnutt (1873–1949)

And now we give you thanks because through him you have given us the spirit of discipline, that we may triumph over evil and grow in grace.

From the Alternative Service Book (1980)

Almighty and everlasting God,
you hate nothing that you have made,
and forgive the sins of all those who are penitent.
Create and make in us new and contrite hearts
that lamenting our sins and acknowledging our wretchedness,
we may receive from you, the God of all mercy,
perfect forgiveness and peace,
through Jesus Christ our Lord. Amen.

Thomas Cranmer (1489–1556), collect for Lent

We thank you, Father, for those days in the desert when, through prayer and fasting, Jesus discovered your will for his life and overcame the temptations of the Evil One.

Help us, during these days of Lent, to come close to you and to listen to your voice. Give us strength to overcome the temptation to please ourselves and live life without you. Teach us your way. For Jesus' sake.

Christ give you grace to grow in holiness, to deny yourselves, take up your cross and follow him.

From the Alternative Service Book (1980)

Mothering Sunday (Mothers' Day)

On Mothering Sunday, which falls in mid-Lent in many countries, families used to worship at the mother church in their area. Sons and daughters came home to visit their mothers, bringing flowers and a cake. Today, many celebrate by giving cards and gifts to their mother and specially remembering all her love and kindness. In some countries Mothers' Day is celebrated on the second Sunday in May.

◆Thank you, Lord, for our mothers. We remember today their loving care, and their ceaseless love for us. May we show them by our gifts, our words and our actions that we love them and care about them too.

Father, we thank you for the family of the church. Thank you for those who are true mothers within our Christian family. May they know your blessing and strength as they care for others. Amen.

Palm Sunday

Jesus, you rode into your city in triumph on this day, receiving the shouts and the welcome of many. Come into this church today. Receive our welcome and our acclaim. Come to rule in the hearts and minds of all who lead our worship and then help us all to go out and to proclaim you as King over all the world and every life.

Dear Master, we remember that many who claimed you as King on Sunday shouted 'Crucify' on Friday. So confirm our faith today that our love for you will never falter or turn to hatred but will remain constant now and for ever. We offer our worship to you, Lord, with all our love. Amen.

From Prayers Before Worship

Good Friday

There is a green hill far away
Outside a city wall,
Where the dear Lord was crucified,
Who died to save us all.

We may not know, we cannot tell
What pains he had to bear;
But we believe it was for us
He hung and suffered there.

Cecil Frances Alexander (1823–1895)

O Lord, who for our sake did endure the bitterness of death and despise the shame and in your cross and passion did draw all men unto yourself: kindle in our hearts the vision of your love and shed abroad the light of your victory in the darkness of the world; who now lives and reigns with the Father and the Holy Spirit and are loved, worshipped and adored, world without end. Amen.

Frederick B. Macnutt (1873–1949)

Tell how Christ the world's Redeemer
As a victim won the day.
Amidst the nations God, saith he,
Hath reigned and triumphed from the tree

Venantius Fortunatus (?530–609)

Not because of your promised heaven
Do I wish to devote my love to you;
Nor from dread of a much-feared hell
Do I wish to cease from offending you.
You touch me, Lord, when I see you nailed—
Nailed on a cross—when I see you mocked;
I am stirred by the sight of your body bruised,
By your sufferings too and by your death.
I am stirred by your love in such a way
That even without hope of heaven I shall love you
And without any fear of hell I shall fear you.
Naught you need give me that I may love you
for even without hoping for the hope that is mine
I shall love you as love you I do.

Sonnet attributed to St Francis Xavier (1506–1552)

◆ Good Friday is a time of sadness,
Easter is a time of gladness.
On Good Friday Jesus died
But rose again at Eastertide.
All thanks and praise to God.

Lord, teach us to understand that your Son died to save us not from suffering
but from ourselves, not from injustice, far less from justice, but from being
unjust. He died that we might live—but live as he lives, by dying as he died
who died to himself.

George MacDonald (1824–1905)

Jesus who died for me,
Help me to live for thee.

O Lord Jesus, as we face the cross today, we wonder at your love for us. We can never deserve what you did for us on this day. Looking at the people who brought about your death we can see so many of the same faults in ourselves and we are sorry for them. By faith we gladly take the forgiveness you offer us from your cross and through the door you pushed open then, we come back into God's family where we really belong.

Leslie Earnshaw

Today he who hung the earth upon the waters is hung upon the cross.
He who is King of the angels is arrayed in a crown of thorns.
He who wraps the heavens in clouds is wrapped in the purple of mockery...
The Bridegroom of the Church is transfixed with nails.
The Son of the Virgin is pierced with a spear.
We venerate your Passion, O Christ,
Show us also your glorious Resurrection.

Eastern Orthodox Church hymn for Good Friday

Verses for meditation:

He committed no sin, and no deceit was found in his mouth.
When they hurled their insults at him, he did not retaliate; when
he suffered, he made no threats. Instead, he entrusted himself to
him who judges justly. He himself bore our sins in his body on
the tree, so that we might die to sins and live to righteousness; by
his wounds you have been healed.

From 1 Peter 2

We implore you, by the memory of your cross's hallowed and most bitter anguish, make us fear you, make us love you, O Christ.

St Bridget (453–523)

This is that night of tears, the three days' space,
Sorrow abiding of the eventide,
Until the day break with the risen Christ,
And hearts that sorrowed shall be satisfied.

So may our hearts have pity on thee, Lord,
That they may sharers of thy glory be:
Heavy with weeping may the three days pass,
To win the laughter of thine Easter Day.

Peter Abelard (1079–1142)

Good Captain, maker of the light
Who dost divide the day and night,
The sun is drowned beneath the sea,
Chaos is on us horribly.
O Christ, give back to faithful souls the light!

Prudentius (348–410), prayer for the kindling of the light on Easter Eve

Easter

O God, who by thine only-begotten Son hast overcome death and opened unto us the gate of everlasting life; grant, we beseech thee, that those who have been redeemed by his passion may rejoice in his resurrection; through the same Christ our Lord. Amen.

From the Gelasian Sacramentary

Spirit of God
we thank you for raising up Jesus.
Though we are yet in the body,
raise us up too into newness of life.

Kate Compston

Be present, O risen Lord,
in this your church's Easter praise;
that its anthems of joy and its proclamation of your victory
may worthily celebrate
both the mystery of your redeeming love
and the majesty of your eternal glory. Amen.

C. N. R. Wallwork

Thine be the glory, risen, conquering Son,
Endless is the victory thou o'er death hast won!

Lo, Jesus meets us, risen from the tomb!
Lovingly he greets us, scatters fear and gloom.

No more we doubt thee, glorious Prince of life;
Life is nought without thee, aid us in our strife;
Make us more than conquerors through thy deathless love.

Edmund Budry (1854–1932),
translated by Richard Hoyle (1875–1939)

◆ Jesus, our Lord, we praise you
that nothing could keep you dead in the grave.
You are stronger than death and the devil.
Help us to remember
that there is nothing to be afraid of,
because you are alive and by our side.

Ascension Day

Almighty God, your Son ascended to the throne of power in heaven, that he
might be Lord over all things for his people: We pray that the worship and
service of the church may be inspired by his presence, and that he will remain
with us always, to the end of the age. Amen.

From Collects with the New Lectionary

Lord Jesus, we remember how you returned to your Father on the first Ascension Day. Although we cannot see you with our eyes, we know that you are still with us as you promised always to be. We thank you for being our constant friend. Help us to remember that you are near and that you will never fail us. Help us to come to you when we are frightened or disappointed, and may we remember to tell you about our joys as well as our troubles.

O Lord Jesus Christ, who after your resurrection from the dead did gloriously ascend into heaven, grant us the aid of your loving-kindness, that according to your promise you may ever dwell with us on earth, and we with you in heaven, where with the Father and the Holy Ghost, you live and reign one God for ever and ever. Amen.

From the Gelasian Sacramentary

Whitsun/Pentecost

O God,
you have graciously brought us to this hour,
the time when you poured out your Holy Spirit
in tongues of fire upon your apostles,
filling them with the gift of your grace;
so, most wonderful Lord,
may we too receive this blessing;
and as we seek to praise you, merciful God,
in psalms and hymns and spiritual songs,
may we share in your eternal kingdom.
For your name is worthy of all honour and majesty
and you are to be glorified in hymns of blessing,
Father, Son and Holy Spirit,
now and for ever, to the ages of ages. Amen.

Eastern Orthodox Church

O God, we cannot do your will unless you help us.
Send the Holy Spirit into our lives to show us how to live.

From Time and Again Prayers

O Holy Spirit, the Comforter, who with the Father and the Son abides one God, descend this day into our hearts, that while you make intercession for us, we may with full confidence call upon our Father; through Jesus Christ our Lord. Amen.

From the Mozarabic Sacramentary

Holy Spirit, mighty wind of God,
inhabit our darkness, brood over our abyss
and speak to our chaos
that we may breathe with your life
and share your creation in the power of Jesus Christ. Amen.

Janet Morley

Harvest

◆We plough the fields and scatter
the good seed on the land.
But it is fed and watered
By God's almighty hand.
He sends the snow in winter,
The warmth to swell the grain,
The breezes and the sunshine,
And soft, refreshing rain:

All good gifts around us are sent from heaven above;
Then thank the Lord, O thank the Lord,
for all his love.

Matthias Claudius (1740–1815)

Father in heaven, all good gifts come from you. You send the sunshine and the rain and it is through your love and care that we can enjoy harvest time. Thank you for providing so richly for our needs and help us to share the good things we have with those who have little or nothing.

Lord we pray for your blessing on every kind of harvest that we enjoy. Thank you for the harvest of the land and the sea. Bless too the harvest of factory, mine and workshop. Bless the harvest of research and of creative art. May we work together with you in every area of life to produce what is worthwhile, good and fruitful. May you be glorified in it all.

◆We dare not ask you bless our harvest feast
Till it is spread for poorest and for least,
We dare not bring our harvest gifts to you
Unless our hungry brothers share them too.

Not only at this time, Lord; every day
Those whom you love are dying while we pray.
Teach us to do with less, and so to share
From our abundance more than we can spare.

Now with this harvest plenty round us piled,
show us the Christ in every starving child;
Speak, as you spoke of old in Galilee,
'You feed, or you refuse, not them but me!'

Lilian Cox

Your people bring you thanksgiving gifts this harvest day, Creator Lord: produce of farm and field, garden and orchard. Stand guard over our worship, eternal God, lest we who come with full hands, leave with empty hearts. Let your creative power, self-evident in harvest plenty, also newly create our faith in Christ to yield a harvest which is eternal. Amen.

From Prayers before Worship

Bring to fruition, Creator God,
the work of your kingdom.
Make us part of that joyful harvest
in which your loving purpose is completed.
Help us to realize
how important the smallest words and deeds are
in the context of eternity.
At harvest time, when we remember your goodness
make us grateful also
for all we have received from the labour of others
who have sown the seeds of faith, hope and love in our lives.

Author unknown

Lord, your harvest is the harvest of love;
love sown in the hearts of people;
love that spreads out
like the branches of a great tree
covering all who seek its shelter;
love that inspires and recreates;
love that is planted in the weak and the weary,
the sick and the dying.
The harvest of your love is the life that reaches
through the weeds of sin and death
to the sunlight of resurrection.
Lord, nurture my days with your love,
water my soul with the dew of forgiveness,
that the harvest of my life might be your joy.

Frank Topping

All this world is God's own field,
Fruit unto his praise to yield;
Wheat and tares together sown,
Unto joy or sorrow grown;
First the blade and then the ear,
Then the full corn shall appear:
Lord of harvest, grant that we
Wholesome grain and pure may be.

Henry Alford (1810–1871)

O Christ who holds the open gate,
O Christ who drives the furrow straight,
O Christ, the plough, O Christ, the laughter
Of holy white birds flying after,
Lo, all my heart's field red and torn,
And thou wilt bring the young green corn,
The young green corn divinely springing,
The young green corn for ever singing;
And when the field is fresh and fair
Thy blessed feet shall glitter there.
And we will walk the weeded field,
And tell the golden harvest's yield,
The corn that makes the holy bread
By which the soul of man is fed,
The holy bread, the food unpriced,
Thy everlasting mercy, Christ.

John Masefield

God stir the soil,
Run the ploughshare deep,
Cut the furrows round and round,
Overturn the hard, dry ground,
Spare no strength nor toil,
Even though I weep.
In the loose, fresh mangled earth
Sow new seed.
Free of withered vine and weed
Bring fair flowers to birth.

Prayer from Singapore

The seed is Christ's,
The granary is Christ's;
In the granary of God
May we be gathered.
The sea is Christ's,
the fishes are Christ's;
In the nets of God
May we all meet.

Irish prayer

◆Father of all the peoples,
We who can eat our fill
Ask as your gift at harvest
A dedicated will.

Show us our hungry brothers,
Teach us that we must care,
Help us to live more simply
Because we want to share.

For you, who fed the hungry,
May we so break our bread
In constant, costly giving
That others may be fed.

Lilian Cox

All Saints

Saints are those who by their life and work make it clear and plain that God lives.

Nathan Soderblom (1866–1931)

O God, throughout the ages you have raised up the great cloud of witnesses from all nations and from all tongues. Grant us to be strengthened in this generation by their testimony, to be witnesses ourselves of your power and your peace, to join with their praise and like them to behold you one day in glory, through Jesus Christ our Lord who lives and reigns with you in the unity of the Holy Spirit for ever and ever. Amen.

Nessie Stranger

Almighty and everlasting God, who enkindles the flame of your love in the hearts of the saints, grant to our minds the same faith and power of love; that as we rejoice in their triumphs, we may profit by their examples; through Jesus Christ our Lord. Amen.

From the Gothic Missal

Almighty God, we offer unto you most high praise and hearty thanks for the wonderful graces and virtues which you have manifested in all your saints and in all other holy persons upon earth, who by their lives and labours have shined forth as lights in the world, whom we remember with honour and commemorate with joy. For these and for all your other servants who have departed this life with the seal of faith, we praise and magnify your holy name; through Jesus Christ our Lord.

From the Scottish Liturgy (1560)

O thou Lord of all worlds, we bless your name for all those who have entered into their rest and reached the promised land where you are seen face to face. Give us grace to follow in their footsteps as they followed in the footsteps of your holy Son. Keep alive in us the memory of those dear to ourselves whom you have called to yourself; and grant that every remembrance which turns our hearts from things seen to things unseen may lead us always upwards to thee, till we come to our eternal rest; through Jesus Christ our Lord.

Fenton John Anthony Hort (1828–1892)

<u>For personal consideration:</u>

Remember your former leaders, who spoke God's message to you. Think back on how they lived and died, and imitate their faith. Jesus Christ is the same yesterday, today, and for ever.

From Hebrews 13

O Almighty God, who hast knit together thine elect in one communion and fellowship, in the mystical body of thy Son Jesus Christ our Lord: grant us grace so to follow thy blessed saints in all virtuous and godly living, that we may come to those unspeakable joys, which thou hast prepared for them that unfeignedly love thee; through Jesus Christ our Lord.

Collect for All Saints' Day (1549)

O Lord, we praise your holy name for all your servants departed from among us in your faith and fear; and we humbly beseech you so to bless us who remain on earth that, being protected from all evil, we may ever serve and please you with quiet minds and thankful hearts and together with those that are gone before may have our refreshment in paradise and our portion in the resurrection of the just; through Jesus Christ our Saviour.

Frederick Temple (1821–1902)

O you who are the God of all the generations of men, we thank you for all who have walked humbly with you and especially those near to us and dear, in whose lives we have seen the vision of your beauty. May we know that in the body or out of the body they are with you. Unite us still, God of our souls, in one household of faith and love, one family in heaven and on earth; through Jesus Christ our Lord.

John Hunter (1849–1917)

O God, who has brought us near to an innumerable company of angels and to the spirits of just men made perfect; grant us in our pilgrimage to abide in their fellowship, and in our heavenly country to become partakers of their joy; through Jesus Christ our Lord.

William Bright (1824–1901)

O Lord our God, who is in every place and from whom no space or distance can ever separate us, we know that those who are absent from each other are present with you. We therefore pray you to have in your holy keeping those dear ones from whom we are now parted; and grant that both they and we, by drawing nearer unto you, may be drawn nearer to each other, bound together by the unseen chain of your love, in the communion of your Spirit; through Jesus Christ our Lord.

Sir William Martin (1807–1882)

Let the glory of the saints, O Lord, illuminate the dullness of our hearts; that following the example of their lives on earth, we may shine with them in the everlasting light of heaven; through Jesus Christ our Lord. Amen.

From Another Day

Almighty God, break the power of darkness, let your glory appear among us and make us sharers of your eternity, with all your saints, through Jesus Christ our Lord. Amen.

From Praise in All Our Days

❖ *Prayers of the Bible* ❖

Your face, Lord, I will seek.

FROM PSALM 27

In the Old Testament, the Book of Psalms is full of prayers, uttered sometimes in crisis and at other times in joyful celebration. In the New Testament, the prayer taught by our Lord himself stands supreme. But there are other prayers, too, scattered throughout Scripture, which put into sublime words the very things we still need to say to God.

Prayers from the Old Testament

I will sing to the Lord, because he has won a glorious victory;
he has thrown the horses and their riders into the sea.
The Lord is my strong defender;
he is the one who has saved me.
He is my God, and I will praise him,
my father's God, and I will sing about his greatness . . .
Lord, who among the gods is like you?
Who is like you, wonderful in holiness? . . .
You, Lord, will be king for ever and ever.

From Exodus 15, Moses' song at the Red Sea

If you do not go with us, don't make us leave this place.

From Exodus 33, Moses' prayer

Please, let me see the dazzling light of your presence.

From Exodus 33, Moses' request

The Lord has filled my heart with joy;
how happy I am because of what he has done!
I laugh at my enemies;
how joyful I am because God has helped me!
No one is holy like the Lord;
there is none like him,
no protector like our God. Stop your loud boasting;
silence your proud words.
For the Lord is a God who knows,
and he judges all that people do...
He lifts the poor from the dust
and raises the needy from their misery...
The foundations of the earth belong to the Lord;
on them he has built the world.

From 1 Samuel 2, Hannah's song of praise

I am not worthy of what you have already done for me, Sovereign Lord, nor is my family. Yet now you are doing even more, Sovereign Lord; you have made promises about my descendants in the years to come... How great you are, Sovereign Lord! There is none like you; we have always known that you alone are God... And now, Sovereign Lord, you are God; you always keep your promises, and you have made this wonderful promise to me. I ask you to bless my descendants so that they will continue to enjoy your favour. You, Sovereign Lord, have promised this, and your blessing will rest on my descendants for ever.

From 2 Samuel 7, King David's prayer

The Lord is my protector;
he is my strong fortress.
My God is my protection,
and with him I am safe.
He protects me like a shield;
he defends me and keeps me safe.
He is my saviour;
he protects me and saves me from violence;
I call to the Lord,
and he saves me from my enemies;
Praise the Lord!...
You, Lord, are my light;
you dispel my darkness ...
O Lord, you protect me and save me...
The Lord lives! Praise my defender!
Proclaim the greatness of the strong God who saves me!

From 2 Samuel 22, David's song of praise

O Lord God, you have let me succeed my father as king, even though I am very young and don't know how to rule. Here I am among the people you have chosen to be your own, a people who are so many that they cannot be counted. So give me the wisdom I need to rule your people with justice and to know the difference between good and evil. Otherwise, how would I ever be able to rule this great people of yours?

From 1 Kings 3, King Solomon's prayer for wisdom

You, Lord, have placed the sun in the sky,
> yet you have chosen to live in clouds and darkness.
> Now I have built a majestic temple for you,
> a place for you to live in for ever...

But can you, O God, really live on earth? Not even all heaven is large enough to hold you, so how can this Temple that I have built be large enough?

Lord my God, I am your servant. Listen to my prayer, and grant the requests I make to you today. Watch over this Temple day and night, this place where you have chosen to be worshipped... Hear my prayers and the prayers of your people when they face this place and pray. In your home in heaven hear us and forgive us.

From 1 Kings 8, King Solomon's prayer at the dedication of the temple

O Lord, the God of Abraham, Isaac, and Jacob, prove now that you are the God of Israel and that I am your servant and have done all this at your command. Answer me, Lord, answer me, so that this people will know that you, the Lord, are God, and that you are bringing them back to yourself.

From 1 Kings 18, Elijah's prayer at Carmel

O Lord, the God of Israel, enthroned above the winged creatures, you alone are God, ruling all the kingdoms of the world. You created the earth and the sky. Now, Lord, look at what is happening to us. Listen to all the things that Sennacherib is saying to insult you, the living God... Now, Lord our God, rescue us from the Assyrians, so that all the nations of the world will know that only you, O Lord, are God.

From 2 Kings 19, King Hezekiah's prayer

Help us now, O Lord our God, because we are relying on you, and in your name we have come out...

From 2 Chronicles 14, King Asa's prayer before battle

O Lord God of our ancestors, you rule in heaven over all the nations of the world. You are powerful and mighty, and no one can oppose you. You are our God... We do not know what to do, but we look to you for help.

From 2 Chronicles 20, King Jehoshaphat's prayer

I praise you, Lord! You were angry with me,
but now you comfort me and are angry no longer.
God is my saviour;
I will trust him and not be afraid.

From Isaiah 12, Isaiah's song of praise

Lord, heal me and I will be completely well; rescue me and I will be perfectly safe. You are the one I praise!

From Jeremiah 17

Lord, you have deceived me,
and I was deceived.
You are stronger than I am,
and you have overpowered me . . .
Lord, I am ridiculed and scorned all the time
because I proclaim your message.
But when I say, 'I will forget the Lord
and no longer speak in his name,'
then your message is like a fire
burning deep within me.
I try my best to hold it in,
but can no longer keep it back . . .

From Jeremiah 20

O Lord, I have heard of what you have done,
and I am filled with awe.
Now do again in our times
the great deeds you used to do.
Be merciful, even when you are angry.

From Habakkuk 3

In my distress, O Lord, I called to you,
and you answered me.
From deep in the world of the dead
I cried for help, and you heard me.
You threw me down into the depths,
to the very bottom of the sea,
where the waters were all round me,
and all your mighty waves rolled over me...
The water came over me and choked me;
the sea covered me completely,
and seaweed was wrapped round my head.
I went down to the very roots of the mountains,
into the land whose gates lock shut for ever.
But you, O Lord my God,
brought me back from the depths alive.
When I felt my life slipping away,
then, O Lord, I prayed to you,
and in your holy Temple you heard me.

From Jonah 2

Even though the fig trees have no fruit
and no grapes grow on the vines,
even though the olive crop fails
and the fields produce no corn,
even though the sheep all die
and the cattle stalls are empty,
I will still be joyful and glad,
because the Lord God is my saviour.
The Sovereign Lord gives me strength.
He makes me sure-footed as a deer,
and keeps me safe on the mountains.

From Habakkuk 3

O God, I am too ashamed to raise my head in your presence. Our sins pile up, high above our heads; they reach as high as the heavens. From the days of our ancestors until now, we, your people, have sinned greatly ... Lord God of Israel, you are just, but you have let us survive. We confess our guilt to you; we have no right to come into your presence.

From Ezra 9

But now, God, make me strong!

From Nehemiah 6

I know, Lord, that you are all-powerful;
that you can do everything you want.
You ask how I dare question your wisdom
when I am so very ignorant.
I talked about things I did not understand,
about marvels too great for me to know.
You told me to listen while you spoke
and to try to answer your questions.

In the past I knew only what others had told me,
but now I have seen you with my own eyes.
So I am ashamed of all I have said
and repent in dust and ashes.

From Job 42

PRAYERS FROM THE PSALMS

Protect me, O God; I trust in you for safety.
I say to the Lord, 'You are my Lord;
all the good things I have come from you.'

From Psalm 16

My God, my God, why have you abandoned me?
I have cried desperately for help,
but still it does not come.
During the day I call to you, my God,
but you do not answer;
I call at night, but get no rest.
But you are enthroned as the Holy One,
the one whom Israel praises...
It was you who brought me safely through birth,
and when I was a baby, you kept me safe.
I have relied on you since the day I was born,
and you have always been my God.
Do not stay away from me!
Trouble is near,
and there is no one to help.

From Psalm 22

The Lord is my light and my salvation;
I will fear no one.
The Lord protects me from all danger;
I will never be afraid.

From Psalm 27

Be merciful to me, O God,
because of your constant love.
Because of your great mercy wipe away my sins!
Wash away all my evil
and make me clean from my sin!

From Psalm 51

Be merciful to me, O God, be merciful,
because I come to you for safety.
In the shadow of your wings I find protection
until the raging storms are over.

From Psalm 57

Hear my cry, O God;
listen to my prayer!
In despair and far from home
I call to you!
Take me to a safe refuge,
for you are my protector,
my strong defence against my enemies.

From Psalm 61

O God, you are my God,
and I long for you.
My whole being desires you;
like a dry, worn-out, and waterless land,
my soul is thirsty for you.
Let me see you in the sanctuary;
let me see how mighty and glorious you are.
Your constant love is better than life itself,
and so I will praise you.
I will give you thanks as long as I live;
I will raise my hands to you in prayer.
My soul will feast and be satisfied,
and I will sing glad songs of praise to you.

From Psalm 63

We give thanks to you, O God,
we give thanks to you!
We proclaim how great you are
and tell of the wonderful things you have done.

From Psalm 75

O Lord, you have always been our home.
Before you created the hills
or brought the world into being,
you were eternally God,
and will be God for ever...
Teach us how short our life is,
so that we may become wise...
Lord our God, may your blessings be with us.
Give us success in all we do!

From Psalm 90

Give thanks to the Lord, because he is good;
his love is eternal!

From Psalm 107

To you alone, O Lord, to you alone,
and not to us, must glory be given
because of your constant love and faithfulness.

From Psalm 115

Lord, I look up to you,
up to heaven, where you rule.
As a servant depends on his master,
as a maid depends on her mistress,
so we will keep looking to you, O Lord our God,
until you have mercy on us.

From Psalm 123

Lord, I have given up my pride
and turned away from my arrogance.
I am not concerned with great matters
or with subjects too difficult for me.
Instead, I am content and at peace.
As a child lies quietly in its mother's arms,
so my heart is quiet within me.

From Psalm 131

I will proclaim your greatness, my God and king;
I will thank you for ever and ever.
Every day I will thank you;
I will praise you for ever and ever.
The Lord is great and is to be highly praised;
his greatness is beyond understanding.

From Psalm 145

Prayers from the New Testament

JESUS' PRAYERS

The prayer Jesus gave to his disciples:

Our Father in heaven:
May your holy name be honoured;
may your Kingdom come;
may your will be done on earth as it is in heaven.
Give us today the food we need.
Forgive us the wrongs we have done,
as we forgive the wrongs that others have done to us.
Do not bring us to hard testing,
but keep us safe from the Evil One.
For yours is the kingdom, and the power, and the glory for ever.
Amen.

From Matthew 6

*(The Lord's Prayer in its traditional form
can be found at the beginning of this book)*

Father, Lord of heaven and earth! I thank you because you have shown to the unlearned what you have hidden from the wise and learned. Yes, Father, this was how you wanted it to happen.

From Luke 10

I thank you, Father, that you listen to me. I know that you always listen to me, but I say this for the sake of the people here, so that they will believe that you sent me.

From John 11

Father, bring glory to your name!

From John 12

Father, the hour has come. Give glory to your Son, so that the Son may give glory to you. For you gave him authority over all mankind, so that he might give eternal life to all those you gave him. And eternal life means knowing you, the only true God, and knowing Jesus Christ, whom you sent . . .

I do not pray for the world but for those you gave me, for they belong to you . . . Holy Father! Keep them safe by the power of your name, the name you gave me, so that they may be one just as you and I are one . . . I pray not only for them, but also for those who believe in me because of their message. I pray that they may all be one. Father! May they be in us, just as you are in me and I am in you. May they be one, so that the world will believe that you sent me.

From John 17

Father, my Father! All things are possible for you. Take this cup of suffering away from me. Yet not what I want, but what you want.

From Mark 14, Jesus' prayer in Gethsemane

PRAYERS FROM THE CROSS

Forgive them, Father! They don't know what they are doing.

From Luke 23

My God, my God, why did you abandon me?

From Mark 15

Father! In your hands I place my spirit!

From Luke 23

PRAYERS OF THE YOUNG CHURCH

Master and Creator of heaven, earth, and sea, and all that is in them! By means of the Holy Spirit you spoke through our ancestor David, your servant, when he said,

> 'Why were the Gentiles furious;
> why did people make their useless plots?
> The kings of the earth prepared themselves,
> and the rulers met together
> against the Lord and his Messiah.'

For indeed Herod and Pontius Pilate met together in this city with the Gentiles and the people of Israel against Jesus, your holy Servant, whom you made Messiah. They gathered to do everything that you by your power and will had already decided would happen. And now, Lord, take notice of the threats they have made, and allow us, your servants, to speak your message with all boldness. Stretch out your hand to heal, and grant that wonders and miracles may be performed through the name of your holy Servant Jesus.

From Acts 4, the church under persecution

Lord Jesus, receive my spirit!
> Lord! Do not remember this sin against them!

From Acts 7, Stephen's prayers as he was being stoned to death

What shall I do, Lord?

From Acts 22, Paul's prayer at his conversion

PRAYERS IN THE LETTERS OF PAUL

May God our Father and the Lord Jesus Christ give you grace and peace.

From Romans 1

May God, the source of patience and encouragement, enable you to have the same point of view among yourselves by following the example of Christ Jesus, so that all of you together may praise with one voice the God and Father of our Lord Jesus Christ.

From Romans 15

May God, the source of hope, fill you with all joy and peace by means of your faith in him, so that your hope will continue to grow by the power of the Holy Spirit.

From Romans 15

May God, our source of peace, be with you all. Amen.

From Romans 15

Let us give thanks to the God and Father of our Lord Jesus Christ, the merciful Father, the God from whom all help comes!

From 2 Corinthians 1

May God our Father and the Lord Jesus Christ give you grace and peace.

In order to set us free from this present evil age, Christ gave himself for our sins, in obedience to the will of our God and Father. To God be the glory for ever and ever! Amen.

From Galatians 1

I... ask the God of our Lord Jesus Christ, the glorious Father, to give you the Spirit, who will make you wise and reveal God to you, so that you will know him. I ask that your minds may be opened to see his light, so that you will know what is the hope to which he has called you, how rich are the wonderful blessings he promises his people, and how very great is his power at work in us who believe.

From Ephesians 1

I ask God from the wealth of his glory to give you power through his Spirit to be strong in your inner selves, and I pray that Christ will make his home in your hearts through faith.

From Ephesians 3

I pray that you may have your roots and foundation in love, so that you, together with all God's people, may have the power to understand how broad and long, how high and deep, is Christ's love. Yes, may you come to know his love—although it can never be fully known—and so be completely filled with the very nature of God.

From Ephesians 3

I pray that your love will keep on growing more and more, together with true knowledge and perfect judgement, so that you will be able to choose what is best. Then you will be free from all impurity and blame on the Day of Christ. Your lives will be filled with the truly good qualities which only Jesus Christ can produce, for the glory and praise of God.

From Philippians 1

We ask God to fill you with the knowledge of his will, with all the wisdom and understanding that his Spirit gives.

From Colossians 1

May the Lord make your love for one another and for all people grow more and more.

From 1 Thessalonians 3

We ask our God to make you worthy of the life he has called you to live. May he fulfil by his power all your desire for goodness and complete your work of faith.

From 2 Thessalonians 1

May our Lord Jesus Christ himself and God our Father, who loved us and in his grace gave us unfailing courage and a firm hope, encourage you and strengthen you to always do and say what is good.

From 2 Thessalonians 2

◆ *Brief Prayers* ◆

Be persistent in prayer, and keep alert as you pray, giving
thanks to God.

FROM COLOSSIANS 4

Jesus warned against long and wordy prayer and some of the most remarkable prayers are 'one-liners'. Perhaps the most famous is Peter's, when he walked to Jesus across the lake and felt himself sinking. He cried out: 'Save me, Lord!'

The things, good Lord, that we pray for, give us the grace to labour for.
Thomas More (1478–1535)

O God, help us not to despise or oppose what we do not understand.
William Penn (1644–1718)

Let this day, O Lord, add some knowledge or good deed to yesterday.
Lancelot Andrewes (1555–1626)

And now, dear God, what can I do for you?
English child

O Lord, that lends me life,
Lend me a heart replete with thankfulness.
William Shakespeare (1564–1616)

O God, I thank you for all the joy I had in life.
Earl Britnoth 991

My dearest Friend, when I forget to speak to you, speak to me until we speak together.
William Hodges

Give us this day our daily discovery.
Prayer often used by Dr Rendell Harris, Quaker

Grant us grace, Almighty Father, so to pray as to deserve to be heard.
Jane Austen (1775–1827)

Lord, help me to say 'yes'.
Michel Quoist

O Lord, never suffer us to think that we can stand by ourselves, and not need thee.

John Donne (1573–1631)

Help us to keep the promises we make to you, O God.

From Family Prayers (1974)

O Lord, let us not live to be useless, for Christ's sake. Amen.

John Wesley (1703–1791)

Thank you, Lord, that even though we fail you, you never give up on us.

Ron Brandon

Come, Holy Spirit, prepare us to enter the hut of others.

Prayer from Africa

O God, thou knowest that I do not want anything else but to serve thee and men, always, all my life.

Temple Gairdner (1873–1928)

O Christ, be with all who are facing death today in fear or loneliness.

United Society for the Propagation of the Gospel

O Jesus, Son of God, who was silent before Pilate, do not let us wag our tongues without thinking of what we are to say and how to say it.

Irish Gaelic prayer

Lord, make me according to thy heart.

Brother Lawrence (1611–1691)

O Lord, thou knowest how busy I must be this day; if I forget thee, do not thou forget me.

General Lord Astley (1579–1652), before the battle of Edgehill

O God, grant that I may do and suffer all things this day for the glory of thy name.

Used by the Curé d'Ars (1786–1859)

You wake us to delight in your praises; for you made us for yourself, and our heart is restless until it reposes in you.

St Augustine (354–450)

Lord, take my lips and speak through them; take my mind and think through it; take my heart and set it on fire.

W. H. Aitken

Lord, make your will our will in all things.

Charles Vaughan (1816–1897)

Lord, give me what you are requiring of me.

St Augustine (354–430)

Square my trial to my proportioned strength.

John Milton (1608–1674)

O Lord, put no trust in me, for I shall surely fall if you uphold me not.

St Philip Neri (1515–1595)

Lord, who has given all for us, help us to give all for you.

G. W. Biggs

Lord, help me never to use my reason against the Truth.

Jewish prayer

Bless, O God, bless my weather-beaten soul.

Prayer of an old man, West Indies

Lord, let thy glory be my end, thy word my rule, and then thy will be done.

King Charles II (1600–1648)

Let us thank God for his priceless gift!

From 2 Corinthians 9

O God, make us children of quietness and heirs of peace.

St Clement (150–215)

I'm tired, Lord, but I'll lift one foot if you'll lift the other for me.

Saidie Patterson

Here, Lord, is my life. I place it on the altar today. Use it as you will.

Albert Schweitzer (1875–1965)

Teach me to pray, pray thou thyself in me.

François Fenelon (1651-1715)

Dear God, be good to me. The sea is so wide and my boat is so small.

Breton fishermen's prayer

Lord, make me what I should be, change me whatever the cost.

Anthony Bloom

Lord, of thy goodness, give me thyself.

Augustine Baker (1575–1641)

To him who is everywhere, men come not by travelling but by loving.

St Augustine (354–430)

Lord, come to me, my door is open.

Michel Quoist

My God and my all.

St Francis of Assisi (1182–1226)

The Lord almighty grant us a quiet night and a perfect end.

From the Office of Compline

Come, Lord Jesus!

From Revelation 22

❖ *Blessings* ❖

May God be gracious to us and bless us
and make his face to shine upon us.

From Psalm 67

Some of these prayers call for God to be blessed and honoured but most of them pray for God's presence and his many blessings to be ours. These prayers also commit us to God's keeping.

May the Lord bless you and take care of you;
May the Lord be kind and gracious to you;
May the Lord look on you with favour and give you peace.

From Numbers 6

The grace of the Lord Jesus Christ,
the love of God,
and the fellowship of the Holy Spirit
be with you all.

From 2 Corinthians 13

May God, the Lord, bless us with all heavenly benediction, and make us pure and holy in his sight.
May the riches of his glory abound in us.
May he instruct us with the Word of truth, inform us with the gospel of salvation, and enrich us with his love,
Through Jesus Christ, our Lord.

From the Gelasian Sacramentary

God the Father, bless us;
God the Son, defend us;
God the Spirit, keep us
Now and evermore.

From Little Folded Hands

The peace of God, which passeth all understanding, keep your hearts and minds in the knowledge and love of God, and of his Son, Jesus Christ our Lord: and the blessing of God Almighty, the Father, the Son, and the Holy Ghost, be amongst you and remain with you always.

Holy Communion (1549)

God be in my head, and in my understanding;
God be in my eyes, and in my looking;
God be in my mouth, and in my speaking;
God be in my heart, and in my thinking;
God be at my end and at my departing.

From a Book of Hours (1514)

The Lord Jesus Christ be near to defend thee, within thee to refresh thee, around thee to preserve thee, before thee to guide thee, behind thee to justify thee, above thee to bless thee; who liveth and reigneth with the Father and the Holy Spirit, God for evermore.

Author unknown (tenth century)

May the eternal God bless and keep us,
guard our bodies, save our souls, direct our thoughts,
and bring us safe to the heavenly country, our eternal home
where Father, Son and Holy Spirit ever reign,
one God for ever and ever.

From the Sarum Breviary

May the grace of Christ our Saviour,
And the Father's boundless love,
With the Holy Spirit's favour,
Rest upon us from above.

John Newton (1725–1807)

Bless all who worship thee,
from the rising of the sun unto the going down of the same.
Of thy goodness, give us;
with thy love, inspire us;
by thy Spirit, guide us;
by thy power, protect us;
in thy mercy, receive us now and always. Amen.

From Divine Worship

The peace of God be with you,
the peace of Christ be with you,
the peace of Spirit be with you
And with your children,
From the day that we have here today
To the day of the end of your lives,
Until the day of the end of your lives.

Celtic prayer

May God in the plenitude of his love pour upon you the torrents of his grace, bless you and keep you in his holy fear, prepare you for a happy eternity, and receive you at last into immortal glory.

Blessing at the consecration of Coventry Cathedral

May the love of the Lord Jesus
draw us to himself;
May the power of the Lord Jesus
strengthen us in his service;
May the joy of the Lord Jesus
fill our souls.
May the blessing of God almighty,
the Father, the Son, and the Holy Ghost,
be amongst you and remain with you always.

William Temple (1881–1944)

May the cross of the Son of God who is mightier than all the hosts of Satan, and more glorious than all the angels of heaven, abide with you in your going out and your coming in! By day and night, at morning and at evening, at all times and in all places, may it protect and defend you! From the wrath of evil men, from the assaults of evil spirits, from foes invisible, from the snares of the devil, from all low passions that beguile the soul and body, may it guard, protect and deliver you.

From The Christarakana Book of Common Prayer,
Church of India, Pakistan, Burma and Sri Lanka

The guarding of the God of life be on you,
the guarding of loving Christ be on you,
the guarding of Holy Spirit be on you
Every night of your lives,
To aid you and enfold you
Each day and night of your lives.

Celtic prayer

May the Lord bless you with all good and keep you from all evil; may he give light to your heart with loving wisdom, and be gracious to you with eternal knowledge; may he lift up his loving countenance upon you for eternal peace.

From the Dead Sea Scrolls

We commend unto you, O Lord,
our souls and our bodies,
our minds and our thoughts,
our prayers and our hopes,
our health and our work,
our life and our death,
our parents and brothers and sisters,
our benefactors and friends,
our neighbours, our countrymen,
and all Christian folk,
this day and always.

Lancelot Andrewes (1555–1626)

May the God of peace provide you with every good thing you need in order to do his will, and may he, through Jesus Christ, do in us what pleases him. And to Christ be the glory for ever and ever! Amen.

From Hebrews 13

The blessing of the Lord rest and remain upon all his people, in every land, of every tongue; the Lord meet in mercy all that seek him; the Lord comfort all who suffer and mourn; the Lord hasten his coming, and give us, his people, the blessing of peace.

Handley Moule (1841–1920)

May the Lord bless you and keep you,
may he show his face to you
and have mercy on you,
may he turn to you and give you peace,
may the Lord bless you, Brother Leo.

St Francis of Assisi (1181–1226)
(On a sheet of parchment, which Brother Leo always carried on his person, he noted: 'The
Blessed Francis wrote this blessing with his own hand for me, Brother Leo.')

May the everlasting Father himself take you
in his own generous clasp,
in his own generous arm.

Celtic prayer

May the God who gives us peace make you holy in every way and keep your
whole being—spirit, soul and body—free from every fault at the coming of
our Lord Jesus Christ.

From 1 Thessalonians 5

The eye of the great God be upon you,
The eye of the God of glory be on you,
The eye of the Son of Mary Virgin be on you,
The eye of the Spirit mild be on you,
To aid you and to shepherd you;
Oh the kindly eye of the Three be on you,
To aid you and to shepherd you.

Celtic prayer

May the blessing of God almighty, the Father, the Son and the Holy Ghost,
rest upon us and upon all our work and worship done in his name. May he
give us the light to guide us, courage to support us and love to unite us, now
and for evermore. Amen.

The Lord bless us and keep us. The Spirit of the Lord cleanse and purify our inmost hearts, and enable us to shun all evil. The Lord enlighten our understandings and cause the light of the truth to shine into our hearts. The Lord fill us with faith and love towards him. The Lord be with us day and night in our coming in and going out, in our sorrow and in our joy. And bring us at length into his eternal rest. Amen.

May our Lord Jesus Christ be near us to defend us, within us to refresh us, around us to preserve us, before us to guide us, behind us to justify us, above us to bless us. Who lives and reigns with the Father and the Holy Ghost, God for evermore. Amen.

Author unknown (tenth century)

To God be glory;
To the angels honour;
To Satan confusion;
To the cross reverence;
To the church exaltation;
To the departed quickening;
To the penitent acceptance;
To the sick and infirm recovery and healing;
And to the four quarters of the world great peace and
tranquillity;
And on us who are weak and sinful may the compassion and
mercies of our God come, and may they overshadow us
continually. Amen.

Prayer from the old Syriac, used by Christians
in Turkey, Iran and South India

May the Lord lead us when we go, and keep us when we sleep, and talk with us when we wake; and may the peace of God, which passes all understanding, keep our hearts and minds in Christ Jesus our Lord. Amen.

Into your hands, O Father and Lord, we commend our souls and bodies, our parents and homes, friends and servants, neighbours and kindred, our benefactors and brethren departed, all folk rightly believing, and all who need your pity and protection. Light us all with your holy grace, and suffer us never to be separated from you, O Lord in Trinity, God everlasting.

Edmund Rich (1170–1240)

> May God shield me,
> May God fill me,
> May God keep me,
> May God watch me,
> May God bring me
> To the land of peace,
> To the country of the King,
> To the peace of eternity.

May God the Father bless us. May Christ the Son take care of us. The Holy Ghost enlighten us, all the days of our life.

The Lord be our defender and keeper of body and soul both now and for ever to the ages of ages. Amen.

Go forth into the world in peace; be of good courage; hold fast that which is good; render to no man evil for evil; strengthen the fainthearted; support the weak; help the afflicted; honour all men; love and serve the Lord, rejoicing in the power of the Holy Spirit.

And the blessing of God Almighty, the Father, the Son and the Holy Ghost, be upon you, and remain with you for ever.

From the proposed 1928 Prayer Book

Deep peace of the running wave to you,
Deep peace of the flowing air to you;
Deep peace of the quiet earth to you;
Deep peace of the shining stars to you;
Deep peace of the gentle night to you.
Moon and stars pour their healing light on you;
Deep peace of Christ the light of the world to you;
Deep peace of Christ.

Scots Celtic prayer

Hear our prayer, O Lord:
bless, protect and sanctify
all those who bow their heads before you.
Through the grace, mercy and love
of your only-begotten Son,
to whom with you and your most holy,
gracious and life-giving Spirit
be blessing now and for ever,
to the ages of ages. Amen.

Eastern Orthodox Church

God the Father bless me, Christ guard me, the Holy Spirit enlighten me, all
the days of my life. The Lord be the defender and guardian of my soul and my
body, now and ever, and world without end. Amen.

From The Book of Cerne (ninth century)

May the Lord himself, who is our source of peace, give you peace at all times
and in every way. The Lord be with you all.

From 2 Thessalonians 3

And now may the blessing of the Lord rest and remain upon all his people in
every land of every tongue. The Lord meet in mercy all that seek him. The
Lord comfort all that suffer and mourn. The Lord hasten his coming, and
now give us and all his people peace by all means. Amen.

Doxologies

A doxology is a short burst of praise to God.

Praise God, from whom all blessings flow;
Praise him, all creatures here below;
Praise him above you heavenly host;
Praise Father, Son and Holy Ghost.

Thomas Ken (1637–1711)

To him who by means of his power working in us is able to do so much more than we can ever ask for, or even think of: to God be the glory in the church and in Christ Jesus for all time, for ever and ever! Amen.

From Ephesians 3

Praise to the Father,
Praise to the Son,
Praise to the Spirit,
The Three in One.

Celtic prayer

All things were created by him, and all things exist through him and for him. To God be the glory for ever! Amen.

From Romans 11

To him who is able to keep you from falling, and to bring you faultless and joyful before his glorious presence—to the only God our Saviour, through Jesus Christ our Lord, be glory, majesty, might, and authority, from all ages past, and now, and for ever and ever! Amen.

From Jude

To the eternal King, immortal and invisible, the only God—to him be honour and glory for ever and ever! Amen.

From 1 Timothy 1

To God the Father, who first loved us
and made us accepted in the Beloved:
To God the Son, who loved us, and washed us
from our sins in his own blood;
To God the Holy Ghost, who sheds the love of God
abroad in our hearts,
Be all love and all glory,
From time and for eternity.

Thomas Ken (1637–1711)

To him who sits on the throne and to the Lamb,
be praise and honour, glory and might,
for ever and ever!

From Revelation 5

Brief Notes on Sources of Prayers

Peter Abelard 1079–1142

Born in Brittany, philosopher and theologian. Famed for his love for Héloïse, his contribution to the mediaeval church was to help reconcile faith and reason.

Alcuin of York 735–804

Christian scholar educated at York, who taught at Charlemagne's court. He wrote extensively and led revision of the Vulgate text of the Bible.

Henry Alford 1810–1871

Dean of Canterbury, hymnwriter.

King Alfred 849–901

King of Wessex and overlord of England, who defeated the Danes. He encouraged learning and translated part of the Bible into Anglo-Saxon.

Alternative Service Book (1980)

The first fully authorized alternative to the *Book of Common Prayer* of the Church of England.

St Ambrose 340–397

Son of the Christian prefect of Gaul, he became a fearless church leader. His first act as bishop of Milan was to give all his money to the poor. He greatly influenced St Augustine.

Lancelot Andrewes 1555–1626

Bishop of Winchester and chaplain to Queen Elizabeth I. He translated part of the Old Testament for the Authorized Version of 1611.

St Anselm 1033–1109

Born in Italy and a monk in Normandy, he became Archbishop of Canterbury. An enlightened and sympathetic thinker, he wrote widely.

Sir Jacob Astley 1579–1652

A supporter of King Charles I in the English Civil War, he commanded the King's forces at the battle of Edgehill.

St Augustine of Hippo 354–430

Born in Algeria of a pagan father and a Christian mother. His mother prayed constantly for him and in time he was dramatically converted. He became a bishop in North Africa. Best known for his autobiographical *Confessions*, his influence on the church has been immense.

Jane Austen 1775–1827

English novelist, author of *Pride and Prejudice*.

William Barclay 1907–1978

Professor of Divinity and Biblical Criticism at Glasgow University. He was a gifted preacher, teacher, broadcaster and scholar. His series of Bible study notes on the New Testament used his own translation from the Greek.

Sabine Baring–Gould 1834–1924

Mediaeval scholar and hymnwriter, probably best known for
Onward Christian Soldiers.

Karl Barth 1886–1968

Swiss theologian, who sought to bring the church back from liberal theology to the fundamentals of faith. He was banished from Germany, where he had lectured, because of his opposition to the Nazis. His most famous work is the outstanding commentary on Romans.

Richard Baxter 1615–1691

Puritan divine, who was excluded from the Church of England and imprisoned for continuing to preach. He wrote *The Saints' Everlasting Rest*.

The Venerable Bede ?673–735

Monk and scholar of Jarrow, his learning and holiness helped to make Northumbria a centre of Christian learning. His *Ecclesiastical History* gave him the name of 'father of English history'.

St Benedict 480–543

From Nursia. He established the Benedictine order of monks, with his own rule for the monastic life which has become the basis of many other rules.

Richard Meux Benson 1824–1915

Founder of the Cowley Brotherhood, an Anglican religious order, based
near Oxford.

Bernard of Clairvaux 1091–1153

Founded the Cistercian house at Clairvaux. He combined deep piety and mysticism with practical activity.

Eugène Bersier 1831–1889

Swiss pastor and historian. He persuaded his breakaway Paris church to rejoin the main Reformed Church of France, for the sake of unity.

William Blake 1757–1827

English poet, painter, engraver and mystic

Jacob Boehme 1575–1624

German Lutheran mystic, whose teaching sprang from his mystical experiences. Most of his life he worked as a shoemaker.

Dietrich Bonhoeffer 1906–1945

German Lutheran pastor who foresaw the danger of Nazi beliefs. He was involved in resistance to Hitler, imprisoned and executed on charges of treason.

Book of Common Prayer

Based on Cranmer's liturgy, it first came into use on Whitsunday, 1549, and replaced the service books of the breviary, missal and manual previously used by clergy. It was revised, withdrawn under Cromwell, and then re-introduced in 1662 on the Restoration of Charles II.

Corrie Ten Boom 1892–1983

With her Dutch father and family, she hid Jews from the Nazis during the Second World War, for which they were sent to Ravensbruck concentration camp. She survived, and preached and wrote widely.

John Bradford 1510–1555

A royal chaplain; sympathetic to the Reformation, he was imprisoned in the Tower and burnt at Smithfield.

Thomas Bradwardine 1290–1349

Archbishop of Canterbury. Nicknamed the 'profound professor' for his ability in mathematics and theology, he was chaplain to Edward III and died from the Black Death.

Nicholas Brady 1659–1726

Irish clergyman and staunch suppporter of the Prince of Orange. With Nahum Tate he wrote a metrical version of the Psalms.

Breviary

Book containing the 'Divine Office' of psalms, Bible readings and prayers for the day, to be recited by priests, monks and nuns.

William Bridge 1600–1670

Nonconformist preacher who served as a dissenter on the Westminster Assembly, which was convened to promote unity among churches.

St Bridget or Brigid 453–523

Abbess and much revered Irish saint. Believed to have founded the first religious community for women among the Irish.

William Bright 1824–1901

Professor of ecclesiastical history at Oxford. He mainly wrote about the Church Fathers, but also wrote some hymns.

Robert Browning 1812–1889

Leading English poet, known for his dramatic monologues.

Edmund Budry 1854–1911

French pastor, who wrote the hymn 'Thine be the glory' (*A toi la gloire*).

John Bunyan 1628–1688

Puritan writer and preacher. He was imprisoned for preaching as a non-Conformist, and wrote *Pilgrim's Progress* in prison.

William Burleigh 1812–1871

American Unitarian reformer, editor and hymnwriter.

Robert Burns 1759–1796

Greatest of Scottish lyric poets.

John Byrom 1692–1763

English poet and hymnwriter, who emphasized the love of God in Christ and the work of the Holy Spirit.

John Calvin 1509–1564

An early Protestant reformer. He established Geneva as a centre of Christian living. His major work is the *Institutes*, a defence of Reformation beliefs.

Peter Canisius 1521–1597

Jesuit reformer of the Catholic church in southern Germany and Austria. Outstanding as preacher, educational reformer, teacher and pastor.

William Carey 1761–1834

English pioneer Baptist missionary to India. He translated the Bible, set up a printing press and established schools, medical work and much more.

Amy Carmichael 1868–1951

Founded the Dohnavur Fellowhip in South India, which rescued children from Hindu temple service. She wrote many poems and books in spite of suffering much ill-health.

Edward Caswall 1814–1878

Hymn writer and Anglican vicar who joined Cardinal Newman at the Oratory, Edgbaston, after becoming a Roman Catholic.

John Cennick 1718–1755

Hymnwriter; he helped John Wesley and Whitefield before becoming a
Moravian minister.

Allen William Chatfield 1808–1896

Classical scholar and clergyman. He specialized in translating early Greek Christian hymns
into English verse.

John Chrysostom 347–407

Bishop of Constantinople, he was nicknamed Chrysostom or 'golden-mouthed' for his
preaching, and his writings have nearly all survived. He suffered persecution
for his integrity and zeal.

Matthias Claudius 1740–1815

German poet, wrote 'We plough the fields and scatter', to meet the need for harvest festival
hymns. It was translated by Miss J.M. Campbell.

Clement of Rome (died 95)

Early Christian leader whose writings were held in great honour in
the second century.

John Colet 1497–1519

Dean of St Paul's and founder of St Paul's School, London. Renaissance thinker and
reformer.

Robert Collyer 1823–1912

Yorkshire born, he was apprenticed to a blacksmith, but studied to became a Methodist
minister. He emigrated to America, where he supported the abolition of slavery, and became
a Unitarian preacher and missionary.

St Columba ?521–597

Abbot and missionary in Ireland and then Scotland. He founded a community on the island
of Iona, and he and his followers evangelized the Picts.

Emperor Constantine ?280–337

The first Christian Roman emperor. He moved his capital from Rome to
Byzantium, and renamed it Constantinople.

Corymeela

The Corymeela Community seeks to bring Protestants and Roman Catholics
together in Northern Ireland.

Bishop Cosin 1595–1672

Bishop of Durham. Deprived of his benefices by the Puritan Long Parliament, he became
chaplain to the Anglican royalists in Paris.

Miles Coverdale 1488–1568

Bishop of Exeter, he first helped Tyndale in his translation and was later responsible for the first printed English Bible as well as the Great Bible.

Thomas Cranmer 1489–1556

First Protestant Archbishop of Canterbury and chief author of the *Book of Common Prayer*. He was burnt as a heretic by the Catholic Queen Mary.

Thomas Cromwell ?1485–1540

Earl of Essex, English statesman, secretary to Cardinal Wolsey and later adviser to Henry VIII. He was responsible for much of the Reformation law but was later executed by the king's order.

Charles d'Arcy 1859–1938

Archbishop of Armagh

Teilhard de Chardin 1881–1955

Roman Catholic Jesuit priest, also a paleontologist, who sought to bring together modern science and Christian theology.

Charles de Foucauld 1858–1916

Roman Catholic missionary and ascetic, born in Strasbourg. His final mission and translation work was in Algeria where he was murdered.

John Donne 1573–1631

Dean of St Paul's Cathedral and leading poet of the Metaphysical school, remembered for his love poetry, holy sonnets and sermons.

Francis Drake ?1540–1596

An English navigator, the first Englishman to sail around the world. He commanded a fleet against the Spanish Armada and contributed greatly to its defeat.

Mary Duncan 1814–1840

Daughter and wife of a vicar, her hymns were chiefly written for her children.

Lord Dunsany 1878–1957

The eighteenth baron, he was born Edward John Moreton Drax Plunkett. He was an Irish dramatist and short story writer.

Eastern Orthodox Church

Probably one sixth of all Christians belong to this church. Most live in Greek or Slavonic lands. It is a family of self-governing churches, which lays great stress on the Trinity and on liturgy.

Ephraem ?306–373

Great classical writer of the Syrian church, nicknamed by the Syrians 'the lyre of the Holy Spirit' for his poetry.

Desiderius Erasmus 1467–1536

An illegitimate son of a Dutch priest, he became the foremost scholar of his age. He wrote against corruption in the church, travelled to Paris and England and finally settled in Switzerland.

St Ethelwold 908–984

Bishop of Winchester. He was a reformer who helped, with St Dunstan, to renew the English church. He translated St Benedict's Rule into English for nuns who knew no Latin.

Venantius Fortunatus ?530–609

A hymnwriter who was born in Italy but lived mostly in Gaul. He became Bishop of Poitiers.

St Frances Xavier 1506–1552

Jesuit missionary to the East Indies and Japan. One of the group who helped Ignatius Loyola to form the Society of Jesus (the Jesuits).

St Francis of Assisi 1182–1226

Love for Christ caused him to leave his well-to-do life of pleasure and embrace 'Lady Poverty'. His followers, later the Franciscan order, lived simply, by faith, as he did.

Richard Hurrell Froude 1803–1836

A scholar and Tractarian (High Church) leader, sometimes known as the 'third man' of the Oxford Movement (Newman and Keble being the other two).

Thomas Fuller 1608–1661

Much acclaimed preacher and historian, said to be one of the first authors to make an income by his pen.

François Fénelon 1631–1715

French theologian and writer. He defended Mme Guyon's *Quietism*, a form of mysticism.

Temple Gairdner 1873–1928

He was a missionary in Egypt, and a gifted linguist who taught missionaries colloquial Arabic. He wrote diversely and loved music, poetry and nature.

Gelasian Sacramentary eighth century

A sacramentary was named after the writer or collector of the prayers. Gelasius was a fifth-century pope but the Gelasian Sacramentary was probably written by nuns at Chelles, near Paris. See *Sacramentary*

General Charles Gordon 1833–1885

British general, administrator and Governor of Sudan. He was killed in the siege of Khartoum.

St Gregory ?540–604

Born in Rome, the first and greatest of the sixteen popes of that name. One of the four great Latin doctors of the church. He sent St Augustine of Canterbury to convert the English.

Stephen Grellett 1773–1855

Born in France. After his conversion he became a Quaker missionary. He introduced Elizabeth Fry to her work in Newgate prison.

John Hamilton 1512–1571

The last Roman Catholic to hold the office of Archbishop of St Andrews. He supported Mary Queen of Scots, and was finally hanged as a traitor.

Gavin Hamilton 1561–1612

Bishop of Galloway

Dag Hammarskjöld 1905–1961

Swedish statesman; Secretary-General of the United Nations and Nobel peace prize winner

Joseph Hart 1712–1768

Independent minister who wrote many hymns following his conversion.

Warren Hastings 1732–1818

British administrator and reformer in India. He was the first Governor General of Bengal.

Frances Ridley Havergal 1836–1870

Gifted in the classics and Hebrew. Her main interest, after her conversion at fifteen, was in writing poems and hymns.

Matthew Henry 1662–1714

Non-conformist Bible expositor and preacher, best known for his seven volume commentary on the Bible

George Herbert 1593–1633

English poet of the Metaphysical school, he was the rector of Bemerton.

Robert Herrick 1591–1674

English lyrical poet and vicar of Dean Prior.

George Hickes 1642–1715

Bishop of Thetford and a nonjuror, that is, one who refused to give his oath of
allegiance to William and Mary.

Hildebert 1056–1133

French writer, who was Bishop of Le Mans, where he built part of the cathedral, and
Archbishop of Tours.

Rowland Hill 1744–1833

English preacher and evangelist, he helped to found the British and Foreign Bible Society.
Rowland Hill, creator of the Penny Post, was named after him.

Fenton John Anthony Hort 1828–1892

New Testament critic and Bible scholar.

William Walsh How 1823–1897

First bishop of Wakefield, known as 'the poor man's bishop'. He wrote fine hymns.

John Hunter 1849–1917

Minister of Trinity Church, Glasgow

St Ignatius of Antioch martyred ?107

Bishop of Antioch, known through his seven letters to churches,
collected by *Polycarp*.

St Ignatius Loyola 1491–1556

Brought up as a soldier, he was converted while he convalesced after battle.
He founded the missionary order of Jesuits.

Bernhardt Ingemann 1789–1862

Professor of Danish language and literature, poet and hymnwriter.

Irenaeus ?130–?202

Bishop of Lyons, with strong links going back to apostolic times. He provided a bridge
between the Eastern and the Western church.

St Jane de Chantal 1572–1641

Foundress of a new order of convents, under the guidance of St Francis de Sales.

Benjamin Jenks 1646–1724

English writer and rector of Kenley.

John Jewel 1522–1571

Bishop of Salisbury. A staunch Anglican, he wrote the first defence of the Church of
England against Rome.

St John of the Cross 1542–1591

Spanish mystic. He worked with *St Teresa of Avila* for the reform of the Carmelite orders, and together they founded the Barefoot Orders. His best known writing is *The Dark Night of the Soul.*

Samuel Johnson 1709–1786

English critic, writer and conversationalist, immortalized in Boswell's biography of him.

J.H. Jowett 1846–1923

English congregationalist preacher in USA and Westminster Chapel London. He wrote many devotional books.

Julian of Norwich ?1342–after 1413

Mystic who lived as an anchoress or hermit in a cell attached to St Julian's church, Norwich. Her writings and life reflect on the revelations she received of God's great love.

John Keble 1792–1866

Parish priest and hymnwriter, he was a leader of the Tractarian or Oxford Movement, a revival of the Anglican High Church.

Thomas Ken 1637–1711

Bishop of Bath and Wells, author of 'Awake my soul, and with the sun' and 'Glory to thee, my God, this night'. He lived out his Christian principles.

Søren Kierkegaard 1813–1855

Danish philosopher. Kierkegaard was an eccentric and melancholy figure, who wrote with brilliant and biting wit. He rejected a lukewarm or hypocritical approach to the teaching of the New Testament.

William Knight 1836–1916

Professor of moral theology. His numerous writings include work on the Lakeland poets and prayers.

John Knox 1505–1572

Scottish reformer and famous preacher, chaplain to Edward VI of England but in conflict with Mary Queen of Scots. He was the main creator of the Scottish prayer book.

Edward Lake 1641–1704

Archdeacon of Exeter

Archbishop Laud 1573-1645

Archbishop of Canterbury, who supported Charles I and high church policies against the Puritans and was executed for treason.

Brother Lawrence 1611–1691

Born Nicholas Herman in Lorraine, he became a soldier. After his conversion to Christianity he joined the Carmelite order as a lay brother, where he worked in the kitchens. He wrote *The Practice of the Presence of God*.

Jane Leeson 1807–1882

Hymnwriter, who also translated hymns from Latin.

Martin Luther 1483–1546

German leader of the Protestant Reformation. Originally a monk, his life changed when he recognized that human justification with God is by faith alone. He laid great stress on the Bible, which he translated into German.

Henry Lyte 1793–1847

Curate at Lower Brixham, Devon, and hymnwriter, best known for 'Abide with me' and 'Praise my soul the King of heaven'.

George Macdonald 1824–1905

Scottish novelist and poet, source of inspiration to C.S. Lewis.

Frederick Macnutt 1873–1949

Provost of Leicester cathedral and chaplain to the King. He wrote sermons and an anthology of prayers.

Sir William Martin 1807–1882

First Chief Justice of New Zealand.

Henry Martyn 1781–1812

Missionary to India. He translated the New Testament and Prayer Book into Hindustani and his Journals are classics of devotional literature.

Hrabanus Maurus 788–856

A mystical interpreter of the Bible who wrote prolifically on both sacred and secular subjects. He studied under Alcuin of York and became Abbot of Fulda and later Archbishop of Mainz.

Mechtild of Magdeburg 1207–1294

A German mystic. She lived a hermit-like existence, writing down her visions.

Philip Melanchthon 1497–1560

German reformer, born Scharzerd, nicknamed 'Melanchthon'—the Greek form of his name—because of his interest in Greek studies. He published Luther's early works and wrote in his defence.

Eric Milner-White died 1963

Dean of King's College, Cambridge, then of York. He wrote many prayers.

John Milton 1608–1674

A great English poet, best known for *Paradise Lost*. He was also a pamphleteer
in Parliamentarian and other causes.

Missal

Book containing the service of the Mass for the whole year.

Thomas More 1478–1535

English statesman, humanist and Roman Catholic saint, executed on a charge of treason for
refusing to recognize Henry VIII's divorce from Catherine of Aragon and the Act of
Supremacy which made Henry head of the Church of England.

Bishop Handley Moule 1841–1920

Bishop of Durham. He wrote hymns, poems, commentaries and devotional works, and was
associated with the Keswick Convention.

Mozarabic Sacramentary

A collection of prayers and liturgies used by Christians in Moorish Spain.

Ogden Nash 1902–1971

American humorous poet

Nestorian Liturgy 5th century

The forms of worship of the Nestorian Church

John Henry Newman 1801–1890

A leader of the Anglican Oxford Movement, he was later received into the Roman Catholic
Church and became a cardinal. His influence in both Churches has been great.

John Newton 1725–1807

Anglican clergyman and writer of, among other hymns, *Amazing Grace*, dramatically
converted after a life involved in the slave trade.

William Orchard 1877–1955

Minister of King's Weigh House Chapel, London

John Oxenham 1853–1941

Born William Dunkerley, he was a novelist and poet and a devout
Congregationalist.

Francis Paget 1851–1911

Bishop of Oxford. He wrote theological books.

W.H. Parker

Baptist hymnwriter.

Blaise Pascal 1623–1662

French mathematician and physicist. He had a deep spiritual experience and his unfinished writings on faith were published after his death.

William Penn 1644–1718

English Quaker who founded the American colony of Pennsylvania, where there could be freedom of expression, as a refuge for persecuted dissenters.

Theodore Philaret 1553–1633

Patriarch of Russia. He brought about social reforms and established theological seminaries and libraries.

St Philip Neri 1515–1595

Born in Florence, he devoted himself to reforming and social work in Rome.

Folliot Sandford Pierpoint 1835–1917

Hymnwriter. He is best known for 'For the beauty of the earth', which was originally a hymn for Holy Communion.

Primer

Prayer or devotional book for lay people, in use before and for some time after the Reformation.

Clemens Prudentius 348–410

Born in Spain, he was a lawyer and civil servant. He wrote Christian Latin poetry.

Walter Rauschenbusch 1861–1918

Born to German immigrant parents in the USA, he was called the 'father of the social gospel in America' because of his deep care for the underprivileged. He was also a pacifist.

Edmund Rich 1170–1240

Archbishop of Canterbury, also known as Edmund of Abingdon. He was a teacher, a preacher, a man of study and prayer and a mystic. He chose Richard of Chichester as his chancellor, to help in practical problems.

Richard of Chichester 1197–1253

Described as 'a model diocesan bishop' he lived a poor and holy life. His grave was a shrine for pilgrims at Chichester.

Martin Rinkart 1586–1649

German clergyman, musician and poet, who supported his people in Saxony during the horrors of the Thirty Years War.

Richard Rolle 1290–1349

Yorkshire hermit, scholar and mystic writer.

Christina Rossetti 1830–1894

Poet and sister of Dante Gabriel Rossetti. She lived a life of Christian
faith and self-denial.

Sacramentary

Early book of offices (services) of the church, with the prayers and forms of words
belonging to the sacraments such as Baptism, Holy Communion and Marriage. See *Gelasian
Sacramentary.*

Albert Schweitzer 1875–1965

German theologian, musician and medical missionary, who wrote *The Quest for the Historical
Jesus.* He founded a hospital in the Congo at Lambarene.

Lord Shaftesbury 1801–1885

Seventh Earl and Member of Parliament. Outstanding evangelical and reformer in many
areas of social need.

Sadhu Sundar Singh 1889–?1929

Brought up as a Sikh, in India, he was converted to Christianity after having a vision of
Jesus. When he was driven from home, he wore the robe of a *Sadhu* (holy man) to evangelize
the Hindus. He disappeared while evangelizing Tibet.

Robert Louis Stevenson 1850–1894

Scottish writer, best known for *Treasure Island.* Many of his prayers were written on the
island of Samoa, where he lived for his health.

Jonathan Swift 1665–1745

Irish satirist and dean of St Patrick's Cathedral, Dublin. His best known satire is *Gulliver's
Travels.*

St Symeon the New Theologian 949–1022

A mystic, venerated in the Orthodox Church of Constantinople, where he was brought up.

Synesius ?375–?430

Bishop of Ptolemais

Rabindranath Tagore 1861–1941

Indian Christian poet and philosopher, and Nobel prize winner for literature

Thomas Tallis ?1505–1585

Considered one of the greatest early composers. He wrote much fine music for church
services.

Nahum Tate 1652–1715

Irish poet and dramatist who became poet laureate. Wrote a metrical version of the Psalms with Nicholas Brady, as well as the Christmas carol 'While Shepherds Watched'.

Jeremy Taylor 1613–1667

Anglican bishop and writer, who pleaded for toleration in an intolerant age. Perhaps best known for his works *Holy Living* and *Holy Dying*.

Frederick Temple 1821–1902

Father of William Temple, headmaster of Rugby School and Archbishop of Canterbury. He was involved in social needs of the time.

William Temple 1881–1944

Archbishop of Canterbury. An outstanding preacher and writer of scholarly and devotional works.

St Teresa of Avila 1515–1582

Spanish noblewoman who became a nun at the age of twenty. After a deep experience of God her life was transformed. She founded the order of barefoot Carmelites and combined mysticism with a practical life of reform.

Thomas à Kempis 1380–1471

German mystic, best known for *The Imitation of Christ*, one of the most widely read Christian books ever written.

St Thomas Aquinas 1225–1274

Born in Italy, he was a scholar and philosopher who became the greatest theologian of the mediaeval church.

Augustus Toplady 1740–1778

Anglican vicar and hymnwriter—he wrote 'Rock of Ages'—who was a powerful Calvinist preacher, opposed to John Wesley.

Lawrence Tuttiett 1825–1897

Gave up medicine to go into the ministry. He was prebendary of St Ninian's Cathedral, Perth and wrote prayer manuals.

Charles Vaughan 1816–1897

Dean of Llandaff, reformed Harrow School as its headmaster. Fine preacher and teacher.

Isaac Watts 1674–1748

Pastor of a London non-conformist church, he is best known for his prolific output of fine hymns.

John Wesley 1703–1791

Great English travelling preacher and founder of Methodism. The world was his parish; his preaching changed the face of Britain.

Charles Wesley 1707–1788

Eighteenth child of Samuel and Susanna Wesley, converted three days before his brother John. He was a preacher and a great hymnwriter who wrote some 7270 hymns.

Brooke Foss Westcott 1825–1901

Bishop of Durham, where he did much for social conditions. Known for his Bible commentaries.

John Greenleaf Whittier 1807–1892

Quaker poet; an important writer in the anti-slavery movement. He wrote religious verse in his old age.

William of St-Thierry ?1085–1148

A Scholastic philosopher and a writer. He was a friend of Bernard of Clairvaux, and Abbot of St-Thierry, near Rheims.

Thomas Wilson 1663–1755

Bishop of Sodor and Man, he brought about many reforms on the island and his books were the first to be printed in Manx.

Catherine Winkworth 1829–1878

A pioneer in women's higher education. She translated a large number of German hymns.

Index of Subjects

This list supplements, and is designed to be used in conjunction with, the main contents list at the beginning of the book.

Index of Authors

Prayers from the Bible

Index of First Lines

Acknowledgements

We would like to thank all those who have given us permission to include prayers in this book, as indicated on the list below. Every effort has been made to trace and contact copyright owners. If there are any inadvertent omissions in the acknowledgments we apologize to those concerned. All prayers except those acknowledged in the main text or listed below have been written by Mary Batchelor. Each figure refers to the page number of a prayer.

Amnesty International: from *The One Who Listens*, 184.
Andrews and McMeel Inc: from *Prayers of Life*, Michel Quoist (US rights) 12,50,86,88,260,362,365.
Anthony Clarke Books: from *Paths to Contemplation*, Yves Raquin, translated by P. Barrett 24.
Baptist Peace Fellowship: from *Prayers for Peace*, 228.
BBC Publications: from *New Every Morning*, 24,28,239,244.
Blandford Press: from *The Infant Teacher's Prayer Book*, 127,293,296 and 293,296.
Canon Michael Botting: 246.
Zinnia Bryan: from *Let's Talk to God*, 137,292,327, from *Let's Talk to God Again*, 298, from *Family Prayers 1974*, 363.
Cairns Publications: from *Prayer at Night*, Jim Cotter, 37,153,157,201,227,231,272,276,277.
Cassell plc: 219.
CCA Youth: from *Your Will Be Done*, 29,153,163,229,254, and 234,235.
Christian Aid: 166,235.
Christian Literature Campaign, Inc: from *Rose from Briar*, Amy Carmichael, 174
Christian Publicity Organization: 111,134,149,150,162,170,175,201,204,205
Church of England Central Board of Finance: from *The Alternative Service Book* (1980),
39,42,75,79,111,112,113,134,165,204,205,323,328,329, from the proposed *1928 Prayer Book*, 170,373.
CMS: from *Morning, Noon and Night*, John Carden, 27,65,80 *All Our Days*, Irene Taylor and Phyllis Garlick, 62, and 80,145,340.
Donald Coggan: 88.
Concordia Publishing House: from *Little Folded Hands*, 367.
Constable & Co Ltd: from *Medieval Latin Lyrics*, Helen Waddell, 105,333, from *More Latin Lyrics*. Helen Waddell, 33.
The Coptic Orthodox Patriarchate: 208,213.
Council for World Mission: from *Mission Pursuit*, 247.
Curtis Brown: from *Prayers From Other Lands*, 132,226,254,259,310, from *Parents Keep Out*, Ogden Nash, 254
Darton, Longman and Todd: from *St Francis at Prayer*, edited by Wolfgang Bader, 125,171,172,371,
from the *Catholic Prayer Book*, 73.
Patrick Dennis: from the Sheffield Diocese *Decade of Prayer*, 84.
Edward England Books: from *A Healing House of Prayer*, Morris Maddocks, 257.
The Episcopal Church of the United States: 282.
Epworth Press: from *A Book of Vestry Prayers*, 67,78,81,325,327,334
Faber & Faber: from *Markings*, Dag Hammerskjöld, 21,49,153, from the *Festal Menaion*, 326.
Faith Press: from *Praise in All Our Days*, 342.
Fleming H. Revell: from *The Practice of the Presence of God*, Brother Lawrence, 32,117.
Forward Movement Publications: from *The Anglican Cycle of Prayer—Partners in Prayer*, 144.
Frederick Muller: from *Hymns and Prayers for Children*, 215.
Friendship Press: from *The Cross is Lifted*, 172.
Geoffrey Chapman: from *A Christian's Prayer Book*, Peter Coughlan, 326, from *Journal of a Soul*, Pope John XXIII, 327.
Gill and Macmillan: from *Prayers of Life*, Michel Quoist, 12,50,86,88,260,362,365.
Girl Guides Association: 310.
Grove Books: from *Collects with the New Lectionary*, 86,334.
Harper and Row: from *Justice and Mercy*, edited by Ursula Niebuhr, 71, from *Prayers of the Spirit*, 159,
from *The World at One in Prayer*, 144.
HarperCollins Publishers: from *Something Beautiful For God*, Malcolm Muggeridge, 284, from *When My Visitors Go*, Rita Snowden,
176, from *Letters and Papers from Prison*, Dietrich Bonhoeffer, 147,158,183,186,262,268, from *More Prayers of the Plain Man*, William
Barclay, 44,45,106,131, from *Be Still and Know*, Michael Ramsey, 48, from *Prayers for Busy People*, Rita Snowden, 52,127,156,266,
269, from *Child Education*, A.W.L. Chitty, 208.
Hodder and Stoughton Ltd: from *New Parish Prayers*, Frank Colquhoun, 14, from *Kathleen*, E.M. Blaiklock, 160, from *I've got to talk
to somebody, God*, 110,165,281,285, Marjorie Holmes, from *God of Our Fathers*, Frank Colquhoun, 29,148, from *Uncommon Prayers
for Younger People*, Cecil Hunt, 312.
John Murray (Publishers) Ltd: from *A Chain of Prayer Across the Ages*, 43.
Brother Kenneth and Sister Geraldine: from *Live and Pray*, 62.
Keston College: 165,188,192, from *The Prisoner's Lantern*, 181,182,185,186,190,192, from *Poems from Communist Prisons*, 183,186,
from *Last Repentance*, 187, from *Miracle of Prayer*, 191.
Kingsway Publications Limited: from *Prayers for Today's Church*, Dick Williams, 78, 298, 291, 294, 295, from *Please God*, Dick
Williams, 48.

Lakeland: from *The Blessings of Illness*, 175.

Longman Group Ltd: from *A Cambridge Bede Book*, Eric Milner-White, 120, from *Meditations and Prayers*, Evelyn Underhill, 121, from *An Anthology of Prayers*, T. Fisher, 290, from *Early Christian Prayers*, edited by A. Hamman, translated by Walter Mitchell, 26, 225, 234.

Lutterworth Press: from *Lord of the Morning*, Frank Topping, 256, from *Lord of the Evening*, Frank Topping, 57,266,272,321, from *Lord of Time*, Frank Topping, 48,129,107,160,161,285,338, from *Lord of Life*, Frank Topping, 70,143,259, from *Family Prayers*, 52.

Nancy Martin: from *Prayers for Children and Young People*, 53,101,121,125,168,173,177,209,211,212,213,215,217, 236,295,297,299.

Mayhew-McCrimmon Ltd: from *The One Who Listens*, 162,173, from *Family Book of Prayer*, Tony Castle, 101,102,104,109,113, 115,277,287,311,312,313,324.

Macmillan Publishers Ltd: from *Collected Poems and Plays*, Rabindranath Tagore, 94,141,207,257, from *Readings in St John's Gospel*, William Temple, 24,95,369.

Randle Manwaring: 155,292.

Methodist Church Overseas Division: from *A World of Prayer*, 17, from *Your Kingdom Come in Prayer*, 63, from *Going and Coming*, 230, from *The Kingdom Among Us*, 125, from *Channels of Prayer*, 126,235,243,from *Prayer Calendar 1983*, 341.

Methodist Church Division of Education and Youth: from *Together in Church*, 319.

Methodist Publishing House: from *Divine Worship*, 368.

Methuen: from *First Prayers for Children*, 123, from *Bees in Amber*, John Oxenham, 146,273.

Moorhouse Barlow Co: from *Help Me God*, 14.

Janet Morley: 336.

Mothers' Union: 115,280.

Mowbray: from *Talking to God*, Ena V. Martin, 59, from *The Prayer Manual*, 328,330, from *God of All Things*, Joan Gale Thomas, 137,297, from *The Lord is My Shepherd*, 132, from *The Orthodox Way of St Symeon*, Bishop Kallistos Ware, 36, from *Intercessions for use with Rite A*, 246, from *Office of Compline—Alternative Order*, 269, 270, from *After the Third Collect*, Eric Milner-White, 26.

National Christian Education Council: from *Prayers Before Worship*, compiled by Hazel Snashall, 161,225,241,242,322,325, 330,337, from *More Everyday Prayers*, 101,103,106,114,118,122,130,148,161,168,171,188,207,212,241,243,317, from *Further Everyday Prayers*, 109,111,150,151,165,166,175,190,202,203,208,210,216,217,219,220,229,238, 245,246,281,282,323,325, from *What Next, Lord?* Lilian Cox, 128,265,340, from *Prayers for Home and Family*, 332, from *Missionary Prayers and Praises*, Hilda I. Rostron, 295, from *Praying with Juniors*, Jack and Edna Young, 298.

National Society for Promoting Religious Education: from *Hymns and Songs for Children*, E. Rutter Leatham, 208.

New City Press, US rights: from *St Francis at Prayer*, edited by Wolfgang Bader, 125,171,172,371

Oxford University Press: from *Enlarged Songs of Praise*, 117, from *Daily Prayer*, Eric Milner-White, 319, from *Collected Poems of J.K. Baxter*, 83, from *Diary of Private Prayer*, John Baillie, 271.

Penguin Books Ltd: from *Prayer and Meditations of St Anselm*, 105.

Prison Fellowship: 189, from *Meditations of a Lifer*, 189,193.

Pro Civitate Christiana: from *Al De La Della Cose*, Charles de Foucauld, 94.

Saint Andrew Press: from *Prayers for Use in Church*, 84, from *Worship Now*, J.L. Cowie, 64, from *Sunday, Monday*, R.S. Macnicol, 294.

SCM Press Ltd: 156, from *Student Prayer*, 94, from *Contemporary Prayers for Public Worship*, 102,233, from *Contemporary Prayers for Church and School*, 28.

Scottish Academic Press: from *The Celtic Vision*, Esther de Waal, 30,98,99,100,137,139,140,199,200,256,270,276,278,323, 369,371,375

Scottish Episcopal Church: from the *Scottish Prayer Book*, 201.

Scripture Union Publishing, US rights: from *Let's Talk to God*, Zinnia Bryan, 137,292,327, from *Let's Talk to God Again*, Zinnia Bryan, 298, from *Family Prayers 1974*,363.

Seabury Press: from *Instrument of Thy Peace*, Alan Paton, 232.

Sheldon Press: from *Sometimes I Weep*, Ken Walsh, 197.

Sidgwick and Jackson: from *The Everlasting Mercy*, 339.

SPCK: from *One Man's Prayers*, 172, from *A Little Book of Prayers*, Lilian Cox, 337, from *A Brownie Guide Prayer Book*, 296, from *Another Day*, 140,146,163,181,184,197,247,343, from *A St Francis Prayer Book*, Malcolm L. Playfoot, 125,167, from *Draw Near*, Margaret Cropper, 36, from *In the Silence of the Heart*, Mother Teresa, edited by Kathryn Spink, 90,228, from *Edges of His Ways*, Amy Carmichael, 15,274, from *Prayers for the World Today*, 51, from *Praying with the Orthodox Tradition*, 54,73,75,95,258,273,275, 335,374, from *Praying with the Jewish Tradition*, 27,28,29,34,138,148,196,207,237,284, from *Praying with St Augustine*, 85,88, from *Praying with St Teresa*, 26,30,32,90,154, from *Manual of Eastern Orthodox Prayers*, Metropolitan Philaret of Moscow, 65,92,260.

The Terence Higgins Trust, London,© 1987 used with permission, 179.

Bernard Thorogood: from *In His Hands*, 280.

From *Lord, It Keeps Happening And Happening*, by Ruth Harms Calkin, © 1984. Used by permission of Tyndale House Publishers Inc. All rights reserved. 100,119,147,185,285. From *Lord I Keep Running Back To You*, by Ruth Harms Calkin, © 1979. Used by permission of Tyndale House Publishers Inc. All rights reserved. 99,110,124,130.

USPG: from *Prayers for Mission*, 21.

United Reformed Church: from *All the Glorious Names*, Stephen Orchard, 139, from *Prayer in God's Household*, 25,60, from *Encounters*, 333.

H.E. Walter, from *Little Prayers for Little People*, Kathleen Partridge, 51.

World Council of Churches: 146,226,233.

BEATRICE PUBLIC LIBRARY
BEATRICE, NE   68310